EXPLORING GREEN CRIME

Exploring Green Crime

Introducing the Legal, Social and Criminological Contexts of Environmental Harm

Matthew Hall

 macmillan education **palgrave**

First published 2015 by
PALGRAVE

Palgrave in the UK is an imprint of Macmillan Publishers Limited, registered in England, company number 785998, of 4 Crinan Street, London N1 9XW.

Palgrave Macmillan in the US is a division of St Martin's Press LLC, 175 Fifth Avenue, New York, NY 10010.

Palgrave is a global imprint of the above companies and is represented throughout the world.

Palgrave® and Macmillan® are registered trademarks in the United States, the United Kingdom, Europe and other countries.

ISBN 978–1–137–31022–4 hardback
ISBN 978–1–137–31021–7 paperback

This book is printed on paper suitable for recycling and made from fully managed and sustained forest sources. Logging, pulping and manufacturing processes are expected to conform to the environmental regulations of the country of origin.

A catalogue record for this book is available from the British Library.

A catalog record for this book is available from the Library of Congress.

Printed in China

For Rosemary

Contents

Figures

Acknowledgements

In such a new and rapidly developing field as the criminological study of environmental crime (and still wider environmental harms), one can scarcely make any progress at all towards writing a book on the subject without drawing on the combined wisdom of the rapidly growing community of green criminologists worldwide. My particular thanks must go to the UK contingent of this undertaking: Nigel South of the University of Essex; Tanya Wyatt from the Northumbria; Angus Nurse from Middlesex University; and Christopher Williams, to name just a few of the many colleagues whose insight, experience and advice have directly influenced this project. Particular thanks must also go to Rob White of the University of Tasmania and Duncan French of the University of Lincoln for their continued advice and support. I would also like to thank the anonymous reviewers whose thoughtful comments on the draft text have improved the finished result no end.

As in all things, I would like to thank my wife Claire, my son Edward and my daughters Kate and Rosemary, whose support and love – as ever – is reflected on every page of this volume.

Any errors or omissions remain my own.

Publisher's Acknowledgements

Article 38 from the Statute of the International Court of Justice is reproduced with the permission of the United Nations. Extracts from Article 11 and the Explanatory Report under Article 11 of the Convention on the Protection of Environment through Criminal Law © Council of Europe are reproduced with the permission of the Council of Europe.

Chapter 1

What Is 'Green Criminology' and Why Study It?

'Green Criminology' is a relatively new and quickly evolving field. Although this development has been proceeding since the early 1990s, there is still much to be clarified about this area, including its theoretical underpinnings, its methodologies, its proper/intended scope, what it is setting out to achieve and even its name. This first chapter will discuss what it means to 'do' green criminology and investigate some of the criticisms that have surrounded its development. The chapter will scrutinise some of the areas green criminologists have already touched upon in the budding literature and propose other issues it may move on to address.

By the end of the chapter readers should:

- Have a firm understanding of the various arguments and meanings attributed to 'green criminology' as a topic.
- Appreciate the conceptual differences between 'green crimes', 'environmental risk' and 'social harms' approaches.
- Appreciate different conceptions/components of 'eco-justice' and how they impact upon the green criminology project.
- Be able to critically assess the potential scope, aims and subject matter of a green criminology.
- Understand how green criminology fits within, and extends the project of, critical criminology.

In recent years, the enduring problem of environmental pollution and climate change has become an accepted reality for most scholars and practitioners working in both the physical and social sciences. At the same time, man-made environmental disasters have become a recurrent topic of extended discussion within academic writing (see, for example, Walters, 2010) and, more pervasively, in the mass media. Major environmental incidents such as the 2010 BP oil spillage in the Gulf of Mexico are still regularly promoting fresh news reports nearly four years after the event (BBC, 2013). This demonstrates not only that 'the environment' has become a pervasive, newsworthy issue (see Anderson, 1997), but also that associated questions concerning individual, corporate and state responsibility for the damage caused to animal life, human life and the ecology of the region (and further afield) are themselves a topic of sustained public concern.

The title of this chapter implies that criminology has become sensitive to such events and their surrounding implications, but an initial question might be why *criminologists* should be concerning themselves with 'green' issues at all? A simple but pragmatic answer might be that in most jurisdictions there exists a body of criminal law concerned with the environment and the sheer volume of environmental laws on the statute book in most countries and at the international level is rapidly increasing (see Chapter 3). In the United Kingdom at least, *criminal* law has arguably been the traditional approach to tackling environmental degradation (Bell et al., 2013). Across the European Union as a whole, EU Directive 2008/99/EC on the protection of the environment through the criminal law (see p.36 for an explanation of 'Directive' in this context) specifically requires EU member states to apply *criminal* sanctions (which are usually used to tackle *public* disputes of concern to the state) to enforce EU environmental law. That said, many commentators in the wider literature now contend that civil mechanisms (usually reserved for more *private* conflicts between individuals) and sanctions offer distinct advantages over the criminal enforcement of environmental standards, and this will be discussed in more detail in Chapter 3 (see Faure and Svatikova, 2012). The question of whether or not the *criminal* law is employed in any given situation – and thus whether the remit of the criminal penalties are expanded to include different kinds of environmental degradations – is a central concern of criminologists, as will be discussed below.

Another reason criminologists might find themselves concerned by green issues, and specifically by climate change, is that – as argued by Hall and Farrall (2013) – climate change caused by atmospheric pollution itself appears to be criminogenic, which is a term used by criminologists in this context to indicate that it leads to more 'mainstream' offending. In particular the authors note how possible reductions in crop yields, rises in food prices and threats to supplies of food and water (often referred to in the literature as food and/or water 'security' (United Nations Food and Agriculture Organization, 2010)) may lead to increased violent behaviour and food riots in the worst affected parts of the world (Ivanic and Martin, 2008). Other crimes may follow, such as adulteration of foodstuffs (that is adding illegal impurities to food) by producers and consumers turning to illegal food markets which themselves may be associated with wider offending activities. Furthermore the *displacement* of peoples prompted by the desertification of farmland has been particularly apparent in recent years in parts of Africa. Several studies have demonstrated that displaced peoples can not only find themselves turning to crime to survive but are also susceptible to people trafficking (Jasparro and Taylor, 2008). Trafficking of all kinds itself tends to be linked with and facilitates other crimes such as smuggling, drug distribution and prostitution in receiving countries (Lee, 2007). The notion that environmental degradation may lead to further crimes will be discussed in greater detail in Chapter 2.

In a sense, much of the above constitutes well-travelled territory for mainstream criminology. However, if 'green criminology' was simply a matter of examining 'new crimes' or other 'new business' for criminal justice systems with traditional criminological theory and methodologies there would be little need for specific books focused on the subject. This being the case, it may be that we can draw distinctions between a 'criminology of climate change' or a 'criminology of pollution' and a true *green* criminology. What I hope to demonstrate during the course of this book is that 'green criminology' often incorporates much wider conceptions of 'justice' (see p.18), 'harm' (see p.15), 'risks' (see p.14) and non-human victimisation (see Chapter 7). It also requires different underlying theoretical positions and differing methodologies than those employed in more traditional areas of criminological thought. Throughout this book, by 'traditional' or 'mainstream' criminology' (and 'victimology') I am referring to usually non-critical criminology ('critical' criminology seeking to problematise the labelling of some activities as crimes while others are not, placing this in the context of societal power inequalities, see p.211) which has historically focused attention on state-defined crimes revealed through police statistics and surveys conducted with crime victims, including property crime, crimes of violence and sexual crime.

It is argued that such traditional forms of criminology have largely excluded environmental issues or questions concerning environmental harm.

That said, an important goal of this volume is to demonstrate why 'green criminology' in fact reflects many of the more recent developments in criminological thought and associated methodologies. As such, it will ultimately be argued that green criminology represents an important constituent of modern criminology as a whole and should not be relegated to a curiosity or specialism considered by only a small subset of dedicated commentators. To begin explaining why this might be the case, let us consider once again the 2010 Gulf of Mexico oil spill.

To a criminologist, disasters like the 2010 oil spill raise intriguing questions, but also represent a considerable challenge. Certainly there are many angles from which the criminologist might wish to approach the event as a topic of study. One might, for example, question whether the actions or inactions leading to the disaster could be classed as 'criminal' or, failing that, at least 'deviant'. If the activities of BP did not in fact constitute officially recognised criminal acts according to the justice system of the state in question, the critically inclined criminologist might question what wider socio-political factors have made this the case. One might proceed to question what mechanisms (criminal, regulatory or otherwise) are in place to address the harms caused, the nature of those harms (including their timescales) and whether those mechanisms have met with success. We might at the same time question whether different forms of *regulation* (which, broadly speaking, is often based on administrative *rules* often defined in statute but not made part of the criminal *laws*) rather than *criminalisation* would achieve more positive outcomes or might even have prevented the spillage in the first place. Further questions then follow. What does 'addressing' the situation 'successfully' mean in this context and what outcomes are desirable and to whom? To the environment affected? To animals and plant life inhabiting that environment? To the people affected socially, economically and physically? To wider society? To the planet as a whole?

The struggling criminologist faced with such questions might resort to a strategy of trying to categorise the issues in terms of more established areas of criminological thought. Perhaps, for example, we can conceptualise the actions and inactions of BP as corporate crime, or white-collar crime (see pp.86 and 90). In looking at the conditions under which BP was and is allowed to operate in the United States and elsewhere, perhaps we might also think in terms of state crime or abuse of power (see p.173). If such standard classifications prove insufficient, however – as will be discussed in each of the proceeding chapters – one might need to employ novel, alternative characterisations of harm and deviance, such as crimes against the 'carrying capacity' of the planet (Mares, 2010), 'ecocide' (Gray, 1996; Foster, 2011; Rivers, 2012; Higgins et al., 2013) or perhaps 'environmental terrorism' (Schofield, 1999) (see pp.64, 63 and 45 of this volume respectively).

As well as the difficulties of formulating an underlying theoretical perspective, environmental damage raises many further (inherently connected) challenges to the criminologist of a practical and methodological nature. Fundamentally the potential breadth of harms, interests and species affected by these issues mean data collection in such cases can never be comprehensive. Uncertainties arise as to where criminologists should be focusing their attention, which perhaps helps explain the marked lack of data presently available on the nature, scope and response to environmental crimes – or 'harms' falling short of crimes – in most jurisdictions. Identifying these significant gaps in our knowledge will become a recurring theme throughout this book. In some cases, such as illegal wildlife tracking, this lack of data is in part attributable to an apparent lack of resources, expertise or interest by relevant authorities, or because those authorities are vulnerable to corruption (Giovanini, 2006; Downs, 2013). The question of who exactly *are* the 'relevant authorities' in such cases is also far from straightforward (see Chapter 6). In other areas, the lack of data might be explained by the fact that transgressions of environmental laws are often dealt with through informal rather than formal means, which do not lend themselves to external scrutiny (Dal Bó, 2006).

Notwithstanding the present lack of research, the question of what *kind* of data we might need to examine the sorts of questions introduced above is far from clear. The answer in fact largely depends on the methodological leanings of the individual researcher. So, for example, the positivistic-inclined criminology researcher (that is, one subscribing to the view that social realities can and should be studied by methods traditionally used in the natural sciences) might seek to identify and gather statistical (so-called quantitative) data concerning the measurable 'impacts' of the environmental event/process in question and the effects of any justice mechanisms stemming from it. Those keen on more qualitative methodologies (emphasising words over statistics) may seek to gather opinion and perspectives from those (humans) involved in the event and its aftermath for the purposes of a bottom-up analysis of the issues and an assessment of the law 'in action'.

Of course this is not to imply that qualitative and quantitative methods are mutually exclusive. Both strategies however bring difficulties and limitations because, fundamentally, up until very recently criminology has been an almost exclusively anthropocentric discipline: meaning it has focused on human needs, expectations and harms. In this book such an approach will be contrasted with a so-called eco-centric perspective, which considers humans alongside non-human animals and the environment itself. 'Non-human animals' is of course a somewhat clumsy term and will mainly be shortened to simply 'animals'. It is acknowledged however that from both an eco-centric perspective and a bio-centric perspective (Halsey and White, 1998) neither term is quite satisfactory: 'animals' suggesting something very different from human life while 'non-human animals' situates humans in the primary position and non-humans as 'the other' (see Beirne, 2007, and p.167 in this volume for more discussion on these points).

Thus the traditional methodologies associated with criminology are arguably not well suited to gathering information about non-human impacts and effects, or even to linking such effects back to human suffering. Indeed this debate can be taken a step further back to question the underlying epistemology (stance on what counts as 'true' knowledge) of any green criminology, the question being what sources of knowledge we are to utilise. For example, many commentators now agree that the production of data even in the physical sciences, and in relation to environmental harm in particular, is far from objective or value-free (Herrick, 2004). Indeed, it is on such an understanding that international environmental law adopts the so-called precautionary principle (Kriebel et al., 2001), to be discussed in more detail in Chapter 5.

Methodological question aside, criminologists have, for their part, received extended criticism for focusing the majority of their attention on those notions of crime and criminal justice espoused by *states* (McBarnet, 1983). Not only has this impeded wider questioning concerning which actions become criminalised in the first place, it has also promoted criminologists (following the lead of most criminal justice systems) to think largely in terms of individual, identified offenders and singular/small groups of *human* victims. Such restrictive terms of reference of course provide the context and boundaries that allow criminologists to know roughly what it is they are trying to measure and explain. In the case of environmental damage however, harm may be widespread, diverse and involve 'mass' victimisation to groups of humans, non-human animals and the wider environment. Perpetrators may not be 'criminals' in the legalistic sense of the word and may not even be readily identifiable.

Take for example the apparent harms falling on the Maldives as a result of rising sea levels, which have arguably been triggered by climate change (Docherty and Giannini, 2009). It is widely (although not unanimously, see

Mörner et al., 2004) argued that damage is occurring to the islands, its fish stocks and, consequently, the human population who rely on these, but who is the perpetrator? Where is the 'crime' and how do we measure its impacts: both on the environment as an object of intrinsic worth and in relation to human concerns?

The above paragraphs essentially map out some of the core questions that have become the preserve of a relatively new field of study now widely termed 'green criminology'. The discussion also highlights some of the difficulties and complexities of approaching the problem of environmental damage from the criminological perspective. Indeed one might question the utility of the whole exercise given that, as hinted above, many of the most environmentally destructive activities witnessed in the world today are not officially recognised *crimes* in many jurisdictions and even when they are recognised as harms, any recourse will often be to civil or administrative procedures. One pertinent example is that of the shipment of e-waste, discussed in Box 1. While research into the illegal shipment and disposal of such waste is rapidly emerging (Gottberg et al., 2006), much e-waste is transported to developing countries from developed nations in a completely legal manner to be disposed of in ways that are themselves entirely legal in the receiving country (although frequently not in the source country). Indeed, arguably the greatest challenge to green criminology comes not from the major environmental disasters alluded to above, but rather from the far more day-to-day activities perpetrated by countries, corporations and individuals which impact negatively upon the environment in its widest sense, and in the long term. The question therefore becomes, what does a so-called green criminology have to offer that is not already covered by other physical and social science disciplines as well as the study of environmental law? The rest of this chapter (and indeed this book as a whole) begins the process of answering these core questions.

Box 1: Electronic waste

With our ever-growing reliance on technological devices such as computers, mobile phones, tablets and so on, the distribution and disposal of waste electronic and electrical equipment (usually known in Europe as WEEE and in the United States as e-waste) has become a key environmental concern (Rothe, 2010). Such waste (especially computers, refrigerators and fluorescent tubing) contains toxic materials such as mercury and hazardous gasses with the potential to cause considerable damage to the natural environment (especially water courses) as well as health problems in human and non-human animals. The problem is heightened by the speedy development of such tech-nologies making older models quickly 'obsolete' in the eyes of consumers in developed countries.

Many Western countries have responded to the challenge posed by WEEE by reg-ulating its storage and disposal. For example, the United Kingdom has implemented the Waste Electronic and Electrical Equipment Regulations of 2006. The difficulty how-ever is that increased regulation has prompted the export of WEEE to other countries where regulation is less stringent. China has been a particularly notable recipient of much of this waste. Ruggiero and South (2010) cite numerous cases of death and illness brought about in areas of the world exposed to hazardous waste materials, including the so-called cancer villages of China, where residents' increased susceptibility to sev-eral classifications of tumours has been directly attributed to their exposure to cadmium and mercury released through the recycling of e-waste (Watts, 2010: p.21). The redis-tribution of e-waste from developed to developing nations represents an example of how 'environmental risks' are essentially being reallocated from the global rich to the global poor (see Bisschop, 2012). In the EU the recent update of the law under Directive 2012/19/EU (see p.36) on waste electrical and electronic equipment is intended to place greater controls on the export of this material beyond Europe, although considerable problems remain with the transport of WEEE even within the EU (Li et al., 2013). In the United States, the Environmental Protection Agency admits:

> While accurate data on the amount of e-waste being exported from the U.S. are not available, the United States government is concerned that these exports are being mismanaged abroad, causing serious public health and environmental hazards, and representing a lost opportunity to recover valuable resources effectively. U.S. laws and regulations are limited in their ability to prevent harmful exports of used electronics to developing countries. (EPA, 2013: unpaginated)

More recently, concerns have been expressed that Ethiopia may prove the next nation to develop significant problems with e-waste (Manhart et al., 2013). Complicating the issues significantly is the fact that in many developed countries an unknown but probably significant proportion of the trade and export of e-waste may in fact be carried out illegally (or semi-legally) by criminal organisations (Bisschop, 2012) and thus the material is difficult to trace and the harms caused become impossible to quantify.

BACKGROUND AND THEORY TO A 'GREEN CRIMINOLOGY'

White (2008a) has characterised green criminology in succinct terms as 'basi-cally refer[ing] to the study of environmental harm, environmental laws and environmental regulation by criminologists' (p.8). This simple explanation however betrays considerable debate in the literature concerning what 'green criminology' is and even what it should be called. Certainly as a field it has taken some time to gain momentum. Lynch and Stretesky (2007) have commented that the lack of development in the criminological study of environmental degradation is particularly apparent in the United States, although it is generally true of the field globally. They note the irony in this, as one of the first true green criminology discussions came out of the United States (Lynch, 1990). In that paper, Lynch argued that the ' "greening" of criminology' was derived from the coming together of at least three separate movements:

■ Firstly, ecofeminists (as Lynch understands this label, see p.52 in this volume) from the mid-1970s began arguing that the effects of environmental degradation fall disproportionately on women compared to men.

■ On a similar theme, Lynch attributes the second foundation of green criminology to growing discussions of what has come to be known as 'environmental racism'. This is the suggestion that the impact of environmental degradation falls disproportionately on some races.

■ Finally, Lynch draws on what he calls 'red/green alliances', by which he means forms of ecological socialism, the adherents of which sought to emphasise the inequalities of wealth and power in society which both lead to increased environmental degradation while also ensuring it is the poor and socially excluded who bear the brunt of its negative effects.

Gibbs et al. (2010) provide an overview of the various classifications and definitions of green criminology, starting with the so-called legalistic understanding of environmental crimes as violations of criminal laws designed to protect the health and safety of people, the environment or both. The legalistic position is contrasted to the socio-legal approach, which acknowledges that the differences between 'crime', 'deviance', 'civil wrongs' and 'regulatory violations' are all socially constructed. Both perspectives are contrasted to the concept of 'environmental justice', which is discussed in greater detail below (p.18). The final classification drawn upon by Gibbs and colleagues is the notion of 'biocentric' or 'deep green' perspectives, which construe environmental crime as 'any human activity that disrupts a biotic system' (p.127).

One of the key assertions made by Gibbs et al. (2010) is that '[g]reen criminology needs an interdisciplinary framework' (p.129), a contention I will return to at the end of this chapter. For these authors, the difficulty with much of the existing literature in this field is that it is value laden and presupposes set conclusions to environmental problems (criminalisation, regulation, etc.). As such, their 'conservation criminology' is research based and draws on three specified disciplines: criminal justice and criminology; risk and decision analysis; and natural resource conservation and management.

Other phrases to be tabled in the literature include Groombridge's (1991) Eco-criminology, which for him draws on 'ethics, religion, politics, economics and feminism'. Lynch and Stretesky (2007) have also commented in some detail on the development in the late 1990s of a field of study known as eco-critical criminology (EEC) (Seis, 1999). EEC is characterised by a tendency 'to connect environmental issues to economic and political structures and hierarchies' and, as such, has much to offer green criminology. In particular, Lynch and Stretesky highlight the attention paid by ECC scholars to the impact of global corporations and, more generally, the global socio-economic context on the development of environmental harms.

Clearly there are conceptual overlaps between all of these differing classifications of study. For Ruggiero and South (2010) (and also for White (2013a)) the question of what to call the field is to some extent settled because:

> for all that it invites criticism as lacking precision and possibly being open to interpretation as aligned with a 'green political party' position, the term 'Green Criminology' has become the most familiar and suggestive term, and also serves well as the most comprehensive conceptual umbrella. (p.247)

That said, not all commentators have been satisfied with this label. Halsey (2004), in criticising an earlier discussion by Lynch and Stretesky (2003), has argued that the label 'green criminology' is in fact too simplistic to adequately reflect the complexities of the issues at hand:

> Indeed, I want to suggest that the term 'green' should be jettisoned from criminological discourse, primarily because it does not adequately capture the inter-subjective, inter-generational, or inter-ecosystemic costs which combine to produce scenarios of harm. (p.247)

As implied by Ruggiero and South (2010a) it has also been noted that 'green' as a label carries political connotations and has links with activism. Another important observation is that 'green criminology' was from the outset conceived as espousing radical criminological principles (Lynch, 1990) and, as such, it might be suggested that rather than constituting a truly 'new' field it in fact largely reflects an extension of Marxist and neo-Marxist criminological thought (see pp.86–87 of this volume and Shantz, 2012). For their part, Lynch and Stretesky (2007) certainly emphasise that '[in]n the green view, the continued existence of environmentally destructive behaviours has a great deal to do with the nature of capitalism' (p.250). This final criticism may however be met with the observation that green criminology in its relatively short history has set out to tackle matters well beyond the traditional Marxist remit, especially in relation to the harms falling on non-human species and the ecosystem itself.

For the reasons discussed in the last two paragraphs, this book will continue to utilise the term 'green criminology' as its conceptual umbrella, albeit that is not to say the brand of green criminology espoused here entirely corresponds with that discussed by Lynch (1990), Ruggiero and South (2010a) or others. Indeed any student of this field should be wary of Kearon and Godfrey's (2007) warning against the academic tendency to 'force social phenomena into false chronologies' (p.30). It is precisely this restrictive approach that has forestalled the development and expansion of criminology along these lines. Labelling a subject area 'green criminology' is useful in that it might signify a set of assumptions, theoretical underpinnings and methodological issues, which the above paragraphs broadly present, but as ever such classifications are just labels, the meanings of which are in constant flux, especially in such a new and rapidly evolving area. Indeed, for his part White (2013a) has recently commented that 'there is no green criminology *theory* as such' (p.22) and that 'those who are doing green criminology define it in ways that best suit their own conception of what it is they are doing' (p.17). For him, therefore, the real benefit of the label lies mainly as a focal point for people interested in environmental crime, harms and risks.

ENVIRONMENTAL DEGRADATION AS 'CRIME', 'RISK' AND 'SOCIAL HARM'?

Environmental 'crime'

Traditionally criminology is conceived as a 'rendezvous discipline' (Rock and Holdaway 1997) comprised of researchers from across the social sciences (principally sociology, law, economics and politics) coming together to examine the nature and causes of crime and criminal justice mechanisms or, as Sutherland and Cressey (1974) put it, 'the study of the making of laws, the breaking of laws, and of social reaction to the breaking of laws' (p.3). From this legalistic perspective, Carrabine et al. (2014) have classified 'green crimes' into two broad categories: primary green crimes, which essentially cause direct environmental destruction and include crimes of air pollution, deforestation, water pollution and crimes against animals; and secondary green crimes, which include 'symbiotic green crime...that grows out of the flouting of rules that seek to regulate environmental disasters' (p.318). Examples of this second category given by the authors include violence perpetrated by the state against green pressure groups and crimes of fraud perpetrated by corporations in an attempt to avoid environmental legalisation (Potter, 2012). A specific example (of the former) is the French government's 1985 bombing of the Greenpeace ship Rainbow Warrior following the ship's involvement in anti nuclear-testing demonstrations.

More recently White (2011) has argued that simply cataloguing lists of green offences as the key constituents of green criminology in itself fails to progress the field. For him it is more helpful to arrange such offences into thematic groupings including crimes related to the transformation of nature; the disposal of waste; global crimes related to worldwide processes and specific crimes related to particular geographical regions. These themes are a useful refinement but it is clear that simply classifying existing or even potential criminal activities which are directly or indirectly related to the environment can only take us so far. One of the first challenges to be faced by green criminology is in fact the truism that many of the individual, corporate and state activities which precipitate environmental damage and associated harms are not in fact 'crimes' recognised by either national or international law. As noted by Skinnider (2011):

> [M]any environmental disruptions are actually legal and take place with the consent of society. Classifying what is an environmental crime involves a complex balancing of communities' interest in jobs and income with ecosystem maintenance, biodiversity and sustainability. (p.2)

Or, as Gibbs et al. (2010) put it:

> A grey area emerges for environmental risks that are not currently subject to regulation or criminal enforcement but where further understanding of the risk may lead stakeholders to argue for regulation and/or criminalization. (p.133)

Box 2: Environmental crime as a 'grey' area?

It is clear that the legality of environmentally questionable and/or destructive activities is frequently open to debate, certainly in relation to the *criminal* law. In the United Kingdom, for example, there has been a lot of argument surrounding genetically modified crops, and what precisely the law in this area allows (Hansen, 2012). Larsen (2013) gives the examples of Norwegian laws on animal welfare, arguing that the legislation is vague and inconsistent on whether animals have intrinsic value. As noted by Larsen, 'Crime as understood by the law is imprecisely defined and reported animal cruelty is always subject to discretion or vague interpretation' (p.54). The strong implication, therefore, is that environmental harm cannot be understood from a purely legalistic perspective. As such, it is one of the potential significant contributions of green criminology to assist in clarifying debates about the nature of green harms and the potential for legal (or extra-legal) redress.

Consequently, if we are to study environmental harm *as criminologists*, we must first accept that one of the roles of criminology (in addition to those set out above) is also to critically evaluate the processes by which some activities become labelled as 'criminal' (and are thus placed within the remit of criminal justice) while others remain beyond the scope of the criminal justice system (with associated harms being left to civil justice or less formal processes). In effect, what this means is that *green* criminology is often also a critical criminology. Critical criminology problematises the classification of 'crime' in the first instance by reference to the political and economic influences that inform and drive this process. Ruggiero and South (2010b) explain how decisions to criminalise given actions are in practice heavily influenced by the power inequalities witnessed in society:

[T]he high status of those causing the most [environmental] harm who (like other powerful offenders) frequently reject the proposition that criminal definitions should apply to them while constantly striving to persuade legislators that the imposition of norms of conduct on them would be detrimental to all. Powerful actors whose conduct impacts on the environment possess the ready-made rationalisation that a law imposing limits to the harm they cause would implicitly endanger the core values underpinning economic development and therefore be damaging to the collective wellbeing. (p.246)

Clearly this reflects the radical critique of Lynch (1990): critical criminology often being seen as overlapping substantially with or comprising radical criminology (see, Carrington and Hogg, 2013). Of course, neo-Marxist critique aside, it is important to appreciate that there are often sound economic and/or political justifications why a company or a state might passively allow harmful and polluting activities to continue, or even to actively promote them (Walters, 2006). This is why Skinnider (2011) refers to the 'complex balancing of communities' interest' in determining what is and is not an environmental 'crime'. To this of course we must add the perspective that, even if the political will is present to legislate against or otherwise restrict a given polluting practice, *criminal law* may not be the most effective solution (see chapters 3 and 7).

Environmental risk

Given that, for the reasons above, green criminology cannot be restricted simply to examining those polluting activities already falling within the remit of a criminal justice process, wider terms of reference are required. One method of achieving this is to think not in terms of *crime*, but of risk. Criminologists became concerned with the concept of risk and risk management largely as a result of the influential work by German sociologist Ulrich Beck and his conception of what he termed 'the risk society'. In short, Beck's (1992) thesis was that Western societies had become organised around the avoidance and management of the risk of future harms occurring, which would include the risks associated with the general rise of atmospheric pollution and the risk of serious environmental disasters like the 2010 Gulf of Mexico oil spill. The application of Beck's ideas has become a common starting point for many green criminologists as well. Indeed, for Gibbs et al. (2010) environmental risk is a key feature of their conception of conservation criminology discussed earlier. Risk here is used as a mechanism of distancing the field of inquiry from the more legalistic understandings of environmental crime noted above.

The risk society thesis received considerable attention in the 1990s, principally by Giddens (1990) who updated the theory to take account of the characteristics of the modern world (modernity). Specifically, Giddens' updated conception acknowledged that risks in modernity were globalised, well known but partially understood and mainly created by man ('manufactured risk') as opposed to coming from nature ('natural risk'). Arguably these additions make the concept of risk even more amendable to application by green criminologists. To illustrate this Newburn (2013), in introducing green criminology, cites the example of the January 2011 earthquake in Japan, which led to a tsunami tidal wave that devastated vast social coastal areas and ultimately damaged the cooling systems at the Fukushima Nuclear Power Plant, creating a risk of meltdown. The event represents how a 'natural risk' of the kind discussed by Beck can be transferred to a 'manufactured risk' as discussed by Giddens. More importantly, Newburn's example helps to demonstrate how green criminologists may concern themselves with an event which was initially an entirely natural disaster, and in relation to which no crime has ever been identified. Furthermore, one of the key precepts of

Beck's thought was that risk had taken over from traditional inequalities of wealth and income as the defining characteristic of society because, while risk was not equally distributed around society, it did affect people according to new patterns and inequalities which are only partially related to income and wealth. Later in this book I will argue that, in reality, environmental harm does in fact appear to fall disproportionately on those of low income and wealth. Nevertheless, applying the notion of risk to green criminological thought moves the debate beyond the radical neo-Marxist critique discussed above.

Environmental 'harms'

A second way of broadening green criminology beyond officially proscribed criminal offences lies in the suggestion made by Hillyard and Toombs in their 2003 book *Beyond Criminology*. They argue that 'social harms' – usually meaning harms that detrimentally affect people's lives but which are not officially proscribed by the criminal law – rather than 'crime' should become the main topic of criminological inquiry. For example, in the United Kingdom, the coalition government recently announced plans to change the law on trespass to assist oil and gas extraction companies tunnelling under people's homes for the purposes of 'fracking' (more properly referred to as 'hydraulic fracturing': this is a process of releasing natural gas and other resources via the injection of high pressure water into shale rocks underground) (Carrington, 2014). This indicates a strong political and legal support for the fracking industry despite the significant concerns voiced by environmentalists about the dangers of fracking to both humans and the environment (see Mooney, 2011). As such, fracking is not only legally permissible in terms of the criminal law, but will also be *facilitated* by changes in the civil law. Any environmental damage caused by such activities would therefore constitute not a green *crime*, but a *harm*. Hillyard and Toombs' argument is thus that such harms should be a focus of criminological enquiry, along with the social, political and legal processes that have seen them fall on the 'legal' side of the debate. More broadly, the authors have argued that, in more recent years, the progress of critical criminology has stalled somewhat from its heyday in the 1960s and 1970s, giving way to an empiricist 'applied science' orientation driven by the political issues of the day. The authors therefore advocate in response to this a return to a criminology based on social harms, and it is in this tradition that the present book situates itself.

Focusing on 'harm' rather than crime has, according to Hillyard and Toombs, several advantages, a number of which seem to have particular resonance with the impacts of environmental pollution and climate change. 'Crime', as argued by Hulsman (1986), is an entirely social construct and hence 'the criminal law fails to capture the more damaging and pervasive forms of harm' (Hillyard and Toombs, 2003: p.12). As criminologists, we may debate the extent to which we agree with the wider implications of such a sweeping statement, but it remains clear that focusing on harm has the potential to include the often legally ambiguous activities that foster environmental damage as well as those which are already covered by civil and administrative systems. Indeed, even when such activities are criminal in the strict legal sense, focusing on harm allows us to account for such activities in cases where whatever mechanisms of justice which are available (at the national, transnational and international levels) fail to adequately prosecute such transgressions.

Another salient point made by Hillyard and Toombs is that the social harms approach allows for the consideration of 'mass harms' covering large areas and large numbers of victims. Again this chimes well with the problems inherent to environmental degradation, where the effects may spiral out to include great swathes of animal, plant and human life. Traditional criminology, on the other hand, has struggled to fully embrace the concept of mass victimisation (certainly in relation to non-humans) and, with the exception of limited inroads into the fields of state crime and corporate crime, has largely remained focused on the individual. For similar reasons, the authors argue that the social harms approach poses a challenge to the still individualistic conceptions of crime grounded around the notions of risk discussed above (Giddens, 1990).

In the existing green criminology literature, White (2008a) also reflects on the concept of harm, offering four groups of key 'considerations of environmental harms' (p.92). The first of these considerations is that of *identifying* the victims of such harm. Criticising more mainstream criminological notions, White makes the important point that victims of environmental harm include the biosphere and non-human animals. It follows again that a further advantage of applying the social harms approach in this field is that it allows commentators to explore the non-human consequences of environmental degradation beyond the highly anthropocentric concept of 'criminal victimisation'.

The second of White's considerations are geographical, encapsulating the fact that environmental harm is often a regional, national, international or even global problem. In a similar vein, White distinguishes geographical considerations from considerations of 'place', by which he means the different types of harm experienced in urban, built-up centres of human habitation, compared with harm caused to natural environments such as oceans, wilderness areas and deserts. Finally, White conceives environmental harm in terms of temporal considerations, meaning that the impact of environmental damage may be short, medium or long term and may have immediate and/or lasting social impacts. There is a key link here to be made with more mainstream discussions of criminal victimisation and the growing acceptance that the impacts of individualistic harms (in this case crimes) vary considerably over time (as well as between individuals) and, with it, the support needs of those victimised (Shapland and Hall, 2007).

White's 'considerations' of environmental harm may in one sense be criticised for failing to 'pin down' the concept to specific human or non-human impacts, although elsewhere White (2007) has categorised such harms into 'brown', 'green' and 'white' groupings encompassing pollution levels, the biosphere and the impact of technological advances respectively. Certainly Hillyard and Toombs (2003) are more explicit in their definition of social harm in that they conceive it as including physical harm; financial/economic harm; emotional/psychological harm and consideration of so-called cultural safety. Of course, once again these are highly anthropocentric classifications. Furthermore, the counter argument can be made that to rigidly define 'harm' would in a sense defeat the purpose of the critical exercise, which is to be inclusive rather than exclusive. As such, for White (2008a) it is important for commentators, especially those concerned with green issues, to move beyond *defining* harm and onto *debating* harm, because only the latter can lead to real-life, operational developments:

> Defining harm is ultimately about philosophical frameworks as informed by scientific evidence and traditional knowledges; debating harm is about processes of deliberation in the 'real world' and of conflicts over rights and the making of difficult decisions. (p.24)

Of course, such a view presents real difficulties for those seeking to develop *legal* systems for addressing environmental harms; as such a system must ultimately be based on concrete and predictable definitions (Williams, 1996). This apparent conflict between predictable legal rules and flexible notions of environmental harm will be another recurring issue throughout this book. Nevertheless, while attributing a precise definition to environmental harm is problematic (certainly with regards to *legal systems*) and perhaps undesirable, the evidence is increasingly clear that whether such harms are criminalised or not, they are a pervasive and significant problem of the modern world.

JUSTICE PERSPECTIVES

Conceiving the subject matter of green criminology as that of 'environmental risk' or 'environmental harms' is a useful means of expanding the scope of the debate beyond simple criminal categories steeped in the unequal power dynamics of the societies that produce them and begging the question of 'why criminal law?' in the first place. Nevertheless, these ideas are still fundamentally anthropocentric, or at least have been in their application in much of the previous criminological literature. Thus, risk usually means risk to humans and social harm usually means harm to humans or, at best, harms which will latter lead to human suffering. This of course fails to acknowledge the perspective that harm to the environment, the animal and the plant kingdoms is destructive as of itself, because animals, plants and the ecosystem have an inherent worth unconnected to what they provide for human beings (see Gray and Coates, 2012). Incorporating such an eco-centric perspective is arguably what distinguishes green criminology from mainstream criminological concerns and certainly in this book I, like Nurse (2013a), include animals and the wider environment within the concept of social harms. As such, green criminology requires different assumptions and different ways of thinking about the nature of justice, which is why 'green criminology' is not just a matter of identifying a new topic for mainstream criminological consideration (a 'criminology of pollution' or a 'criminology of climate change', for example).

A growing body of literature has focused on various conceptualisations of 'justice' as a means of encapsulating this wider assembly of eco-centric concerns for green criminology. Like green criminology itself there is little agreement as to what precisely constitutes justice in this context (and the pursuit of a definition of 'justice' itself is of course an ancient philosophical endeavour) although the broad term 'eco-justice' has been used to encapsulate all their differing ideas under one label (White, 2013b). For example, much reference is made in the literature to so-called environmental justice that emphasises the involvement of people and communities in decisions that might impact upon their environment. This by itself however remains an anthropocentric concept, albeit one that defines the environment broadly to include cultural norms, values, rules, regulations and behaviours (Bryant,

1995: p.6; see also Čapek, 1993; Hofrichter, 1993). Environmental justice is also often considered to include notions of interpretational justice, whereby present generations owe a duty to ensure subsequent generations can enjoy and benefit from the environment in the same manner they have (Hiskes, 2008).

White (2008a), in following a more holistic approach, has criticised this understanding of environmental justice, ignoring the wider issues of *ecological* justice (acknowledging that humans are just one part of a complex ecosystem) and also *animal* and *species* justice (acknowledging the intrinsic right of non-human animals to be free of abuse).

It is beyond the scope of the present book to delve too deeply into the vast philosophical literature on the nature of justice or even the still extensive (if relatively more recent) component of that literature which examines 'justice' as it relates to the environment. In Box 3 I set out an example of such a discussion from Benton (2007), who debates the green challenge to concepts of social justice.

Box 3: Ted Benton – Ecology, community and justice: The meaning of green

In this discussion Benton examines the implications of the 'green agenda' for varying conceptions of 'social justice'. Taking four key components of the green challenge – natural limits on the scale of human activity imposed by nature; the drive for animal/human continuity; non-anthropocentric values and notions of ecotopia – Benton evaluates the implications of these challenges for both formal (equated here with Rawlsian; see Rawls, 1999) and communitarian theories of justice. His analysis demonstrates the multiple challenges posed to existing conceptions of justice, but also how justice principles challenge the foundations of the green agenda. He concludes that 'If anything, the green challenge requires us to give still more attention to the question of justice, as well as providing new work for the concept and principles of justice to do . . . the requirement to conceptualise justice across species is perhaps the most testing of all' (p.29).

Fundamentally most writings in this area adopt either an environmental justice perspective, discussed above, or what White (2007) has broadly termed ecological justice encompassing 'conservations of specific environments, animal rights and preservations of the biosphere generally' (p.39), or some combination thereof. White proceeds to set out the difficulties in reconciling these two positions and ultimately sees this as one of the fundamental questions for green criminology (which is also implied by the work of Benton discussed Box 3). For White an important step towards bridging these two perspectives is to promote the concept of ecological citizenship, which for him would incorporate both environmental justice and ecological justice concerns, placing humans as part of (but equal to) the environment around them. We will see in Chapter 8 that, ultimately, the brand of 'justice' adopted is inherently linked with the notion of environmental rights. This also effects the questions we want answered as green criminologists and the methods we adapt to pursue those answers. Consequently, the issue of ecological vs environmental justice will be another running theme throughout this book.

WHY 'DO' GREEN CRIMINOLOGY?

In the above discussion I have set out some of the theoretical and methodological complexities inherent to the notion of 'green criminology'. This discussion has also demonstrated a distinction I wish to draw between 'criminologists looking at environmental crime' and 'green criminology' with its much wider conceptions of harm, risk and non-human victimisation and different underlying theoretical positions. To highlight this distinction, in the remainder of this book each chapter will begin by examining a core issue of importance to green criminology from the perspective of more midstream criminological classifications: state crime; corporate crime; human rights and so on. The goal of each chapter will then be to demonstrate how such traditional classifications are insufficient and thus introduce into each debate a more genuinely 'green' perspective. The chapters will then each comment on associated methodological issues to offer a way forward in progressing the study of each area, and with it green criminology as a whole.

Of course, that is not to say we should jettison the entire canon of traditional criminology in pursuance of the green agenda. In fact we have seen above that criminology's embrace and development of concepts like 'risk' and 'harm' are vital components of a green criminology. It is in fact criminologists' familiarity with such issues that makes their contribution to the study of environmental harms as a whole so significant. Furthermore, given the increased recognition of environmental harm and the growing understanding of its costs, mainstream criminologists will increasingly find themselves obliged to examine environmental offending because, like other forms of deviance, man-made environmental degradation is quickly becoming a holistic, pervasive social problem. As we have seen, green issues also quite neatly exemplify certain 'missing elements' to mainstream criminology which have long formed the basis of the radical and critical schools. In order to fully meet the challenge posed by these perspectives, the continued development of green criminology is vital.

Criminologists therefore have much to offer and indeed much to gain from study of environmental harms. As well as risk and social harm, concepts of labelling, procedural justice (see p.200), state and corporate crime all have their role to play albeit, as we will see in the remainder of this book, most of these few of these subject areas have up till now embraced a more eco-centric. That said, it is also vital to the development of this field to appreciate the need for the interdisciplinary framework discussed by Gibbs et al. (2010). While criminology certainly brings plenty to the table in the effort to comprehend and meet the challenges posed by environmental degradation (or even recognised environmental *crimes*), full answers to many of the questions posed by this chapter will only come by drawing expertise from across the social and physical sciences, embracing also a strong inter-sectorial component.

The virtues of an interdisciplinary approach are of course in recent years widely touted in most academic fields (see Matthews and Ross, 2010), and for good reason. Drawing from a variety of sources and perspectives almost inevitably provides a broader understanding of any given subject of the research exercise as well as providing the scope for transposing ideas and solutions between subject areas (see Lury and Wakeford, 2012). The virtues of an interdisciplinary approach are also well recognised by criminologists (Dupont-Morales, 1998; Walsh and Ellis, 2007).

The study of environmental harms will inevitably draw on a complex array of data, ideas and practices from across the social and physical sciences. For example, it calls into question the interface between science and law, which Houck (2003) describes as a 'tale from a troubled marriage' (p.1926). Economic matters are also clearly raised by such discussions (Helm and Hepburn, 2009). Perhaps more subtly, economic impacts of environmental harm are often inherently linked with more cultural and social factors, at which point we move into the domains of sociology and anthropology. Thus, the loss of the fishing industry in the Maldives, discussed earlier, is as much a tale of cultural destruction as it is of ecological damage and (perhaps) corporate or even state criminality. As such, criminologists require the input of cultural experts in order to fully appreciate and incorporate such events. Studies of environmental victimisation also inevitably touch upon healthcare issues (Chivian et al., 1993), the politicisation of the 'green agenda' (Helm and Hepburn, 2009) and the provision of insurance to those affected (IASIE, 2009). I have argued elsewhere that a key component of any 'green victimology' will also be a close interaction between victimologists (i.e. those interested in criminal victimisation and the role of victims of crime in criminal justice) and international legal scholars (and practitioners): environmental pollution so often constituting a cross-border issue (Passas, 2005). That said, given the breadth of possible contributors and perspectives relevant to the debates at hand, the idea that *law* (much less *criminal law*) can or should constitute the *sole* solution to the problems of environmental harm is surely wrong. On this point it is interesting to note in passing the gradual development of so-called environmental mediation processes, which in many cases boast many of the features of restorative justice (Amy, 1983). Very little work has yet been carried out to assess the merits of such schemes (to be discussed in Chapter 3), posing yet another challenge to green criminologists.

'GREEN' QUESTIONS?

What then are the guiding questions that can inform the progression of green criminology? Various authors have set out typologies or 'road maps' for the development of the field, including White's (2007) colour classifications noted above. South (1998) and Carrabine et al. (2014) have also reflected on various typologies of issues of interest to green criminologists. Producing a definitive list of green criminological themes would be impossible but we can derive from the prevailing ligature several major issues including, represented in Figure 1.1.

Of course, while road maps and typologies are useful, especially for a burgeoning field, it is important such lists do not constrain or restrict the development of the area but rather constitute a useful *starting point* to begin thinking about identifying and exploring relevant issues. For example, one key question not specifically articulated above is the need for green criminology to identify 'the limits of law' in addressing environmental harm. This will be discussed in more detail in Chapter 3 but, as already noted in this chapter, in general the proposition that *criminalisation* may be incapable of fully addressing environmental harm will be an important theme of this book. Finally, I have elsewhere advocated the development of a parallel (sub) field of 'green victimology' (Hall, 2013). The study of victims of mainstream crimes (and wider social harms) has progressed markedly in the last 30 years

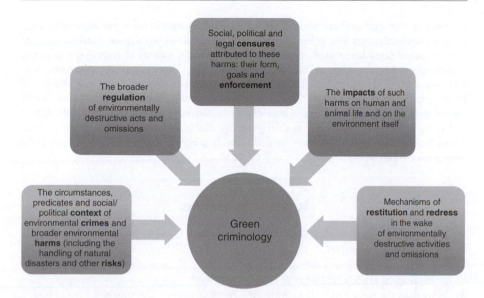

Figure 1.1 Key issues and questions in green criminology

but in many respects still lags behind the vanguard of criminology. The focus of green criminology on the *harms* caused, as opposed to stringent, legal classifications, makes the advent of victimology even more central to this area because it begins the analysis with the *outcome* (victimisation) rather than the classification of the preceding event as 'criminal'. Just as traditional criminology is anthropocentric, so too is traditional victimology and, as such, Chapter 7 will explore ways by which the wider ambit of non-human victims can be addressed by those in the field.

Summary

Although still at a relatively early stage of maturity, 'green criminology' in its short history has already begun to develop a cogent agenda and identifiable theoretical underpinnings (albeit these are not universally shared by all those identifying themselves as 'doing' green criminology). More recently such discussion has progressed beyond neo-Marxism to embrace concepts of risk, social harm and various models of justice. Although, as in any vibrant field, there is little consensus, it is clear that much of green criminology so far has been heavily influenced by the critical criminological school. The incorporation of wider notions of harm and suffering (specifically non-human harm) plus the need to adapt tried and tested criminological methods elevates the area beyond simply constituting 'another' area of mainstream criminological attention. That said, the recognition of an increasingly wide array of environmental harms and 'green crimes', plus the possible criminogenic consequences of environmental degradation itself, means 'the environment' is unlikely to remain the exclusive preserve of a specialist subgroup of criminologists for long. There is a wealth of environmental issues that could form the subject of a green criminological analysis, and the challenge will be in adapting mainstream criminological ideas to this end. Furthermore, green criminology cannot exist in vacuum, as the green issue clearly cuts across traditional academic disciplines and to sectors beyond. As such, green criminology needs to work closely with other disciplines from the physical and social sciences to truly progress itself and to have meaningful impact on the real world.

Review questions

1) How can we conceptualise 'green criminology'? How does it differ from more 'mainstream' criminology?
2) In what ways could green criminology be considered an extension of the critical/radical criminological schools and what does it add to these?
3) How does the notion of 'risk' fit within the remit of green criminology?
4) What kinds of questions should green criminologists concern themselves with?

Further reading

Gibbs, C., Gore, M. and Rivers, L. (2010), 'Introducing Conservation Criminology: Towards Interdisciplinary Scholarship on Environmental Crimes and Risks', *British Journal of Criminology*, 50(1): 124–144.

- Offers a useful introduction to the debate surrounding difference conceptions and labels attached to green criminology.

Lynch, M. (1990), 'The Greening of Criminology', *Critical Criminologist*, 2: 1–5.

- A classic piece setting out the need for the development of criminology along environmental lines.

Mares, D. (2010), 'Criminalizing Ecological Harm: Crimes Against Carrying Capacity and the Criminalization of EcoSinners', *Critical Criminology*, 18: 279–293.

- Offers important insights into the broad nature of environmental harm on a global scale.

Ruggiero, V. and South, N. (2007), 'Critical Criminology and Crimes Against the Environment', *Critical Criminology*, 18: 245–250.

- Contains important insights into the unequal impact of environmental harm at a local, national and international level.

Snider, L. (2010), 'Framing e-waste Regulation: The Obfuscating Role of Power', *Criminology and Public Policy*, 9(3): 569–577.

- Important discussions of how power inequalities impact on law-making and the regulatory process.

Students are also advised to take look at the international green criminology website at http://greencriminology.org/, which hosts various texts including the Green Criminology Monthly Newsletter.

Chapter 2

Environmental Degradation, Social Change and Crime

Having set out some of the key theoretical concepts potentially linking the environment and environmental harm to key areas of criminological debate in the last chapter, this chapter will apply such theories to establish the links between environmental degradation, crime and social harms more explicitly, and with reference to real-life examples. In particular it will examine how the increased attention and social censure of environmentally destructive activities has the potential to promote a 'net widening effect' in the criminal law. At the same time, it will be shown that the social changes prompted by environmentally destructive practices and events can be linked to a wide variety of other offending behaviours (meaning such degradation is criminogenic (see glossary)) and to wider social harms affecting humans, animals and the wider ecosystem. In so doing the chapter will demonstrate the breadth and complexity of inter-related issues which might form the basis of green criminological analysis and, in so doing, argue that the breadth and complexity of this will require criminologists to think in new ways and adopt fresh methodologies.

By the end of the chapter readers should:

■ Appreciate how criminal law has been used to tackle environmentally destructible behaviours across many jurisdictions.

- Appreciate the difference between 'new crimes' created as a response to environmental degradation and existing crimes precipitated by it (or by authorities' responses to it).
- Understand the links between climate change, displacement of peoples and human trafficking.
- Be aware of the economic impacts of pollution and the resulting crime and social harms.
- Understand the concepts of 'food' and 'water security' and 'environmental security'.
- Begin to understand the methodological difficulties and possible solutions inherent to researching the links between environmental degradation, harm and crime.

In the last chapter it was suggested that environmental degradation might be linked to officially recognised criminal activity in two key ways. Firstly, a number of jurisdictions are at present still expanding the number of environmental crimes and the harshness of penalties attached to them on the statute books, creating 'new' crimes and 'new' criminals: albeit much of this will be *existing* activity only recently being *labelled* as 'criminal'. A key example is the expansion of animal protection law witnessed in numerous jurisdictions (see Nurse, 2013a), as well as restrictions on the use of genetically modified crops (De Geer, 2002). Secondly, it was suggested that environmental degradation might be criminogenic (see p.2), in the sense that it leads to other types of crime. The purpose of this chapter is to discuss these possibilities in more detail. In so doing, it will demonstrate how the social changes brought about through environmental degradation (whether specific 'disaster events' or the more creeping impacts of systemic polluting activities and climate change) will inevitably change the face of crime and criminal justice as well as fostering wider social harms.

Of course, examining the labelling of new crimes and the social factors that prompt criminal behaviour are to some extent basic tenants of mainstream criminology. As the discussion develops, however, it will be demonstrated how the complex interaction of topics and impacts raised by the issues at hand will require criminologists to think in new ways and adopt fresh methodologies beyond their traditional remit. As such, ultimately it will be shown that if criminologists are to achieve a genuine understanding of environmental crime, and certainly 'environmental harm' (in line with the critical perspective set out in Chapter 1) they will need to look beyond traditional criminological theory and method. One of the goals of this chapter is therefore to demonstrate how mainstream criminological perspectives can be enriched (when applied to the environment) by arguments informed by the broader understanding of 'green criminology' discussed in Chapter 1 and, in particular, introduce eco-centric perspectives alongside more traditional anthropocentric views.

THE ENVIRONMENT AND SOCIAL CHANGE

Fundamentally, this chapter sets out to demonstrate the links between changes in the physical environment, crime and the recognition of new forms of social harm. Criminologists have long argued that crime is a product of the social world in the sense that it has no reality separate from human society (Hulsman, 1986). From the perspective of legal theory, this represents a social constructivist view of the (criminal) law whereby law is seen as 'an aspect or field of social experience, not some mysterious force working on it' and that law and social ordering are therefore 'mutually constituting' (Cotterell, 2006: p.25). The implications of this ontological position for the selection of methods when researching this area will be returned to later in the chapter.

In *crime* terms, the perspective outlined above should not be mistaken for an outright dismissal of the rational choice perspective of offending: implying that fundamentally motivated potential offenders weigh advantages and disadvantages before *choosing* whether or not to commit an offence. Indeed, the debate between proponents of rational choice theories of criminality versus more deterministic ideas (suggesting criminal actions are predetermined by social or biological factors beyond the individual's control) still drives much of mainstream criminology (Kroneberg and Kalter, 2012). The observation is rather that many authors have questioned the thesis of natural law (the idea that law, or at least some law, is universal and determined by nature), preferring instead the notion that law (especially criminal law) is the product of complex social processes and interactions, and thus adapts itself along with social change (Burr, 2003). A simple example from recent history is the previous criminalisation of homosexuality in many jurisdictions and its still more recent decriminalisation, reflecting developed social attitudes on the issue (see Asal et al., 2013). Indeed Jones (2013) has argued that it is in fact very difficult to identify *any* human activity that has been universally deemed 'criminal' by all societies at all times in history. A more pertinent example for the present discussion rests in the expansion of animal rights laws, even in parts of the world traditionally lacking such regulations (see Park and Singer, 2012). We saw in Chapter 1 that debate often exists as to whether such legislation is truly eco-centric, recognising animals as having *inherent* worth beyond their service to human needs (Nurse, 2013b), but clearly these laws do reflect greater social censure of animal abuse in many jurisdictions in line with conceptions of animal rights (see Chapter 8) and the notion of species justice discussed in Chapter 1.

Of course, many legal philosophers have defended the natural law perspective (George, 2001; Moreno-Riaño, 2005; Finnis, 2011) and it is not the purpose of this chapter to draw in-depth conclusions in this regard. What can be said however is that, at the very least, social change has a large impact on those activities which make it onto the statute books as officially recognised crimes and those which do not, and indeed even those covered by civil and regulatory regimes (see glossary). Even if social harms do not become recognised as 'official' crimes or covered by regulation, society neverthe-less may acknowledge such harms (like animal abuse) as being undesirable. On this point we might look to the philosophy of Hans Boutellier (2000) who argues that, as the processes of globalisation and secularisation go on, common standards of morality decline but common appreciation and sym-pathy for the impacts on those who have suffered harm remains, and that this becomes a barometer for shared moral values. Boutellier refers to this as the 'victimalization of morality'. Boutellier's thought is anthropocentric (based on the suffering of *humans*) but as green criminologists we might see the effect he describes extending to societal condemnation of harm to the environment itself and to non-human animals regardless of the official *criminalisation* of such activities (see Nurse, 2013a).

In sum, as changes in the natural environment continue, this is likely to affect the societies who live in that environment and therefore lead to changes in both official crimes and more generalised views on what is 'harmful'. For these purposes, I include within the concept of 'social change' devel-opments in scientific knowledge itself and society's reactions to the potential harms these developments can bring or, as Giddens (1990) would have it, the man-made risks. The development of nuclear energy was discussed in Chapter 1. More recent examples might include the development of fracking technologies (see p.15 and Chapter 4) and notions of 'Biopiracy' (see Box 1).

Box 1: Biopiracy

In recent years increased attention has been paid to the subject of pharmaceutical and bio-technology companies exploiting the properties of plants either for medical purposes or to produce genetically modified crops. There are generally two aspects to this. Firstly, the anthropocentric aspect is the concern that companies take knowledge developed for generations by marginalised cultures and exploit these for financial gain without the permission of those communities and certainly without any recompense Von Lewinski, 2008). De Geer (2002) gives the example of a traditional nutritious drink called *pozol* passed down for generations by the Mayan people of Mexico. In 1999, the Dutch corporation Quest International in conjunction with the University of Minnesota patented the chemical structure of the active component of the drink and then refuse to recognise the Indigenous knowledge used to develop it. The more eco-centric concern is that these practices represent a threat to biodiversity, either because the geneti-cally modified crops produced dominate other varieties or because it leads to the over-farming of the natural resource (Shiva, 1997).

The chief response of the international community has been the 2011 Nagoya Pro-tocol on Access to Genetic Resources and the Fair and Equitable Sharing of Benefits

Arising from their Utilization (ABS) to the Convention on Biological Diversity of 1992. The Convention and the Protocol (see p.125 for an explanation of these instruments under international law) have prompted legislation in signature countries and the coining of the term 'biopiracy' to describe such activities (although the term 'biopiracy' does not appear within the documents themselves; the term was actually first coined by Rural Advancement Foundation International in 1991, during the Uruguay round of negotiations towards the General Agreement on Tariffs and Trade (Shiva, 1997)). In practice the *criminal* law has not always been utilised to implement either the Convention or its Protocol, but the use of the term 'piracy' is an interesting indication of the crime-like impressions that have developed surrounding such activities.

In a major test case – being called the first prosecution for biopiracy (Laursen, 2012) – Indian officials have recently begun a prosecution of the major bio-tech giant Monsanto for allegedly using local eggplant varieties to develop a genetically modified version (Bt Brinjal) without prior approval of the competent authorities under India's Biological Diversity Act of 2002. The example of biopiracy therefore demonstrates a situation in which scientific development itself has led to new social problems (with anthropocentric and eco-centric implications) and thus new forms of crime.

The general proposition that environmental change impacts on harm and crime via social changes is illustrated in Figure 2.1.

This chapter and Figure 2.1 in particular present the outcome of this process as '*changes* in crime/regulation/harm' because it is important to appreciate that environmental change is not likely to equate simply with 'more crime' or 'more harm'. So, for example, the *amount* of crime committed may well change but so too may rates of *reporting* (environmental and other) crimes. In addition, environmental change may lead to different *patterns* of crime and offending and also to change in public sensibilities to environmental harm and how it should be dealt with (for example whether through civil or criminal mechanisms or through public or private law, see p.33).

The remainder of this chapter will be split into three broad components. Firstly it will offer a relatively brief discussion of some relevant examples of

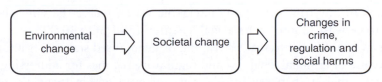

Figure 2.1 Environmental change and changes in crime and harm

how *more* crime relating directly to environmental degradation is being created on statute books in individual jurisdictions and internationally. More detailed discussion of the problems of criminalising such action, along with comparisons between criminal, civil and administrative regimes (see glossary) in this respect, will follow in Chapter 3. For now the point will simply be made that, despite recent trends towards greater use of civil and administrative remedies in environmental cases in many jurisdictions, society's changed views of the environment have nevertheless resulted in a great deal of new criminal legislation as well as increased penalties being attached to existing environmental crimes. Secondly, this chapter will examine three case studies of 'social change' brought about as a result of alterations to the environment and discuss how these may (and already do) lead to crime and to wider social harms. The case studies will be changes in population distributions, economic changes and changes in perceived levels of security. The chapter will then conclude with some discussion of how (green) criminologists can best study these changes and the (adapted) methods they will need to do so.

ENVIRONMENTAL CHANGE AND THE CREATION OF 'NEW' CRIMES

Although the widespread criminalisation of environmental harms is a relatively new legal phenomenon, it is not without historical antecedents. McMurry and Ramsey (1986) for example describe how 'In fourteenth century England the Crown prescribed capital punishment for Englishmen who defied a royal proclamation on smoke abatement' (p.113). Furthermore, Roughton (2007) has discussed how religious scholars have begun to rediscover and reapply environmental precepts of centuries-old Islamic (shariah) law. In modern times, the imposition of criminal liability for environmental harms has existed in the United Kingdom at least since the Forestry Act of 1967. In the United States, one can trace the criminalisation of environmental harms back to the Refuse Act of 1899, which prohibited 'the dumping of material of any kind in any place on the bank of any navigable water, or on the bank of any tributary of any navigable water, where the same shall be liable to be washed into such navigable water' (33 USC s.407).

It is in fact difficult to make sweeping or generalised statements about the relative use of criminal, civil law and regulatory regimes for addressing environmental matters between jurisdictions, or even within them. Frequently such legal regimes have in fact overlapped. So, for example, while Bell et al.

(2013) are almost certainly correct to argue that, in the United Kingdom, the *criminal* law has been the 'traditional' means of addressing environmental degradation (only recently giving way to the use of more civil sanctions) the *application* of criminal law in that jurisdiction has frequently been to punish breaches of *administrative systems*, especially licensing regimes (Mandiberg and Faure, 2009). In many other jurisdictions criminal law has thus far played a more secondary role to administrative sanctions and civil penalties in the environmental sphere, including in the United States (Woods and Macrory, 2003). Debates concerning the relative use and merits of criminal, civil and administrative systems in the area of environmental degradation will be discussed in greater detail in Chapter 3.

Most authors seem to agree that an expansion of officially recognised environmental crime gathered significant pace in many jurisdictions through the 1980s, 1990s and into the 2000s, marked in the United States by the establishment in 1982 of the EPA's Office of Criminal Enforcement (see Marzulla and Kappel, 1991). Such developments took place in the context of developing scientific and social recognition of the present and future problems brought about through environmental degradation, pollution and climate change. According to the UK House of Commons Environmental Audit Committee (2004) there were around 10,000 criminal prosecutions for environmental crimes annually in England and Wales by 2003. Bell and McGillivray (2008) cite 17 distinct environmental offences on the statute books in the United Kingdom by 2007. In May 2011 the UK Environment Agency announced that its successful prosecutions for waste crimes resulted in fines totalling £3 million in 2010, this amount having doubled over the previous five years.

In illustrating an upward trend in the use of criminal sanctions for environmental cases throughout the 1990s Kubasek et al. (2000) draw examples from the United States, Canada, the Netherlands, Ireland and Spain, concluding that 'the increasing use of criminal sanctions to encourage compliance [with environmental law] worldwide seems to be an undisputable trend' (p.158). The importance (and costs) associated with such criminalisation have been exemplified recently by the criminal prosecutions levied at Walmart by the US Department of Justice for violations of the Clean Water Act (constituted by illegally handling and disposing of hazardous materials at its outlets) and also for violations of the Federal Insecticide, Fungicide and Rodenticide Act (FIFRA) (as a result of failures to properly handle pesticides). In pleading guilty to all charges, Walmart was fined $110 million (see Indian Express, 2013).

Despite their broad conclusions, Kubasek et al. (2000) in fact restrict their analysis to Western jurisdictions, but a trend towards criminalisation is still in evidence further afield in to the 21st century. In China, the National People's Congress Standing Committee has recently introduced criminal sanctions, including heavy fines and prison sentences, to anyone prosecuted of adding poisonous or harmful ingredients during the production of food (CNTV, 2011). At the time of writing, both Japanese and Russian authorities have recently announced plans to increase criminal penalties for wildlife crimes and, in the case of Russia, introduced a crime of wildlife trafficking (WWF, 2013). Box 2 further examines recent moves in China to promote at least the *rhetoric* of serious criminal penalties being attributed to environmental transgressions.

Box 2: Environmental crime in China

In June 2013 The Supreme Court of the People's Republic of China issued a joint statement with the Procuratorate (the body responsible for criminal prosecutions and investigations in the country) laying out a new judicial interpretation concerning the enforcement and punishment of breaches in environment-related laws and regulations. The statement acknowledged previous 'lax and superficial' enforcement of such laws and called for 'harsher punishments' which 'in the most serious cases' could include the death penalty (RT, 2013). The announcement met with considerable criticism from human rights organisations (Environmental Leader, 2013) and the move represents a significant departure by China from its traditional stance of softer regulation and little criminalisation in the environmental sphere. Interestingly for the purposes of the present chapter this followed reports of a growth in public interest and condemnation of China's pollution record within the country itself, which had resulted in recent protests (New York Post, 2013). While it must be acknowledged that this statement may be pure rhetoric, the change in approach by the Chinese government also represents an acceptance that the benefits to the state of continued growth should be balanced by environmental concerns, an issue which will be discussed in more detail in chapters 4 and 5.

To take another example, in South Africa the government now runs a dedicated 'Environmental Crimes and Incidents Hotline' and has in recent years raised awareness of environmental crime and its reporting thorough high-profile publicity campaigns (Environment, 2013). More recently, Walters and Westerhuis (2013) in their discussion of the widening use of 'environmental courts' in New South Wales have noted how 'judicial processing of environmental or "green" crimes is rapidly developing across many jurisdictions' (p.279) and that Australia in particular has played a lead role in this development.

Of course, the fact that previously legal activities (albeit in some cases subject to licensing) are now defined and processed as 'criminal' means more people, companies and bodies are being brought within the ambit of the criminal law, a process often associated with the criminological term 'net-widening' (Cohen, 1985). As such, such changes are not (necessarily) reflective of a true 'increase' in the number of environmentally harmful activities taking place in any given jurisdiction, but rather constitute a reclassification of existing activities in response to changed societal views. Of course, in keeping with the radical criminological critique discussed in Chapter 1, it is important to acknowledge that any 'societal views' reflected by changes to legislation (or enforcement practice) are unlikely to represent the perspectives of *all* members of any given society democratically, but rather will be dominated by the concerns of that society's most powerful interest groups who have the facilities and influence to effect change.

The expansion of the *criminal* law in this area has also occurred in response to international instruments and the development of what is now a discrete area of international environmental law (Braithwaite, 2000a). Key examples include the 1992 Basel Convention on the Control of Transboundary Movements of Hazardous Wastes and Their Disposal, the United Nations 1992 Framework Convention on Climate Change (UNFCCC) and the 1992 Rio CBD Convention on Biological Diversity, along with its 2010 Protocol on Access to Genetic Resources and the Fair and Equitable Sharing of the Benefits Arising from their Utilization (2010) (see p.125 for an explanation of such instruments under international law). More generally at the international level, Walters and Westerhuis (2013) have discussed the proliferation of international policing initiatives set up to tackle environmental crime such as the Interpol Environmental Crimes Committee, the United Nations Development Goals, the Lusaka Agreement, the Asian Regional Partners Forum on Combating Environmental Crime (ARPEC) and the Partnership Against Transnational Crime through Regional Organized Law Enforcement. In addition, international NGOs such as TRAFFIC (the wildlife trade monitoring network) have been very active in holding governments to account for failures in their domestic regulations concerning the trade of animals and plants. Indeed a joint report by TRAFFIC and the World Wide Fund for Nature (WWF) into the legal structures available in Russia directly prompted recent reform to the criminal law, mentioned earlier in this chapter, concerning wildlife trafficking (TRAFFIC, 2013).

Across Europe, the proliferation of criminal offences for environmentally damaging activities has been prompted by the introduction of EU Directive (see glossary) 2008/99/EC on the protection of the environment through the criminal law (for an in-depth review of this development see Mullier, 2010). Directives are key legislative tools of the EU in the sense that they require member states to achieve the objectives set down in them, although they do not proscribe the exact means by which these objectives must be achieved. Thus they must be transposed in national law by individual legislation in member states (as opposed to EU Regulations (see glossary), which are directly enforceable in domestic courts). Thus, the 2008 Directive requires Member States to create legislation which criminalises certain breaches of existing EU environmental law, when previously Member States had the sole responsibility to determine the appropriate sanction. As studies for the European Commission on this issue make clear, there was high variability in both the nature (criminal, civil or administrative) and severity of sanctions imposed, which the Directive was intended to address. More detailed discussion of the content and impact of the Directive will follow in Chapter 5.

Of course, to a criminologist or criminal justice scholar the increase in criminal law and the 'on paper' expansion of criminal liability concerning environmental harm is perhaps less significant than the development of *attitudes* towards the issue. This includes the general acceptance that such activities are serious enough to warrant criminal charges and the willingness of prosecuting bodies (and indeed individual prosecutors) to pursue such cases. Thus, methodologies that prioritise the examination of 'unwritten' working practices within the criminal justice system may be of greater significance here to the green criminologist than black-letter legal analysis (see Holdaway, 1983; Hall, 2009; Reiner, 2010).

Questions concerning the enforcement of environmental law will be discussed in greater detail in Chapter 6. Clearly though the perceived seriousness of these 'new' crimes is also reflected by the fact that they often take the form of 'strict liability' offences (see glossary), meaning no moral blameworthiness, 'guilty frame of mind', negligence or fault on the part of the defendant or operator need be proven. A widespread example is that of road traffic offences like speeding, where the offence is committed regardless of what the offender was thinking while committing the offence, or even knew whether the offence was being committed. While this is perhaps understandable in the domain of corporate crime (see Brickey, 1982), the majority of such environmental prosecutions in the United Kingdom at least are in fact carried out against individuals (Bell and McGillivray (2008). The issue of corporate crime further illustrates a point made by Mullier (2010) that environmental criminal law necessitates a marked development of the whole concept of corporate liability. Thus, the increase in crime as a result of such measures derives not only from the number of offences created, but also from changes in attitudes as to the *kinds of bodies* which should be held criminally responsible for their actions. As such, the concept of corporate liability for environmental crime will be discussed in more detail in Chapter 4. Looking further ahead, and into the fields of transnational and international law, such development might result in notions of state crime and state liability for polluting nations becoming more accepted, and indeed there is already a significant literature in the field of international environmental law on this point (Beirne et al., 2009) that will be discussed in Chapter 5.

Of course, sociological considerations may also *limit* the number of polluting activities defined as criminal, as well as expand them. At present the dark figure of environmental crime (i.e. those crimes which are missed by official statistics) is thought to be much greater than that associated with most other forms of criminal activity (Simon, 2000). Bell and McGillivray (2008) explain this discrepancy with the observation that, although there are significant numbers of known breaches of environmental legislation, the proportion of prosecutions or other enforcement action is very low. The authors go on to describe the different enforcement strategies employed by agencies charged with environmental regulation and prosecutions, which range from the formal to the informal, and the cooperative to the sanctioning. As the authors conclude:

> This is not merely a theoretical consideration: the extent to which pollution or other environmental harm is viewed as a 'crime' by operators, regulators, and the general public is a factor that influences such things as whether to enforce and how to sanction or punish offenders. Thus, the moral opprobrium that attaches to environmental crime influences the exercise of discretion in taking enforcement action – that is, which power to exercise or whether to prosecute – and in sanctioning pollution by taking into account mitigating factors when sentencing. (Bell and McGillivray, 2008: p.259)

Thus, the old criminological standpoint that *law* does not make crime, but rather *attitudes* make crime, appears to hold true for the environmental sphere (Schur, 1969). The question then becomes how such attitudes will change in the face of growing certainly as to the causes of environmental deprivation and the practical impacts this will have on increasingly scarce resources.

THE CRIMINOGENIC NATURE OF ENVIRONMENTAL DEGRADATION

The creation of new 'environmental crimes' on paper, even when coupled with the effects of changes in attitudes in favour of more robust enforcement, is likely to constitute only the tip of the iceberg when it comes to social harms and indeed criminal activities linked with changes to the environment. As already noted in this chapter, changes to the environment will impact on society in many diverse ways. This section sets out three such changes brought about by environmental degradation and discusses how they might lead to further harms and further officially recognised crimes, and indeed how this process is already well underway.

Population changes, migrations and human trafficking

The impacts of environmental degradation, and in particular here the effects of climate change, on migration patterns constitute an illustrative example of the process illustrated in Figure 2.1 whereby changes in the environment have a knock-on effect for society and ultimately to crime/social harms or, in this case, the *perception* of crime and disorder. The relevance of immigration here stems from the expected increase in displaced people and forced migrations, as well as a general increase in poverty, in the parts of the world which are hardest hit by climate change (McAdam, 2012). Especially pertinent examples are the areas of Africa bordering the Sahara where usable croplands are being eroded by the marked encroachment of the desert (Odorico et al., 2013). Consequently, population shift from these regions to northern Europe is a real possibility, and indeed already constitutes a recognised social phenomenon (Goff, 2012).

Recent studies of the relationship between immigration and crime have suggested that, rather than being associated with increases in offending, immigration in fact appears to reduce crime (Sampson, 2008). However, while crime rates may go down, public *perceptions* of disorder and the *fear* of crime may rise. Put simply, people would appear to assume that disorder goes hand in hand with concentrations of minority groups when the opposite is in fact true. As such, Sampson also found that the concentration of Latinos in a neighbourhood was strongly related to perceptions of disorder, regardless of the actual amount of disorder in that neighbourhood. Similarly, Chiricos et al. (1997) found that perceptions of the racial composition of a neighbourhood and levels of reported anxiety about crime were related to one another. Relatedly, research into punitive attitudes has suggested that the percentage of African Americans in the county is a significant predictor of support for capital punishment in the United States (Baumer et al., 2003) while areas with large or growing minority populations tend to show growing support for right-wing politicians (Giles and Buckner, 1993).

If environmental refugees are socially and geographically excluded from towns and cities (either deliberately or because the institutions and organisations of civil society are unable to cope with the level of demand), this may see increase in 'shanty towns' on the edge of cities (or at key border points), as has recently been witnessed in Greece (Squires and Anast, 2009). Under such conditions, we might speculate that values of multiculturalism and assimilation may be seriously challenged, possibly leading to increases in racism and xenophobia, all surrounded by concerns related to the preservation of cultures and identities (see Keith, 2005). As well as increased immigration to Europe, there may well be increased migration within Europe, partly as a 'knock-on' effect, but also as a result of some parts of Europe becoming uninhabitable or less desirable.

In sum, increased community tension and a rise in anxiety prompted by immigration (Norgaard, 2006) may express itself as 'fear of crime' (Farrall et al., 2009) and other associated social harms, increasing pressures for punitive sentences. Evidence from criminology literature also suggests that while crime may actually go down as a result of escalating climate change, anxiety about crime, punitive attitudes and intolerance may all increase in countries receiving a mass influx of immigrants.

A further significant change in the landscape of crime and harm promoted by the displacement of peoples/forced migrations lies in the links that have been drawn in more recent years between this and human trafficking (see Lee, 2007). Indeed, returning to an African example, it has been reported that Masaai parents in the Mar region of Kenya, where climate change is already having noticeable effects on crops, are selling their young underage daughters to a group of human traffickers posing as foreign tourists (Women's News Network, 2010). The disproportionate impact of this and other forms of 'environmental victimisation' on women will be discussed in greater detail in Chapter 7.

The United Nations University's Institute for Environment and Human Security (Warner et al., 2008) has drawn specific links between migrations *forced by environmental factors* and a susceptibility of these displaced individuals to human trafficking. Jasparro and Taylor (2008) have also commented on the links between climate change and human trafficking and wildlife trafficking arguing that:

> Southeast Asian livelihood and social systems will be pressured, while state and civil society capacity will be strained. This will intensify existing vulnerabilities to non-state security threats and raise the overall level of vulnerability and risk to both human and state security. (p.1)

In Europe too human trafficking is already a high concern for Member States (Shelley, 2007). It is submitted that the effects of climate change are likely to create a further pull in the direction of stringent collaborative action, with implications for the human rights of those trafficked – many of whom end up working in illegal and poorly regulated sectors of the economy, once again impacting upon levels of crime (see Lee, 2007). Notably, Jasparro and Taylor (2008) also link climate change to trafficking in illicit firearms and drugs. In the later case a recent example from Italy – where 49 Latin Americans stood trial for allegedly force-feeding packaged cocaine to dogs that were then killed and dismembered on arrival in Italy – reminds us that such harms always have the potential to extend beyond humans (AoL Travel, 2013).

Overall it seems clear that, as a major upheaval for any society, a shift in population prompted by environmental degradation has significant potential to foster actual (i.e. officially criminalised) offending behaviour as well as a variety of wider social harms in the form of increased fear and panic about crime and disorder. Understanding the complexities of these links will require a range of expertise from economists, geographers and political scientists as well as criminologists, sociologists and lawyers. Once again therefore green criminology needs to adopt a firmly interdisciplinary stance.

Economic changes

Environmental degradation may well challenge the viability of some communities not only because their means of physical subsistence (crops, water supplies, etc.) are compromised but also via a number of other economic routes, not least of which is the impact on local industries. This in turn may have criminogenic impacts, which will be examined below. Certainly in the business world, studies have indicated a likely negative impact of climate change on a wide variety of industries ranging from paper production (Jaggi and Freedman, 2006) to the wine industry (Nemani et al., 2001); tourism

(Berrittella et al., 2006) and fishing (Perry et al., 2005). Following from the above discussion firms may in any event decide to relocate to different parts of the world if security (or practical) issues become pressing enough, especially if the situation reaches the level of a significant breakdown in law and order.

Perhaps the more pressing concern, however, is that the increase in environmental regulation and criminalisation of environmentally damaging activities discussed above and in the last chapter will make certain businesses unviable. In the first instance this may of course lead to an increase in what Carrabine et al. (2014) call secondary green crimes (see Chapter 1), meaning crimes resulting from the avoidance or ignoring of environmental laws, in an attempt to avoid the costs of such regulation. In the United States, for example, it is widely acknowledged that criminal organisations are heavily involved in the avoidance of environmental regulation, particularly in relation to waste dumping (D'Amato and Zoli, 2012) and that the distinction between 'legitimate' companies and criminal organisations in this area is decisively blurred (a point to be returned to in Chapter 4).

If some firms are unable to compete given the increased costs of such regulation, this has led some commentators to argue that a trade-off exists between employment levels (at the national and local levels) and increasing environmental standards and associated regulations or criminalisation (see Stewart, 1993). Such effects have been the source of particular contention in the United States, following the original enactment of the Clean Air Act in 1963 and through its subsequent amendments (Morss, 1996). Assuming for the moment that increased environmental regulation may lead to unemployment, linking this to changes to *crime* of course raises the very old criminological question as to whether *unemployment* and crime levels are related. This is not a debate the present chapter will enter into in any great detail but certainly one of the most recent major studies on this issue (Hooghe et al., 2011) concluded from empirical work carried out in Belgium that unemployment did lead to upsurges in crime. Indeed, in this project the robustness of the results made the authors able to expand their conclusions beyond all previous work in this area:

> Unemployment is positively associated not just with property, but also with violent crime. The impact of unemployment therefore might even be larger and more pervasive than Lin (2008) already argued and certainly this is a relation that needs to be investigated further in future research. (p.14)

Of course, in some parts of the world, local unemployment may lead to those out of work entering into more profitable illegal businesses such as, for example, wildlife trafficking (see Nurse, 2013a). Clearly secondary green crimes also have implications for the environment itself. As such, the resulting criminal activities discussed in this chapter are not exclusively human-centred.

The impact of environmental regulation on employment levels is however a highly contested issue, with Goodstein (1994) dismissing the alleged trade-off as a 'myth'. There is indeed increasing evidence to support the dismissal of this link, although again much of this research has been confined to the United States. Levinson (1996) for example offers statistical evidence to the effect that 'interstate differences in environmental regulations do not system-atically affect the location choices of most manufacturing plants' (p.5). In the United States, Northeast States for Coordinated Air Use Management (2011) has argued that, far from causing unemployment and economic degradation in the northeast/mid-Atlantic region, the introduction of programmes to pro-mote clean transportation fuels will in fact create tens of thousands of jobs each year:

> The results of the analysis suggest that the transition to lower carbon fuels could pro-vide important energy security, climate change, and economic benefits in the region. For example, electricity, advanced biofuels, and natural gas are low carbon fuels not yet widely used in the region for transportation. A gradual transition to one or more of these fuels would reduce carbon emissions and those of other harmful pollutants, enhance energy independence and reduce vulnerability to price swings in imported petroleum, and create jobs in the region. (p.9)

Furthermore, a review of studies published by The Lancet Series on Cli-mate Change (Watts, 2010) suggests similarly positive outcomes of attempts to address environmental polluting activities when any negative economic impacts are weighed against the benefits to health:

> The threat of climate change has generated a global flood of policy documents, sug-gested technical fixes, and lifestyle recommendations. One widely held view is that their implementation would, almost without exception, prove socially uncomfortable and economically painful. But as a series of new studies shows, in one domain at least – public health – such a view is ill founded. If properly chosen, action to com-bat climate change can, of itself, lead to improvements in health. The news is not all bad. (p.2)

There has been some counter-argument that those advocating such a positive view of environmental regulation and its effect on industry and employment are also those with more eco-activist credentials (see Vogel, 2003). By contrast, for example, Davies (2013) has recently presented a detailed case study of impacts to the local community of Lynemouth in the United Kingdom following the closure of a major smelter plant run by Rio-Tinto Alcan (one of the world's largest producers of aluminium). The closure followed economic assessments by the parent firm which, in short form, concluded that the costs of complying with increased environmental regulatory regimes made the plant economically unsustainable. The plant had been the major local employer for the community and Davies uses this study to illustrate the tensions that often exist in practice between notions of 'ecological justice' and 'social justice' (see Chapter 1). This ongoing debate serves as a good illustration of a point made by White (2011) that the 'objective' nature of 'science' and 'knowledge' in this area must always be subject to scrutiny when 'doing' green criminology.

Crime resulting from the avoidance of environmental regulation or following increased levels of unemployment may not be the only criminogenic effects in evidence following a shift in economic pressures fostered by changes in the environment. Hall and Farrall (2013), for example, have highlighted how the increase in regulatory processes to tackle environmental crime also bring increased costs for the local and national governments charged with enforcing them, which are likely to be passed on to the taxpayer. Indeed, a form of so-called eco-tax is already in operation in Germany and in parts of the United States (Jackson, 2000). In the United Kingdom, increased taxation on polluting industries was a contentious issue in the first years of the present Conservative/Liberal Democrat coalition government (Harvey, 2011). Since many people may not wish to pay increased rates of taxation, so rates of taxation avoidance may increase as a response, especially when such taxes are politically unpopular and are met with suspicion by the electorate (see Brown, 2008). Thus, in contrast to the social attitudes in favour of prosecuting polluters in criminal courts, those same public attitudes may not consider the avoidance of taxes intended to fund environmental projects as representing 'real' criminality. This will not just have consequences for those services provided for by taxation, but will also see increases demands placed upon those who regulate and police taxation systems.

Another example of the broader economic impact of environmental degradation lies in the insurance sector. In 2009 the International Association for the Study of Insurance Economics acknowledged that climate change would inevitably lead to higher costs 'largely due to socio-economic factors such as value concentrations in coastal areas' (International Association for the

Study of Insurance Economics, 2009: p.42). Higher costs may lead to an erosion of confidence in the insurance sector, and to widespread mis- or over-claiming among consumers. In 2004, Karstedt and Farrall (2006) asked citizens in England & Wales about the extent to which they trusted their insurers to make them a fair offer during a claim; around 20% said that they did not. They also asked people if they had ever been offered less by their insurer than they felt that were entitled to; 27% said that this had happened at least once to them. When asked if they were worried about being left out of pocket on an insurance claim some 39% said that they were very or fairly worried about this possibility. Five percent said that they had deliberately cheated on an insurance claim. Insurance may seem like an odd service to highlight in a discussion of the consequences of environmental degradation for crime and social harms. However, for many people who see themselves as 'non-criminal' or 'non-deviant' insurance claims offer one arena in which they can extract (an illegal) profit without feeling that they are offending. As insurers become more selective about who or what they are prepared to cover and how much of an excess they are prepared to request, so insurance clients may seek to gain redress via such scams.

The above subsection has demonstrated the complex interaction between changes in the environment, the economy and crime and other social harms. It is of course impossible to cover *all* means by which economic changes may result in crime and victimisation (on which, see Chapter 7). Nevertheless, approaching the question from an economic angle is useful in that it allows judgements to be made regarding the cost-effectiveness of mechanisms intended to reduce environmental degradation and also systems of regulation or criminalisation. Indeed, attempts by collaborations of economists, criminologists and victimologists to express the impacts of more traditional crimes in economic terms have recently gathered pace (Loomes, 2007; Cook et al., 2012) and is only likely to continue as green criminology becomes more established.

Changes in security

In recent years, ideas regarding 'security' have been increasingly linked to environmental concerns to produce a distinct literature on 'environmental security' (see Hough, 2012). Definitions of environmental security differ, with no overarching understanding yet agreed upon (see Heckler, 2011), but generally the concept tends to link environmental degradation and the associated scarcity of resources with human conflict at individual, group and state levels. Brunnèe (1995) conceives it as 'the prevention and management of conflicts precipitated by environmental decline' (p.1742). Although typically limited to the field of armed conflicts, some understandings of environmental security incorporate a wider body of threats to the natural environment (Ullman, 1983). Furthermore, Hsiang et al. (2013) have recently presented evidence that changes in the climate are associated with increased violence and conflict:

> A rapidly growing body of research examines whether human conflict can be affected by climatic changes. Drawing from archaeology, criminology, economics, geography, history, political science, and psychology, we assemble and analyze the 60 most rigorous quantitative studies and document, for the first time, a remarkable convergence of results. We find strong causal evidence linking climatic events to human conflict across a range of spatial and temporal scales and across all major regions of the world. (p.2054)

In recent years the concept of environmental security has led some commentators to speak of 'environmental terrorism', which Chalecki (2001) defines as 'the unlawful use of force against in situ environmental resources so as to deprive populations of their benefit(s) and/or destroy other property' (p.3). Schofield (1999) adds to this the use of the environment as a conduit for destruction (such as poisoning the water supply of an urban centre). While this is a contested topic, Schwartz (1998) discusses how environmental terrorism has gained considerable public, political and academic support since the early 1990s, even before the terrorist attacks in the United States of September 2001. Thus, by 2008, New York City was spending a $12 million grant from the US Environmental Protection Agency on its Water Security Initiative, a pilot programme to develop and evaluate a contamination warning system for its drinking water distribution network. There have also been marked concerns voiced regarding the possibility of terrorist attacks on oil pipelines in Russia and Central Asia. Schwartz also called for the creation of a new international crime of 'ecocide' to reflect the social condemnation of such deliberate acts of wasteful environmental destruction, which is a cause gathering some momentum in the literature and among NGOs (see generally Agnew, 2013).

For the purposes of this present discussion, the important observation is that, as natural resources become restricted by the various impacts of climate change and wider environmental degradation, this is likely to make such resources increasingly precious to states and therefore increasingly attractive to terrorist groups seeking to achieve symbolic victories. In keeping with the above discussion, the response of governments is again likely to be increased regulation and the rollout of harsher penalties (and new crimes) for environmental terrorists, just as the scope of 'terrorism' itself was expanded in many jurisdictions in the light of the 2001 US terrorists attacks (Mythen and Walklate, 2006). In sum, once again, the proliferation of environmental degradation shows itself to be criminogenic.

While the impact of threats to environmental security in general are very real, for many they are perhaps less immediate or widespread than the dangers posed by the more specific threat to 'food security'. Food security has been defined by the World Food Summit of 1996 as existing 'when all people at all times have access to sufficient, safe, nutritious food to maintain a healthy and active life' (United Nations Food and Agriculture Organization, 2010). The concept is usually understood as including both physical and economic access to food that meets people's dietary needs as well as their food preferences (Pinstrup-Andersen, 2009). At present much of the literature and policy attention in various countries has focused on the immediate health and humanitarian implications of food (and water (Bakker, 2012)) security coming under threat (see Box 3), however the legal and criminogenic implications are also beginning to be assessed. MacLeod et al. (2010) for example have written at length on the introduction of regulative frameworks intended to preserve food security. This chapter has already noted the tightening of regulation concerning the production of food in China (CNTV, 2011) and such adjustments have also been commented on in Bangladesh (Ali, 2013) and in India (Indian Express, 2010), where adulteration of food has been a major health concern. Across Europe anti-adulteration legislation was largely rolled out due to the so-called Food Hygienic Package of regulations introduced by the European Commission in 2004.

Box 3: Water Security in Chile

Chile (along with South Africa) faces some of the greatest challenges in the world concerning water security. This has been defined as an acceptable level of water-related risks to humans and ecosystems, coupled with the availability of water of sufficient quantity and quality to support livelihoods, national security, human health and ecosystem services (Bakker, 2012). Geographically Chile is the longest north/south trending country in the world, meaning climate conditions vary quite dramatically. Thus, while Chile has large water reserves in the South, the North faces considerable threats to water security. According to Global Water Partnership (2013), the key threats to water security in the country derive from:

- Water pollution from raw sewage.
- Active volcanism due to more than three-dozen active volcanoes along the Andes Mountains.
- Tsunamis.
- Widespread deforestation and mining threaten natural resources.
- Severe earthquakes.
- Air pollution from industrial and vehicle emissions.

Notably this list represents a combination of man-made and natural threats, demonstrating the point made in Chapter 1 that distinguishing between these two categories of risk is one of the hallmarks of green criminological debate.

Chile is particularly noted for its response to these problems in the form of the 1981 and 2005 Water Codes, in which water rights are protected as transferable private property. This system has fostered much debate within the country itself and in the wider literature. In particular, prior to the 2005 reform speculative acquisition of water rights by big businesses (notably Endesa Chile, the country's largest electricity generator, at one point accumulated 80% of the country's non-consumptive rights) impeded growth by smaller firms and restricted supplies generally. As summarised by (Azzopardi, 2012):

> A market system [of water rights] only works if there are enough rights to go around and this is not the case in much of Chile. Rapid economic expansion over the last three decades has seen water consumption skyrocket in some valleys. A couple of years of below average rainfall have left large areas of central and northern Chile in crisis, with fruit withered and livestock dying. The situation is likely to worsen as demand continues to rise and global climate change makes Chile hotter and drier. Rising temperatures are already reducing the amount of snow and ice that accumulates in the Andes Mountains during the winter and spring. (unpaginated)

More recently there have been calls to nationalise water in Chile, ostensibly to reduce speculation, although it has been suggested that the backers of this proposal (an alliance of environmentalists and legislators) have ulterior motives such as limiting the expansion of hydropower or exercising greater control of key industries by restricting access to water. In sum, the situation in Chile demonstrates how environmental change and the regulation of the environment remain value-laden, political issues.

It had been widely predicted that the impact of climate change on crop levels would lead to a drop in supply and therefore a rise in the price of food, with obvious implications for food security (see Schanbacher, 2010). This effect was confirmed by Lobell et al. in May 2011. Of course, a rise in the price of food itself has many criminogenic implications. Clearly given such a situation there is a concern that the poorest people will turn to the illegal food markets. As well as being criminal as of themselves, such illegal markets will undoubtedly be run by those who will be willing to use threats or actual violence to ensure that they get their price they want for the goods they sell, and who may also be involved in other allied trades (such as the supply of weapons, drugs and the control of prostitution). 'Grey' markets may also arise wherein food producers, under pressure to maintain both high supply and low prices, find themselves under increased pressure to cut corners or to adulterate their product (Mandalia, 2005). This is another secondary green crime which may extend beyond anthropocentric impacts if resulting (illegal) use of pesticides damages the sustainability of crop verities (Walters, 2006) or if, for example, meat producers cut costs by reducing standards of care for animals raised for slaughter and consumption (Grandin, 2006).

Lack of food may also lead to localised violence and riots about food prices, as demonstrated by the unrest felt across some 20 countries in 2008, when world food prices reached crisis levels (Ivanic and Martin, 2008). In the African context, Takemura (2007) asserts that there is a 'deepening anger and resentment among people at the bottom of society, fostered by a rise in food prices, which could threaten stability in developing countries' (p.273). This is of course is the same effect discussed above in relation to forced migration and, indeed, the author asserts:

> The great threat is global warming. The vast Sahara Desert is encroaching slowly but steadily into cropland. One-third of Sub-Saharan Africans live in drought-prone areas. The effects of global warming are serious indeed because food production relies more than 90 per cent on rainwater. (p.247)

The violence that has been predicted to come as a result of food insecurity may well have already found expression, with some suggesting that food prices helped to trigger the unrest in Tunisia and Egypt in early 2011 (Evans-Pritchard, 2011). Historically food riots are also not alien to the United Kingdom, where they occurred in the 18th century (Thompson, 1991), or to the United States, where the 1862 'Bread Riots' were precipitated by droughts, leading to a reduction in grain and other basic foodstuffs, exasperated by the pressures of the civil war (Steinberg, 2008). Mares (2010) argues that while this may all sound somewhat extreme, there is ample historical evidence that some previous civilisations literally ran out of 'dirt' and collapsed. In short, 'the exhaustion of soil resources across the globe has great potential to create substantial future human insecurity and harm' (p.283).

Environmental degradation therefore undermines security in a number of ways, which have the potential to exert major consequences for human beings and animals in terms of their health, safety and continued prosperity. As such, it can also be gleaned from the above that threats to security may prompt increased deviance, criminal activities and social harms.

SOCIAL CHANGE, ENVIRONMENTAL HARMS AND METHODS FOR GREEN CRIMINOLOGISTS

The above, diverse, discussion is intended to demonstrate the complex inter-action of factors linking environmental change to social change and changes in crime and other social harms. As noted at the beginning of this chapter, a fair proportion of this discussion has raised more traditional criminological ideas about the factors that lead to the creation, committing or reporting of crimes old and new. To some extent, therefore, this is 'the criminology of the environment' rather than 'green criminology' (see Chapter 1). It is nonethe-less important to empathise that much of the 'deviant' behaviour discussed above falls into the legal 'grey area' introduced in Chapter 1, particularly when discussing issues like food adulteration and avoidance of environmen-tal regulatory regimes. Thus, while it can be persuasively argued that the social changes discussed in this chapter will lead to changes in *crime* it is also clear that this will result in changes in wider social harms not neces-sarily recognised as 'criminal', or even civil or administrative, wrongs and expanding well beyond direct environmental degradations. This chapter took three particular case studies of 'social change' to illustrate this effect: changes in population, changes in the economy and changes in security. It will be realised that all three of these areas in fact overlap and – as with other areas of green criminology – strict lines of demarcation are difficult to draw, and in any case are probably undesirable. The point is well made by Walters (2006) in his discussion of genetically modified food and its impact on food security and bio-diversity:

> The production and trade of GM food are important issues for green criminology that provide a mandate for broadening the critical gaze and opening up the debate to alternative avenues of analysis that examine the issues within social, cultural and political frameworks. (p.1)

Furthermore, while the above discussion has focused on environmental degradation leading to different kinds of offending (or otherwise deviant) behaviour it must also be recognised that criminal activities, which on the face of it are not 'environmental', in nature themselves may lead to environmental damage. Liddick (2010) highlights the particularly damaging environmental impacts of illegal drug production:

> The cultivation of illicit crops like the opium poppy and the coca plant has serious environmental consequences, including soil pollution, water pollution, and deforestation ... The refinement of heroin and cocaine also precipitates the dumping of toxic chemicals and other waste by-products into streams and rivers (or the waste is buried, contaminating the soil and groundwater sources) ... Each year in Colombia, 20 million liters of ethyl ether, acetone, ammonia, sulphuric acid, and hydrochloric acid used to produce cocaine are dumped from jungle laboratories into the headwaters of the Amazon and Orinoco rivers. Again, the effects can be devastating. (p.141)

The challenge for the green criminologist wishing to understand the links between the environment, society, social harms and crime therefore lies in taking this wide array of issues and developing research designs which can take our understanding forward in a way that incorporates the broader ideas of eco-centralism and environmental justice highlighted in Chapter 1. In commencing that process, one clear theme that emerges in all the above examples is that new crime and new harms may be fostered by environmental degradation in what may at first be quite unexpected, certainly *indirect*, ways. Furthermore, it is clear from this discussion that the boundaries between notions of 'the environment', 'crime', 'civil wrongs' and 'harm' are in constant flux.

In methodological terms impressions like those discussed in the last paragraph seem to support the adoption by criminologists of a constructionist approach to questions of environmental crime and harms (Strauss et al., 1963). Such an approach acknowledges that social phenomena are being constantly revised and thus reflects the fast-paced changes witnessed in the criminalisation and wider censure of environmental harms displayed above. In terms of epistemology, the above discussions might further imply that an interpretist position must be adopted, rather than the positivist stance that arguably still dominates much of mainstream criminology and will be discussed on p.51 (Vito and Mahhs, 2012). In contrast to the positivist quest for objective measurement, an interpretist position is concerned with *understanding* a *process* whereby environmentally destructive activities come to be thought of as criminal, harmful or perhaps 'deviant' and how this also promotes other harmful activities, rather than trying to *explain* a fixed social phenomenon (Bryman, 2012).

Methodwise the above positions suggest we need to employ techniques that better reflect the dynamic nature of the subject matter. It follows that documentary analysis of (criminal and other) legal instruments and policy discussions related to the environment can only take us so far because, fundamentally, these are *static* representations. That said, the above discussion does generally suggest other qualitative methodologies that tap into the lived experience of environmental degradation (from both anthropocentric and eco-centric perspectives) and its subsequent effects. This might imply qualitative surveys, interviews and focus groups carried out in affected communities. The notion of environmental harm *as a process* also suggests the use of narrative analysis, focused on how people make sense of their experiences through narrative accounts (Maines, 1993) to reflect this temporal component.

A serious shortcoming presents itself at this point if such methods are to be used as the tools of *green* criminology, because all such methods are by their nature anthropocentric. Indeed, this criticism may be levied at the constructivist perspective itself given that to speak of 'the environment' and 'nature' as socially constructed concepts bounds up the whole issue in *human* perceptions of harm and *human* narratives. The question asked by many commentators in the field therefore is how approaches like those outlined above can reflect a more eco-centric perspective, giving a voice to the environment itself and to animals. On this point there have been numerous texts (grounded in philosophy and physical science) arguing that it is possible for humans to derive some genuine understanding of what it is like to be an animal (Nagel, 1974; Daston and Mitman, 2005) or a plant (Stone, 2010). Nevertheless, as criminologists it is clear those non-human aspects of the ecosystem cannot be interviewed or put in a focus group. One might argue that incorporating the work of or interviewing 'experts' in various forms of environmental degradation, animal rights and so on might to some extent stand as proxy but, by definition, this remains the *human* view and as White (2011) observes the objectivity of even traditional scientific knowledge grounded in positivism must be questioned in this area.

The methodological issues raised in the above paragraph will recur throughout the remainder of this volume. For now, perhaps one way to begin addressing these is to acknowledge that the *values* of the researcher inevitably impact upon the nature of the research exercise and its products. Again such an acceptance moves away from the traditional positivistic approach to research dominating much of mainstream criminology during the 20th century but is nevertheless becoming more widely accepted (House and Howe, 1999). That said, in many instances a degree of subjectivism is still often presented in the literature as a 'necessary evil' and something we would prefer not to be the case, chiefly because such values inevitably constitute a form of bias (Bailey, 1994). In the case of environmental harms however it may be argued that the views and values a researcher brings with them are – when appropriately acknowledged, and when steps are taken to ensure the research remains robust – in fact very valuable.

Certainly much of the literature in green criminology at present is clearly influenced by the more eco-centric values of the researchers who tend to become involved in the area. With environmentalism sometimes being labelled as a 'religion' (Maintenay, 2013) this is perhaps unavoidable. While this is indeed a form of bias, it also ensures such eco-centric perspectives are at least reflected in the research despite the anthropocentric tradition of many qualitative methods. Arguably therefore it in fact enhances the research for the researcher to be consciously aware of his or her own values and their influence on the research exercise. It is a perspective that has previously been argued to apply to feminist study: Mies (1993) going so far as to argue that 'value free research' is not only impossible but also manifestly undesirable in this area. Her argument is thus that feminist work should be written *for women* by researchers who are indeed 'consciously partial'. This perspective has bridged feminist and environmental issues in the ecofeminist literature, where a normative (i.e. value-based) standpoint is frequently defended. Nor does research that accepts and even promotes the acceptance of values as a contributor to the research exercise necessarily equate with a sacrifice in quality. On this point Burke and Onwuegbuzie (2013) argue:

> We agree with qualitative researchers that value stances are often needed in research; however, it also is important that research is more than simply one researcher's highly idiosyncratic opinions written into a report. Fortunately, many strategies are recognized and regularly used in qualitative research (such as member checking, triangulation, negative case sampling, pattern matching, external audits) to help overcome this potential problem and produce high-quality and rigorous qualitative research. (p.17)

Thus, certainly in terms of qualitative methodologies, there are many options available to counter the more negative implications of allowing values into our research. In sum, therefore, adapting traditionally anthropocentric, qualitative, research methods grounded in constructivist ontology to the service of green criminology arguably necessitates researchers approaching their topic consciously from a more eco-centric stance. Such researchers then need to fully acknowledge this to be the case and actively pursue further strategies to ensure the robustness of the findings.

The above paragraphs notwithstanding, it is important not to dismiss more positivistic-inspired methodologies as forming part of the repertoire of green criminology (although it must here be noted here that qualitative methods can also be grounded in positivism (Lin, 1998). Quantitative data analysis may in fact constitute another means whereby a more eco-centric perspective can be injected into the exercise: in that while we cannot ascertain the view of, for example, birds whose flight patterns are affected by wind farms (Marris and Fairless, 2010; Drewitt and Langston, 2006), we can derive statistical estimates of how many birds are affected and to what extent. Of course, ultimately such statistics are generated by human 'experts' and thus we must be wary of any claim (as is ever the case) that they in fact present an objective reality, much less an eco-centric one. Nevertheless, quantitative methods are also very good at establishing connections between different variables. So, returning to an example from earlier in this chapter, quantitative analysis may hold the key to determining whether increased environmental regulation ultimately leads to unemployment and then to increased crime levels. So long as the researcher is aware that such statistical insights do not necessarily paint the whole picture – for example, even if employment does not go down the social changes evident above may lead to crime and harms in many other ways – it seems there is a real case for both perspectives in green criminology even though, as a matter of methodological theory, they are grounded in very different epistemological and ontological positions.

On this last point, it is important in closing this section to emphasise the growing acceptance of so-called mixed methods research across the social sciences, which essentially discounts traditional divides between qualitative and quantitative research and argues against an unduly rigid focus on epistemological and ontological differences. Burke and Onwuegbuzie (2004) for example argue strongly in favour of such methods. More recently, Campbell et al. (2011, p.377) highlight the utility of mixed-methods approaches in examining 'complex phenomena in real-world settings whereby the use of one single method would be unlikely to reveal a complete picture' (p.377). In this sense, the 'correct' methods to use in different situations may reflect the principles of pragmatism (see Robson, 2011). It is interesting to note here that, while 'green criminology' is a new and developing area, this methodological direction in fact reflects more recent ideas concerning methods seen in wider criminology (see Fielding, 2010).

Summary

This chapter has demonstrated that environmental changes, changes in crime and changes in social harms are inexorably linked. Not only has the greater social censure of environmental degradation resulted in the expanded criminalisation of such activities (and harsher punishments) in some jurisdictions, environmental degradation in itself appears to foster more crime and wider social harms (some feeding back to the environment, some not). These are not just harms to humans, but impacts on animals, plants and the ecosystem as a whole. The chapter provided three key examples of the social impacts of environmental change and demonstrated how they have already lead to social harms, and in all likelihood will continue to do so. The examples themselves – population changes, economic changes and changes in security – are illustrative only and by no means constitute a definitive list of relevant social changes potentially of interest to green criminology or indeed to the criminologies of the environment, climate change and so on.

In moving green criminology forward as a subject area, the preceding discussion suggests the focus should be on social constructivist methodologies as a means of understanding the fluid links between environments, harm and crime: although it was acknowledged that these methods themselves are often anthropocentric. In order to address this shortfall (from the green perspective) it was suggested that (following the lead of some feminists and ecofeminism) green criminology might exploit the positive aspects of the researcher's values affecting research outputs. In particular, through the conscious acknowledgement of such values and adapting strategies to mitigate their less desirable effects on a project the researcher can strive towards greater balance between eco-centricity and the anthropocentric. It was also argued that green criminology needs to embrace the recent trends towards mixed methods research. Thus, in generally moving away from positivism (albeit still utilising more positivistic methods when pragmatic to do so), embracing constructivism and acknowledging less concern about objectivism in its ontological position, researchers can take more mainstream criminological methodological standpoints and move beyond them in a way that begins to address the wider question posed by green criminology. That said, it is relevant to note that all these changes are to some extend being witnesses in mainstream criminology already. In that sense, green criminology perhaps represents part of the vanguard of modern criminological thought as a whole, rather than a curious 'subgroup' of researchers interested in the environment.

Review questions

1) What other areas of industrial, state and individual activity have received more attention from the criminal justice system in recent years as a result of growing concerns about environmental degradation?
2) In what ways can we link the environment with economic factors and crime?
3) How do the issues of food and water security in fact overlap with that of displacement of peoples and resulting crime/fear of crime? Apart from the examples noted in this chapter what other parts of the world have been affected by these issues?
4) How can researchers in green criminology address the challenge that their work is influenced by their own generally more eco-centric values?

Further reading

Croall, H. (2007), 'Food Crime'. In P. Beirne and N. South (eds.), *Issues in Green Criminology: Confronting Harms Against Environments, Humanity and Other Animals*, Collumpton: Willan, 206–229.

• Excellent introduction to a still under-researched issue and some good points for the student about food security.

Smith, P. (2007), 'Climate Change, Mass Migration and the Military Response', *Orbis*, 51(4): 617–633.

• Examines in particular the inequality if impact of environmental harm on a global level.

Drumbl, M. (1999), 'War Against the World: The Need to Move from War Crimes to Environmental Crimes', *Fordham International Law Journal*, 22: 122–153.

• Discusses the overlap between traditional war crime and environmental destructive practices during wartime.

Chapter 3

Environmental 'Crime': Conceptions, Limitations and Alternatives

This chapter examines more closely the concept of 'environmental crime' and exposes the difficulties of importing environmental harms within standard criminal justice models. As such, the chapter discusses the relative merits of criminal versus civil and administrative resolutions (see glossary) to unlawful environmental degradation. Various new conceptions of criminal activity will also be discussed including the notions of endangering 'carrying capacity' and 'ecocide'. The chapter will then discuss how green criminology can contribute to these debates and argue that, given the advent of environmental risk assessments and the modern prevalence of risk in mainstream criminology, green criminology is in fact well positioned to offer real added value to such discussions.

By the end of the chapter readers will:

- Understand the difficulties of criminalising environmentally destructive activities in terms of standards of proof (see glossary), causation and criminal process.
- Be aware of the relative advantages and disadvantage of criminal justice when applied to environmental degradation compared with more civil and administrative-based mechanisms.
- Appreciate in particular the growth in the use of civil-based resolutions and penalties in this area.

■ Understand the importance of 'risk' in relation to forming strategies of regulating environmental harm.
■ Know various strategies by which criminology and green criminology might contribute to these debates.

So far this book has concerned itself largely with the theoretical and method-ological underpinnings of environmental 'crime' as a concept without delving too deeply into the more instrumental questions raised by the prospect of criminalising or otherwise regulating environmentally destructive practices. This chapter looks more explicitly at the notion of environmental degrada-tion *as crime* to pose questions about the difficulties of incorporating this concept within the main criminal justice process and question whether in fact this is the most effective means of addressing such issues. As such, the chapter will also examine some of the possible alternatives to criminalisa-tion including administrative regulation and the use of civil sanctions, which are now on the increase in a number of jurisdictions. Such discussion is in keeping with the critical approach taken to green criminology discussed in Chapter 1, whereby extended debate is called for concerning which activities become labelled as 'crime' in the first place. The points raised in this chapter will also feed into the next two chapters on holding corporate actors and then state actors to account for environmental degradation and how green criminologists might approach these issues.

CONCEPTUALISING 'ENVIRONMENTAL CRIME'

Various commentators have offered concise definitions of 'environmental crime'. Comparing some of these can help us understand the important ques-tions that are raised by this proposition. For example, Bell et al. (2013) cite the definition of Situ and Emmons (2000) who view environmental crime as:

> An unauthorized act or omission that violates the law and is therefore subject to criminal prosecution and criminal sanction. This offence harms or endangers people's physi-cal safety or health as well as the environment itself. It serves the interests of either organizations, corporations or individuals. (p.3)

Notably this definition exhibits a marked anthropocentric slant, requiring the harm or endangerment of humans *as well as* the environment. Thus, harm to the environment alone is not expressly covered or, at least, the meaning is somewhat ambiguous. The insertion of the word 'unauthorized' implies that some environmentally destructive activities which would otherwise be criminal might be subject to permissive licensing: a system generally utilised across many jurisdictions in this area (Faure and Svatikova, 2012). The requirement that the perpetrator seeks business or personal advantage would seem to discount the lone fly-tipper, for example, who derives little to no monetary gain from dumping, although one might argue that the convenience of this option constitutes an advantage. Consider, for comparison, this understanding of environmental crime put forward by the US Department of Justice:

> Most environmental crimes require proof of a pollution event (i.e. discharge of a pollutant into a water of the United States, emission of an air pollutant, or dumping of waste on land) and proof of criminal intent. In most cases, the government proves that intent by showing that the defendant acted 'knowingly.' That is, the government must show voluntary and intentional conduct, not conduct that is the result of an accident or mistake of fact. (US Department of Justice, 2013: unpaginated)

This definition is more eco-centric in that it does not envisage humans necessarily being harmed (although it also does not expressly state that *harm* need befall the environment). This definition does specify the highest degree of moral blameworthiness in the form of an intention on the part of the perpetrator to cause harm. By contrast, many of the environmental crimes found on the statute books across jurisdictions are in fact strict liability offences (see glossary) (Brickey, 2013), meaning they require no guilty frame of mind on the part of the offender, often because they are based on breaches of administrative rules (see below). Both the above two definitions also imply that environmental crimes are not crimes of *negligence* or even (to employ a term from the English law to describe negligence fitting of criminal censure) *gross negligence*. As such, firm lines are drawn here between *criminal* and *civil* wrongdoing (see p.68 for an explanation of the traditional distinction). By comparison, according to the US Environmental Protection Agency, its Criminal Enforcement Programme 'focuses investigative resources on cases that involve *negligent*, knowing or wilful violations of federal environmental law' (EPA, 2012: unpaginated, emphasis added).

To give another example, in the United Kingdom the local government websites states that:

> Environmental crime includes littering, abandoned vehicles, graffiti, fly posting, dog fouling, fly-tipping, dumped business waste, vandalism, abandoned shopping trolleys and noise nuisance. (Gedling Borough Council, 2014: unpaginated)

The Australia Federal Police, for its part, states that:

> Activities that may constitute an environmental crime under Commonwealth law include actions that have a significant impact on matters of national environmental significance, namely: World Heritage properties; National Heritage places; wetlands of international

importance; threatened species and ecological communities; migratory species; Common-wealth marine areas; nuclear actions (including uranium mining). (Australian Federal Police, 2014: unpaginated)

By comparing these last two definitions one can appreciate the vast scope of potential environmental offending and the very different aspects that can be prioritised or highlighted in different contexts. Contrast these two very specified understandings with the very wide definition used by the Royal Borough of Greenwich in the United Kingdom:

Environmental crime is crime that adversely affects the environment. Any action that has a negative effect on our surroundings is considered an environmental crime. (Royal Borough of Greenwich, 2014: unpaginated)

Interestingly none of these definitions or their parent documents elaborate on what constitutes 'the environment' or indeed what concepts like 'harm' or 'adverse effect' might entail.

In sum, therefore, we can see that understandings of what consti-tutes 'environmental crime' vary tremendously between jurisdictions and within them (see Bisschop, 2010). It is perhaps partly for this reason that criminology has been slow to incorporate such concepts even within its more mainstream theories. Indeed, in Chapter 1 it was noted that criminology has been criticised for dwelling too long on stereotypical understandings of crime and offending, which often emanate from the state. The core difficulty with environmental crime, it is submitted, is that many of its characteristics differ from more 'traditional' forms of offending dealt with by criminal jus-tice systems around the globe and therefore (in line with the reproach from the critical school) typically considered by criminologists. Brickey (1982) for example contends that environmental damage is not compatible with the criminal law:

environmental crime is relatively new to the criminal law lexicon, there is widespread pub-lic support for environmental criminal enforcement. Notwithstanding that support much of the environmental legal community considers criminal enforcement of environmental standards unfair. This concern derives from the belief that environmental law has distinc-tive characteristics not found in other regulatory frameworks. Because of the perceived lack of congruence between these distinctive features and core criminal law concerns, environmental law critiques maintain that vigorous enforcement of the environmental criminal provisions is inappropriate. (p.487)

Indeed, despite the developments in criminal law in many national and inter-national jurisdictions alluded to in the last chapter, conceptually ascribing *criminal* blame for an environmentally destructive activity remains a challenging proposition. For example, it is often difficult in such cases to ascribe direct (or even indirect) causation between the actions/inactions of a specific party (or state) accused of bringing about environmental harm and the undesirable outcomes themselves (Du Rées, 2001). This can be particularly difficult given the typically longer *timescale* of environmentally destructive activities and their consequent impacts compared with most traditional forms of criminality. This has prompted Farber (2007) to argue that criminal justice is unlikely to be flexible enough to encompass the possibility of *future* harm to the environment as a whole or to humans and animals specifically as a result of environmental harms occurring in the present, and that the better solution is likely to be an administrative system based on risk (see below). Furthermore, as noted by Bell and McGillivray (2008), the extended range of perpetrators of environmental crime can seem hopelessly wide:

> A diverse range of individuals and corporate bodies carry out the activities that lead to breaches of environmental law, from solo fly-tippers, to huge multinational corporations. (p.264)

In the absence of a generally recognised 'human right' to a clean and unpolluted environment in most jurisdictions and the often ambiguous status of animal rights in many criminal justice systems (see below and Chapter 8) the basis of any criminal liability for such activities and their resulting harms at a jurisprudential level is often unclear. Indeed, Passas (2005) has highlighted the particular difficulty in relation to cross-border practices which are legal in one country but not in another:

> Cross-border malpractices make the best candidates for crimes without any lawbreaking whatsoever. Whether the offenses and offenders cross domestic state lines or international borders is immaterial. Asymmetries in legal definitions and law enforcement enable corporations to do what is prohibited at home in other jurisdictions without breaking any laws. Processes of globalization have multiplied the opportunities for that. (pp.773–774)

Although Passas is not primarily concerned with *environmental* crime or harm, it is clear that the asymmetries he speaks of are precisely what seem to render specific parts of the world and specific groups within society especially vulnerable to environmental victimisation (Mendelsohn et al., 2006). This point will be returned to in Chapter 7. While on the topic of environmental victimisation, however, it is important to note that the majority of criminal justice systems across the world are not geared up to deal with mass (human) victimisations of the kind that are often a feature of environmental offending. Furthermore, the wide and eclectic scope of possible harms that can be associated with environmental victimisation (economic, social, health, security-wise) go well beyond those with which criminal justice systems are traditionally concerned, or indeed, some might argue, *can ever* be concerned given the necessarily high standard of proof required to convict defendants in a criminal court (Hall, 2013). The situation appears even further removed from traditional criminal justice principles if one approaches the issue from a less anthropocentric perspective to consider the victimisation of non-human animals, the ecosystem and so on (see Cazaux, 1999; Zimmerman, 2003).

Given the above difficulties in fitting environmental degradation into standard notions of criminal justice, a number of commentators have worked to develop theoretical models for conceptualising environmental crime. One example is that of Mandiberg and Faure (2009) who describe four models in terms of their relationship with administrative mechanisms. Thus, their first 'abstract enforcement' is in fact grounded in administrative regulatory systems but imposes criminal sanctions for failure to comply with such mechanisms. Often this involves going beyond the boundaries of activities licensed under the administrative regime. As the authors explain: 'In essence, the Abstract Endangerment Model merely adds criminal law to the enforcement mechanisms available to ensure compliance with monitoring, paperwork, licensing, and other rules meant to regulate pollution producing activities' (p.454). Notably, criminalisation is not based on any environmental harm caused per se but rather on the breach of the administrative rules themselves. In fact, the authors argue, no actual contact between the pollutant and the environmental needs to have occurred under this model. The authors then describe administrative based systems requiring proof that the unlawful activity involved a *threat* of harm to the environment ('concrete endangerment') and then *actual* proof of harm occurring (concrete harm crimes with administrative predicates) before reaching the point of imposing criminal liability entirely divorced from any administrative regimes.

As well as becoming more divorced from administrative regimes, these models also represent a continuum ranging from less eco-centric values to more eco-centric values. Thus, in effect the Abstract Enforcement model actually has little regard for the environment itself, given what is being criminalised is the breach of administrative procedures/rules or the terms of a licence. One might argue that the administrative rules themselves ultimately safeguard more eco-centric values however, as the authors argue:

> an entity in compliance with all administrative rules can still cause environmental 'harm.'
> For each parameter—air, water, soil—the administrative agency will set a baseline of

'acceptable' contact between a pollutant and the environment. This baseline will often reflect a compromise among such considerations as the pollutant's effect on the environment, society's need for the polluting activity, and the existence (and cost) of technology that can be used to mitigate the damage. Thus, even if a facility is discharging or emitting pollutants within the baseline, its compliance with other administrative rules does not equate to no environmental 'harm.' (p.456)

As such, it is clear that criminalising polluting and environmentally harmful activities is not a straightforward matter. In response to such observations, some authors have proposed more novel approaches than the traditional criminal law seems able to provide. For example one suggestion, with a growing literature behind it, is to develop a new crime of 'ecocide' at the international level. This is discussed in Box 1.

Box 1: A new crime of 'Ecocide'

One proposed solution to the complexities of criminalising environmentally destructive actions proposed by activists and academics is to take the matter to the international level and the Rome Statute of the International Criminal Court. Specifically, advocates argue for the insertion of a new crime of 'ecocide' within this legal framework. Ecocide has been defined as:

> The extensive destruction, damage to or loss of ecosystem(s) of a given territory, whether by human agency or by other causes, to such an extent that peaceful enjoyment by the inhabitants of that territory has been severely diminished. (Eradicating Ecocide, 2012)

As we have seen in previous examples of environmental crimes, the anthropocentric or eco-centric balance of this definition depends largely on whether the 'inhabitants' mentioned are restricted to *human* inhabitants. Generally however the notion of ecocide is usually presented as representing eco-centric values (Foster, 2011). For example, Higgins et al. (2013) have discussed how in April 2010 a proposal for an international law of ecocide was submitted to the United Nations Law Commission by United Kingdom-based lawyer, Polly Higgins. Higgins' definition noted that:

> Ecocide is the extensive damage to, destruction of or loss of ecosystem(s) of a given territory, whether by human agency or by other causes, to such an extent that peaceful enjoyment by the inhabitants of that territory has been severely diminished. (p.8)

This is clearly more eco-centric, specifically requiring the loss of eco-systems and indeed including man-made *and* natural events. Gray (1996) has argued that all the components of an international crime of ecocide, namely (1) serious, and extensive or lasting, ecological damage, (2) international consequences, and (3) waste, can already be identified as established principles of international law and therefore, he contends, ecocide is itself not such a radical proposition (see Chapter 5 for more discussion on these points). He further postulates that ecocide can be identified on the basis of the deliberate or negligent violation of key state and human rights.

Although largely theoretical at present, the workability of an international crime of ecocide was tested in September 2011 at a mock trial conducted in the Supreme Court of the United Kingdom. The experiment has been called a success both in terms of its signifying the feasibility of such a crime while also demonstrating that *restorative justice* options (see glossary) may be particularly appealing when it comes to the sentencing phase (Rivers, 2012). In addition, the University of Essex has also held a mock ecocide trial in 2012, based on restorative principles. This involved representatives acting for nature (birds, wild spaces, etc.) in a restorative justice forum with actors representing oil and industry polluters. Higgins et al. (2013) similarly conclude that both restorative justice and ecocide are important developments in the manner in which environmental destruction is addressed. Indeed the authors use ecocide not only as an important development in its own right but as a useful illustration of the continuing power of law to affect broader change:

> A law of Ecocide will be more than a lifeline – it will impose a legal duty of care upon all nations to pre-emptively help. The implication of such a law for many Small Island States is huge: not only does such a law abate the threat of climate-driven ecocide it puts in place a legal duty of care to assist. The power of law to act as a mechanism to encourage transformation to a green economy is also underestimated. Using law to prioritise the adoption of technologies that are benign and renewable on a world-wide basis and to prohibit dangerous industrial activity while imposing a legal duty of care, will all redirect investment into clean technologies and a green economy. (p.263)

Another, more eco-centric, approach is that proposed by Mares (2010), who presents a different conceptual framework for understanding the criminalisation of environmentally destructive acts. For him, the harm caused by polluting activities is ultimately reflected by a reduction in the so-called 'carrying capacity' of the planet (that is, its ability to sustain a given amount of human, plant and animal life). In this sense, for Mares, any person, corporation or state which allows, facilitates or engages in behaviour or actions that undermine the future means of existence for life on Earth carries a degree of responsibility for reducing the earth's carrying capacity and therefore engages in a crime against the planet (by which he appears to also mean animal and plant life) and humanity at large. As the author continues, the notion of carrying capacity is a fundamental omission from the majority of modern legal systems:

> Most legal systems have highly specific laws that regulate only the most severe forms of ecological damage (toxic dumping, illegal logging practices, selling unsafe foodstuff, depriving people of food), but none recognize the harm done by individuals or human societies to the future sustainability of the earth. This is glaringly obvious when examining actions that are considered critical to the economic and social wellbeing of current residents. (p.287)

Although somewhat broad-brush, from the perspective of critical criminology the inclusion of corporate and state offenders within this conceptual framework is appealing. That said, central to Mares' conception is the notion that the use of *legal* systems to address environmentally destructive activities (even ones based on notions of carrying capacity) is in fact likely to fail. As an alternative the author calls for a more fundamental cultural shift towards a shaming approach in environmental cases:

> It remains to be seen whether criminalization of ecological harm is a fruitful avenue in anything but the clearest and most outrageous cases. Part of the problem is that the connection between offender (human) and victim (nature) is not clear cut; the human damages to carrying capacity are simply too complex . . . Rather than relying on strict criminalization of behaviors harming our carrying capacity, I would suggest that we emphasize both collective and individual responsibility for our actions and that we underline their negative impact by employing a shaming approach. (p.289)

While there is much to commend this approach in the long term, the difficulty recognised by criminologists is that the kind of wholesale cultural change Mares envisions is unlikely to be achieved in the short or medium term (see Myhill and Brandford, 2013). There are clear parallels to be drawn here between Mares', and others', (see South, 1998) arguments in favour of a shaming approach in cases of environmental harm (or, in his language, threats to carrying capacity) and those who advocate restorative justice as a solution to the problems faced by the 'mainstream' criminal justice system (see Dignan, 2004). Later in this chapter we will see how such ideas have translated into trials of 'environmental mediation' processes in some jurisdictions.

The above arguments notwithstanding, as noted in Chapter 2, it is clear that a number of jurisdictions around the world have increasingly turned to criminal justice as a way of tackling environmental harm. The EU Directive 2008/99/EC on the protection of the environment through criminal law lists in its preamble a number of justifications for adopting the criminal justice system in this context, summarising the main rationale in the following terms:

> Experience has shown that the existing systems of penalties have not been sufficient to achieve complete compliance with the laws for the protection of the environment. Such compliance can and should be strengthened by the availability of criminal penalties, which demonstrate a social disapproval of a qualitatively different nature compared to administrative penalties or a compensation mechanism under civil law.

Thus the justifications for increasing the ambit of criminal law in this area are said to be primarily an increase in *compliance* with existing environmental laws as well as demonstrating social disapproval of polluting activities. Indeed, this notion of expressing greater social condemnation for these activities though the criminal law tallies well with the suggestion from the victimological literature that human crime victims gain greater symbolic benefits from having their victimisation acknowledged by a *criminal* court as opposed to an administrative body or even a civil court (Shapland et al., 1985). From a more eco-centric perspective (at least in terms of outcome), the symbolic impact of having such matters taken seriously as a matter of criminal law may equally influence social attitudes in favour of the inherent worth of the environment, animals and the significance of issues like carrying capacity. Moreover, as the European Court of Justice (the highest court of the European Union, tasked with interpreting European Law) noted in 2005 in judicial proceedings brought over the correct legislative base for the Directive, criminal law has a clear role to play in environmental matters:

> As a general rule, neither criminal law nor the rules of criminal procedure fall within the Community's competence ... the last-mentioned finding does not prevent the Community legislature, when the application of effective, proportionate and dissuasive criminal penalties by the competent national authorities is an essential measure for combating serious environmental offences, from taking measures which relate to the criminal law of the Member States which it considers necessary in order to ensure that the rules which it lays down on environmental protection are fully effective.

Elsewhere in the preamble to the Directive the document mentions increasing the *effectiveness* of investigation and assistance between Member States in the light of environmental offences, and the *protection* of the environment through a greater deterrent effect on would-be polluters. As such, the range of acts which now require the imposition of criminal liability now include instances of pollution, the generation, disposal and other activities related to hazardous waste, nuclear materials and radioactive waste and the operation of a plant in which a dangerous activity is carried out, but in all cases only where they 'cause ... or [are] likely to cause death or serious injury to any person or substantial damage to the quality of air, the quality of soil or the quality of water, or to animals or plants'; (ii) the illegal shipment of hazardous waste; (iii) the destruction of wild fauna and flora and habitat; (iv) trading in protected specimens of wild fauna and flora or parts or derivates thereof; and (v) the various production, transit and marketing stages involving the sale of ozone-depleting substances' (Article 3).

Notably such actions become criminal under the Directive when they are 'unlawful and committed intentionally or with at least serious negligence' (Article 3). Unlawful here refers to falling under existing EU environmental legislation (which is mainly administrative in nature, see p.203). Thus the forms of liability being imposed by the Directive in fact varies between Mandiberg and Faure's (2009) suggested models discussed above, depending on whether harm has been caused, whether harm is likely to have been caused or where no so such actual environmental harm need be identified (in the case of illegal shipment of hazardous waste).

ARE CRIMINAL PENALTIES AN EFFECTIVE WAY TO TACKLE ENVIRONMENTAL DEGRADATION?

Given the problems discussed above concerning the criminalisation of environmentally destructive activities, many commentators have explored and advocated the key alternative of administrative and civil sanctions. As argued by the UK Environmental Law Association:

> criminal prosecution is often too rigid an approach for all but the most serious offences. It focuses on achieving punishment rather than prevention, and the application of strict liability often leads to the imposition of unwarranted criminal blame for a pollution incident which has been caused by an oversight rather than an intentional act. (Woods, 2005: p.5)

In practice, much environmental regulation is in fact civil in nature in many jurisdictions. It is nevertheless important to emphasise that, certainly from the critical criminological perspective, the distinctions between these different mechanisms are not always clear-cut as fundamentally they are all set up to address or at least respond to social harms or, as we will see below, manage environmental risk (see Mann, 1992). Indeed, Skinnider (2011) points out that while the term 'environmental crime' has raised much debate in many jurisdictions, the Canadian courts have established that the nomenclature of environmental 'crimes' or 'offences' or 'regulatory offences' is irrelevant for the purposes of guaranteeing the Canadian Charter of Rights and Freedoms. This means that regulatory provisions that amount to actual prohibition of blameworthy conduct are found to be constitutional under the criminal law.

Bell et al. (2013) argue that the utilisation of civil resolutions in environmental cases is on the increase in many jurisdictions and markedly in the United Kingdom, where a system of civil sanctions as alternatives to environmental prosecutions was rolled out in January 2011:

> The criminal law, as a means of supporting traditional forms of regulation, is to an extent being supplemented by what are more administrative methods of law enforcement the use of environmental civil sanctions being central here. (Bell et al., 2013: p.265)

More recently, the further extension of civil sanctions is presently a key strategy of the UK Law Commission's strategy concerning Wildlife Crime, with similar approaches also in evidence in Australia (Ogus and Abbot, 2013) and New Zealand (New Zealand Law Commission, 2012). Across Europe, the development of civil sanctions for environmental harms was prompted by the introduction of the long-anticipated EU Environmental Liability Directive (2004/35/EC), although this measure has been criticised both for a lack of precision in it mechanisms of determining the extent of injuries to natural resources (Paradossos, 2005) and because it fails to establish any genuine EU-wide civil liability regime (Bell et al., 2013).

Specific civil mechanisms for resolving environmental cases will be reviewed in more detailed when we come to focus on questions of enforcement in Chapter 6. In general terms the primary arguments in favour of civil sanctions in environmental cases are that they allow for greater flexibility and are generally thought to be cheaper to apply than criminal prosecutions (Mann, 1992). Of course, against this the argument can be put that civil resolutions do not convey the same social censure or have the same deterrence effect as criminal law (see Uhlmann, 2011; Tabbach, 2012). Furthermore, it may be argued that the nature of civil remedy is that it *responds* to environmental harm but arguably does little to prevent it. Indeed, as noted by Tabbach (2012) paradigmatically civil law is usually geared around compensating private injuries or disputes between individual citizens rather than defending public norms. Indeed this 'public/private' distinction is still a central, if somewhat debated, feature of legal scholarship. Thus there is a question here as to whether civil sanctions, while representing managerial and administrative benefits to the justice system, can also represent eco-centric values for the environment itself.

The above notwithstanding, while in theory criminal sanctions convey greater social censure, the core difficulty identified by a number of authors in practice is that criminal laws are often not rigidly *enforced* in the environmental field. Faure and Svatikova (2012) for example have recently argued:

> Law and Economics scholarship has pointed to the fact that this leads de facto to many cases where the criminal law is effectively not applied at all as a result of which no sanctions follow. This results in under-deterrence. (p.2)

The authors go on to draw conclusions concerning the relative merits of criminal and administrative/civil sanctions in environmental cases based on a study of four European jurisdictions: the Flemish Region and the United Kingdom (which have traditionally favoured the criminal route) and Germany and the Netherlands (which have traditionally used civil sanctions). Their conclusion is that the most efficient system is one that combines criminal prosecutions for the most serious environmental transgressions and administrative or civil sanctions for the majority of other cases. Such a combined system, they argue, can achieve greater deterrence effects than either system on its own. That said, this conclusion comes with some important health warnings:

> one has to be careful with generalising the conclusion that systems that allow for a more balanced use of the criminal law (by combining it with administrative law for minor or moderately serious violations) are more efficient than systems, which merely rely on the criminal law. After all, our data did not allow us to test the overall effectiveness of the differing approaches as far as the effect on environmental quality is concerned, nor on compliance with environmental regulation by firms. Moreover, economic literature has equally indicated that administrative law systems may have the disadvantage that enforcing agencies could enter into a collusive relationship with the regulated firms as a result of which also administrative agencies could not always impose efficient sanctions. (p.33)

Thus, the authors note in particular that they cannot demonstrate actual benefits to the environment itself as a result of this combination of systems. The issue of regulatory capture (where regulating bodies begin serving the interests of the organisations and industries they are regulating) is also alluded to in this statement and will be discussed in more detail in Chapter 6.

The above caveats notwithstanding, the mounting evidence that criminal sanctions alone cannot adequately address society's problems with environmentally destructive actives is quite persuasive. Indeed, given the complexities of the links between environmental change, changes in society and changes in crime and social harms discussed at length in the last chapter, it would be surprising if this were the case. Of course, the wide variance in the types of cases falling under the banner of 'environmental transgressions' mean one can never draw all-encompassing conclusions. Indeed, criminal penalties, and in particular criminal-based restitution, have on occasion proven a more strategically and beneficial option for the recovery of monies from environmental offenders than civil sanctions (Richardson, 2010). The example of the 1989 Exxon oil spill off the coast of Alaska is given in Box 2.

Box 2: Benefits of criminal prosecution in environmental cases?

On 24 March 1989 the Exxon Shipping Company oil tanker *Exxon Valdez* collided with a reef in the Prince William Sound off the coast of Alaska. As a result, some 10 million gallons of crude oil was spilled into the sound, causing widespread ecological damage, especially to local wildlife. The US federal government sought recovery of natural resource damages to Prince William Sound 'not by pursuing a civil claim against Exxon...but by filing criminal charges' (Richardson, 2010: p.4). As such, the Exxon Shipping Company was charged with criminal violations of the Migratory Bird Treaty Act (having caused the death of protected birds) and the Refuse Act. Significantly, both these crimes carried penalties that would require restitution to injured parties. In this case the injured party was deemed to be the United States, for damage to its natural environmental. The criminal route was chosen because the relevant legislation in the United States imposed significant limitations on the amount that could be claimed from polluters under civil law. The outcome was that Exxon pleaded guilty and a settlement was reached through negotiation with the government that involved significant financial payments to the United States for use to restore the environmental damage (Richardson (2010). Thus, certainly from an eco-centric perspective criminal law *in this case* proved the better option.

Of course, if green criminology is to offer anything new to such debates it may be necessary to move the question of environmental regulation beyond the traditional 'criminal vs civil/administrative' dichotomy. One group of possibilities, which has received relatively little attention up till now in the literature are the attempts that have been made in some jurisdictions at 'environmental mediation' based on restorative principles, which will be discussed in the next section.

A third option: Restorative and mediation approaches?

This chapter has already touched upon the suggestion that, instead of formal legal processes (whether civil *or* criminal), one way of addressing environmentally destructive activities is to draw inspiration from the considerable interest evident among criminologists at present in restorative justice mechanisms. Restorative justice has been variously defined, with one of the most widely used understanding coming from Marshall (1999):

> Restorative justice is a process whereby all the parties with a stake in a particular offense come together to resolve collectively how to deal with the aftermath of the offense and its implications for the future. (p.5)

We can also see elements of this approach in Mares' (2010) discussion of 'carrying capacity' discussed above. Of course, while Mares talks of 'shaming' environmental offenders, restorative justice is often conceived as the very antithesis of 'shaming' (in an exclusionary sense). For present purposes however the point is that both arguments advocate a move away from formal criminal or civil justice processes, as they are traditionally understood. Of course, many advocates of restorative justice retain in their theorising a place for more traditional forms of criminal case disposal (see Dignan, 2002; Braithwaite, 2002). As ever, therefore, in all likelihood what is needed is a *combined* approach drawing on criminal and civil resolutions as well as mediation techniques.

Information concerning the application of restorative processes to cases of environmental harm is scant and mainly anecdotal in nature, but there is a small but growing literature on what has been variously termed 'environmental mediation' and 'environmental alternative dispute resolution' (ADR) (see Edwards, 1985: 'alternative' in the sense of an alternative to more formal court-based resolutions). Interestingly, much of the literature that is available on such processes comes from attempts to galvanise support for such schemes in the early 1980s. As with 'mediation' as applied to restorative justice options, the term is variously defined, although one concise definition is provided by Amy (1983):

> Put most simply, environmental mediation is a process in which representatives of environmental groups, business groups and government agencies sit down together with a neutral mediator to negotiate a binding solution to a particular environmental dispute. (p.1)

From the green criminological perspective, this understanding immediately raises questions concerning how 'the environment' could be represented in any mediation dispute. Even in more anthropocentric terms, we will see in Chapter 7 that the extent to which 'environmentalists' or 'environmental groups' represent the *real* victims of environmental harm (whether human or animal) is a moot point. Furthermore, one of the few studies to examine environmental ADR empirically suggests that when environmental (human) victims engage representation, or collectively group together in an effort to increase bargaining power, this in fact complicates the process to the extent that it becomes more cumbersome:

> Far from the conventional expectation that representation hastens the resolution of environmental disputes, our empirical results suggests ADR becomes less effective when many agents are involved. (Matsumoto, 2011: p.665)

Generally speaking the key advantages of mediation or alternative dispute resolution in environmental cases is said to be considerably lower costs compared to criminal *or civil* justice resolutions, as well as shorter timescales (see Mernitz, 1980) although in fact very little detailed empirical evaluation has been done to test these claims. One exception is that of Sipe (2007) who demonstrates via quantitative analysis that environmental mediation does produce a statistically significant increase in settlement rates, when compared to civil law actions, but no difference in compliance rates compared with administrative sanctions.

Much of the literature concerning environmental mediation is United States-based, which of course is a disadvantage when trying to draw more generalised conclusions. Nevertheless, in one of the first test cases, Gerald Cormick and Jane McCarthy of the University of Washington's Environmental Mediation Project were appointed by the governor of Washington State to serve as mediators in a dispute among environmentalists, farmers, developers and public officials over the damming of the Snoqualmie River as an alternative to seeking either criminal prosecutions or utilising administrative and civil sanctions. According to Shmueli and Kaufman (2006), 'the resulting agreement illustrated one of mediation's main assets – its capacity to generate creative solutions that satisfy the interests of all parties involved' (p.17). Certainly the adaptability of mediation and other restorative options is a big plus because, as noted by Shmueli and Kaufman (2006):

> Each environmental conflict has a unique cast of characters, a history unlike any other except in broad strokes, a singular pattern of resources, interrelationships among parties,

a special set of issues and a unique set of moves that defies simple classification and comparison. (p.20)

In particular, the above example also demonstrates how mediation can amalgamate public and private disputes in a way that is both efficient and provides an outcome in which both sides of the case are accounted for. On the 'private' side of the equation Matsumoto (2011) notes that mediation is a fitting solution for a situation in which, as in many environmental pollution disputes, 'the polluter and its victims are located near each other and will remain in place and maintain an on-going relationship after their dispute is resolved' (p.660). Of course, this amalgamation of private and public disputes is in some quarters controversial, particularly in European legal systems (Burley and Anne-Marie, 1993). Elsewhere however the divide has never been so strict. Hence Merryman (1968) notes that in the United States 'law students are not taught about a division of law into those fields; they do not find the vision employed in statutes, decisions or doctrines' (p.4). In fact this question raises a far larger question for green criminology in the sense that this area may represent, like restorative justice before it, a longer-term trend towards co-existing public and private systems for delivery of criminal justice. Criminologists have already had to tackle such questions of a public ordering of criminal justice in relation to the expanded focus on victims of crime in recent decades (Fenwick, 1997). It has already been noted that civil law is usually employed for private disputes. Thus, again green criminology may well represent part of the criminology vanguard in this sense.

Positive features notwithstanding, environmental mediation does nevertheless also bring difficulties, not least of which is the fact that 'those who have the time and resources to participate in a mediation process are not necessarily representative of the interest groups affected by the decisions issuing from this process' (Shmueli and Kaufman, 2006: p.21). This might be especially true given the economic and social standing of many human victims of environmental harm discussed in Chapter 7. In fact, examples of environmental mediation in the United States seem to differ from Japan in this regard, where Matsumoto (2011) cites statistics indicating that 82.44% of complaints are filed by a personal victim affected by environmental degradation or by his or her family members. That said, in Japan a system of environmental mediation has been adopted by the public authorities, whereas in the United States these are usually private schemes, consequently access to solid data concerning the former jurisdiction is more forthcoming. Amy (1983) has further discussed the opinion expressed in some quarters of environmentalism that mediation of any kind in fact panders to the benefit of big industry and the polluters themselves. Thus, the author contends, most environmental mediation actually takes place in a context of palatable political bias, power imbalance and the illusion of voluntariness. For example, Dryzek and Hunter (1987) have suggested that in the aftermath of the 1984 Indian Bhopal disaster – in which highly toxic methyl isocyanate gas was released from a gas plant in Bhopal (India) owned by the Texas-based Union Carbide corporation (see Chapter 4, Box 1) – the corporation was in fact very keen to engage in attempts by Environmental Mediation International to establish a good compensation scheme rather than going down more legalistic (criminal or civil) routes. While Amy (1983) is generally more hopeful for the overall benefit of mediation in these cases than the worst of these concerns suggests, he still injects a note of caution into his conclusion:

> There is no simple answer. As a rule, it would benefit environmentalists to have a healthy suspicion of mediation, especially when the offer to mediate comes from their opponents. (p.19)

Of course, this is a rather pessimistic interpretation of the motives of corporations wishing to enter into environmental mediation. An alternative suggestion is that mediation and alternative dispute resolution is in fact the usual manner in which corporations resolve conflicts with each other, and thus it may simply be the route with which they are most familiar. More discussion of this issue will follow in Chapter 5.

Overall, the cause of environmental mediation is at present severely held back by a lack of quite basic empirical data concerning the nature of the settlements (including much information about the compensation agreements reached), the processes used and the effectiveness/enforcement of these agreements. Without such information, it is very difficult to test the more alarmist claims of power imbalances and so on. It is also problematic that the majority of information we have comes only from developed countries that do not bear the brunt of environmental harms (see Chapter 7).

There is also a further complication in that the literature that exists on environmental mediation has not yet addressed the problem of *competing interests* not just between polluter and public bodies, but between public bodies, environmental groups, human and animal victims ostensibly sitting on the 'same side' of the table (Hall, 2013). That said, it was noted earlier in this chapter how the recent mock-ecocide trial experiment staged at the Supreme Court of the United Kingdom has indicated the suitability of restorative justice as means of sentencing offenders for environmental crime. On this point Rivers (2012) notes:

> The experiment proved that there is real potential for using restorative justice in conjunction with ecocide. It enables dialogue, understanding, healing and creativity to emerge. It is about making whole again rather reinforcing separation and fragmentation through punishment of perpetrators and exclusion from the process of victims. (p.18)

The future potential for further development of the restorative approach, particularly in regard to case disposal, is therefore clear. As noted by Higgins et al. (2013):

> restorative justice ... is now seen to hold considerable promise as a means to resolve responsibility and agree recompense for crimes against the environment and the human and non-human beings affected. (p.255)

Given the background of criminologists in examining restorative options for criminal activities, it is submitted that there is also a significant opportunity for green criminology specifically to make a substantial contribution to this literature.

EXAMINING ENVIRONMENTAL CRIME AS GREEN CRIMINOLOGISTS

Where does the above discussion on the complexities of addressing environmental degradation through criminal law leave the development of green criminology? Certainly it would seem that the traditional focus of criminology on (officially labelled) crime and criminal justice is not up to the task of representing all relevant perspectives in this debate. On the other hand, it has been noted that most of the commentators who advocate a move away from criminal-based responses to activities which foster (unlawful) environmental harm acknowledge that criminal law remains a viable option, perhaps even the preferable option for the most serious cases. While this remains the case, arguably (critical) criminologists will have an important role to play in helping inform judgements as to the point at which the threshold of culpability has been crossed into 'criminal' territory. When this does occur, criminological analysis will also be instrumental in determining what challenges exist in pursuing such criminal prosecutions and informing debates as to the kinds of resolution(s) criminal justice might offer. Perhaps this is merely 'the criminology of the environment' although, in fact, whether an environmentally destructive activity is thought of as 'serious enough' to necessitate the response of the criminal justice system is closely tied with how anthropocentric or eco-centric that system has become. Green criminology, in attempting to balance anthropocentric and eco-centric perspectives to a far greater degree than traditional criminology, may therefore have an important role to play in its own right in addressing these debates.

Notwithstanding the current predominance of (public) civil and administrative actions in the environmental sphere, arguably green criminology still has much to contribute given its theoretical groundings in critical criminology and specifically in notions of *risk* (set out in Chapter 1). Increasingly the general trend in most jurisdictions is for public authorities to view environmentally destructive activities as an exercise in the management of risk. For example, the Netherlands has been using environmental risk assessments as the basis of public policy in this area since at least the early 1990s (de Jongh and Morissette, 1996). In the United States, according to the Environmental Protection Agency:

> EPA uses risk assessment to characterize the nature and magnitude of health risks to humans (e.g. residents, workers, recreational visitors) and ecological receptors (e.g. birds, fish, wildlife) from chemical contaminants and other stressors, that may be present in the environment. Risk managers use this information to help them decide how to protect humans and the environment from stressors or contaminants. (EPA, 2012: unpaginated)

The UK Environment Agency similarly emphasises the significant influence of risk-based (or 'proportional') approaches:

> We develop methods for screening risk to allow the most important ones to be identified and placing each risk in its true context. When all risk are known, they can be prioritised to determine which to address first. (Environment Agency, 2014b: unpaginated)

In these terms the debates presented throughout this chapter boil down to a basic question of what combination of civil, administrative, mediation-based, criminal justice or other approaches to the issue of unlawful environmental harm will minimise the risk of such harm occurring (or reoccurring). We will see in Chapter 6 that risk-based calculations are also highly influential when public bodies are deciding whether to pursue prosecutions, enforce administrative sanctions and so on in individual cases.

Environmental risk assessments (ERAs) have thus become the key basis on which regulatory mechanisms are developed around industrial or other activities with the potential to cause damage to the ecosystem or affect the health of animals and human beings (see Kasperson and Kasperson, 2013).

The role of (green) criminology in debating responses to environmental harm may ultimately lie in its potential to inject a more sociological perspective on these risks and on the mechanisms that can be used to negate them. So, while traditional ERAs tell us a great deal about the risk of environmental damage occurring, they typically offer little in terms of how different justice resolutions might negate future risk and promote compliance in practice: taking into account factors such as, for example, the occupational cultures of policing and enforcement bodies (see Chapter 6). Thus, criminologists can contribute by assessing the real life (constructivist) interactions between notions of risk and its social context, both in terms of the criminal or civil justice systems and concerning issues like public reaction and confidence in such systems.

Given that green criminology is concerned with social harm, the fact that the *criminal* law may not always be involved (or constitutes but one of several options) is not problematic. Indeed, the key precedent in mainstream criminology is the study of restorative justice mechanisms. Although in such cases the initial harmful action under scrutiny is often officially defined as criminal (but note here the use of restorative justice in cases of anti-social behaviour falling below the threshold of criminal activity (Crawford et al., 2013)) in fact much of this criminological attention has focused on how such *non-criminal* mechanisms measures up against more traditional criminal justice solutions (Shapland et al., 2011). Arguably green criminologists are the best placed to produce similar findings in relation to the regulation of environmental harms.

Of course, environmental risk assessments are often seen as objective scientific instruments, grounded in a positivist epistemology that is very different from the more interpretist approach to green criminology set out in Chapter 2. Indeed, for some criminologists the same positivist approach is taken to their handling of 'risk' (Feeley and Simon, 1994). Nevertheless, in reviewing the advent of risk as part of mainstream criminological thought, O'Malley (2009) notes that:

> For some [criminologists] risk specifically is the use of statistically predictive techniques to minimise harms. For others (e.g. Rose 2000) it refers to a broader, preventative orientation including 'uncertainty' (i.e. the use of non-statistical techniques). (p.1)

As such, there is arguably plenty of scope for green criminology to approach the question of environmental risk and environmental regulation from the more interpretist and constructivist viewpoint set out in Chapter 2. Indeed, contrary to the assumption of scientific certainty implied by the more positivist approach taken to ERAs, many authors have contributed discussions on how policymakers are forced to deal with scientific *uncertainty* in the environmental field and beyond (Harrison and Bryner, 2004). For example, at the time of writing there is considerable scientific debate underway over the potential *or lack of* danger from thawing permafrost warming the Artic Ocean and leading to a huge release of trapped methane gas in the next decade, with a significant impact on global warming and, from an anthropocentric perspective, an alleged $60 trillion price tag for the world economy (Dyupina and van Amstel, 2013). Green criminology therefore has much to offer towards strengthening the science–policy interface. This includes discussion of knowledge brokering (Van Kammen et al., 2006) and the interface between science and law, which Houck (2003) describes as a 'tale from a troubled marriage' (p.1926). This is indeed often a difficult relationship given that lawyers look to scientists to provide certainty while scientists look to lawyers to provide the same, frequently neither party being satisfied with the outcome. Such interactions recall the concepts of 'policy networks' and 'policy communities' (Jordan et al., 2005), which I and other criminologists have previously applied to the development of public policy aimed at more traditional victims of crime both nationally (Hall, 2009) and internationally (Hall, 2010) and essentially 'connotes a cluster of actors, each of which has an interest, or "stake" in a given ... policy sector and the capacity to help determine policy success or failure' (Peterson and Bomberg, 1999: p.8).

In sum, risk-based approaches have pervaded criminology since at least the 1970s (O'Malley, 2009). What this means is that while environmental degradation is often not addressed though criminal justice mechanisms, the grounding of such public policy debates in notions of risk makes this familiar territory for many criminologists. That is not to suggest that the business of green criminology is simply to inform environmental impact assessments but in contributing to discussions about the relative merits of criminal versus other sanctions attached to environmental harms the discipline has much to offer. As discussed in Chapter 1, green criminology is after all a critical criminology, and thus it needs to be constantly reassessing the interrelated nature of 'crime' 'harm' and 'civil wrong'. There is much synergy between these fundamental questions and the issues raised in the above discussion. As such criminology, in the context of a truly multidisciplinary approach called for in Chapter 1, has much to offer in these debates.

Summary

Although criminal sanctions arguably signify the greatest social censure of environmentally destructive practices, in fact the use of the criminal law in this area is generally declining across many jurisdictions. This is largely an acknowledgement of the considerable problems in many instances of environmental harm in establishing causation to the criminal standard and because in practice the lacklustre enforcement of environmental criminal law in many jurisdictions has been shown to significantly reduce the deterrence effect on polluters compared to a more rigidly enforced regimes of civil sanctions. Furthermore, from a green criminological perspective, traditional criminal justice systems are almost entirely anthropocentric in their outlook. Thus, although the trend was for increased criminalisation of environmental harms up until the late 2000s, there is a general impression that in many jurisdictions administrative systems backed by *civil* sanctions are increasingly being utilised, albeit with the retention of criminal sanction for the 'worst' cases. Helping inform debate as to what constitutes those 'worst' cases of course is part and parcel of the green criminology project. The trend in mainstream criminology towards discussion and analysis of risk arguably is in line with the same risk-based approach now being applied in environmental impact/risk assessments and thus the construction of environmental regulatory regimes. What green criminology has to offer such debates are more sociological, interpretest, insights on how such risks interact with their social context and thus their different enforcement options.

Review questions

1) Why is criminal law of limited use in the case of environmental harms? Is this due to fundamental difficulties in criminal law as a concept or more to do with application of such rules in practice?
2) How closely aligned should criminal law be with wider regulatory and administrative systems for addressing unlawful environmental harm?
3) Need 'green criminology' restrict itself to examining criminal law and criminal justice?
4) What parallels exist between the use of 'risk' as a concept in criminology and its use in assessing environmental regimes?

Further reading

Du Rées, H. (2001), 'Can Criminal Law Protect the Environment', *Journal of Scandinavian Studies in Criminology and Crime Prevention*, 2: 109–126. In: R. White (ed.), *Environmental Crime: A Reader*, Cullompton: Willan Publishing, 638–655.

  • Excellent introduction to the complex questions raised by the proposition of criminalising environmental harm.

Higgins, P., Short, D. and South, N. (2013), 'Protecting the Planet: A Proposal for a Law of Ecocide', *Crime, Law and Social Change*, 59: 251–266.

  • Offers key debates in the formation of a crime of 'ecocide'.

Nolon, S. (2012), 'Do We Need Environmental Mediators? Indigenous Environmental Mediation: Exploring New Models for Resolving Environmental Disputes', *Indigenous Environmental Mediation: Exploring New Models for Resolving Environmental Disputes*, January 25.

- Useful introduction to the alternative response of environmental mediation, also useful to help the student appreciate the differing *cultural* impacts of environmental harm.

Uhlmann, D. (2011), 'After the Spill Is Gone: The Gulf of Mexico, Environmental Crime, and the Criminal Law', *Michigan Law Review*, 109: 1413–1425.

- Another useful overview of the difficulties posed by criminalising environmental harm.

Chapter 4

The Corporation and Environmental Harms

In practice, environmental harm of the kind discussed in this book may often come about as the direct or indirect result of industrial-scale activities carried out by large transnational corporations. As was discussed in earlier chapters, some of these environmentally destructive activities may be illegal (whether in the criminal, civil or administrative sense), but many are not, and still more may fall into a nebulous 'grey area'. In any case, concepts such as 'corporate', 'white-collar' or 'business crime' have already exerted and will inevitably continue to exert a significant influence on the development of green criminological debates. This chapter examines how mainstream criminology has developed its approach to what Sutherland (1949) called the 'socially injurious' acts of corporations (and individuals) and how this approach might apply to the issue of environmental harms specifically and indeed be adapted to the green criminological perspective more generally. In doing so the chapter will discuss the application of criminological theory and criminal law to the corporation before examining the place of the corporation in the development of green criminology.

By the end of this chapter readers should:

- Have a working knowledge of the concept of 'corporate crime' and how it relates to environmental degradation.
- Understand how criminological theories have been adapted and applied to the corporation, and the limitations of these from the green perspective.

- Appreciate that the activities and regulation of large, transnational corporations is infused with power inequalities.
- Understand the difficulties of distinguishing between 'legal' and 'illegal' corporate actions impacting on the environment in some industries.
- Appreciate the links between some corporate polluting activities and organised crime.
- Understand how developments in the economics literature surrounding the piercing of the corporate veil and corporate social responsibility may be utilised by green criminologists to further our understanding of this area.

In examining the development of green criminology over its roughly 20-year history it is clear that much of the attention so far has focused on the conduct and activities of big business and major international corporations (Ruggiero and South, 2010a). This focus might be the subject of criticism. Certainly from an environmentalist perspective there is still an important debate to be had concerning the relative contribution to changes in the environment and to climate change of big business versus more individualised 'daily' polluting activities carried out by large proportions of the population in the developed world (see Young et al., 2010; Agnew, 2013). Indeed, the question or whether blame for environmental harms can be laid on individuals (be they the directors of major businesses or independent consumers) rather than corporations as separate legal entitles will be discussed later in this chapter. Certainly, Bell et al. (2013) cite figures implying that, in terms of criminal prosecutions for environmental crimes within the United Kingdom, individual offenders in fact appear more numerous than corporate offenders.

Nevertheless, it is clear that industrial-scale polluting activities of big corporations carried out in the pursuit of financial gain continue to attract significant attention both in the academic commentaries, and arguably from the public at large (via the lens of mediatisation). This is especially the case in relation to large-scale industrial 'accidents' like the BP Gulf of Mexico Oil Spill and the Fukushima Daiichi nuclear disaster (see Adam et al., 2003). It is perhaps with good reason that this is the case. Indeed, the above points notwithstanding, Bell et al. (2013) acknowledge the important point that although there may be fewer corporate defendants the environmental offences for which they are (occasionally) prosecuted will tend to be at the serious end of the spectrum of environmental harm. The authors also argue that there will be many more companies who are in breach of environmental regulations, but not prosecuted (see Chapter 6).

As such, while it remains debatable whether corporations themselves are in fact responsible for the 'majority' of lawful and/or unlawful environmentally destructive activities, certainly it tends to be industrial practices that have the greatest environmentally destructive potential in terms of their scale and duration (whether or not these actions are illegal). Thus, whether we are discussing oil drilling on the Nigerian Delta by Royal Dutch Shell (Pegg and Zabbey, 2013), fracking in the Canadian oil sands by Trican Well Service (Krzyzanowski, 2012) or bioprospecting by Monsanto in India (Ritchie et al., 2012) and South Africa (Hirko, 2012), such corporate practices have in the past led to the biggest single isolated environmentally destructive events on record and therefore – certainly from a social constructivist perspective – have prompted considerable legal and social development, debate and discussion.

One classic example is that of the Bhopal Gas disaster described in Box 1, which has prompted commentaries from legal (Dhavan, 1985) criminological (Pearce and Tombs, 1990) anthropological (Khare, 1987) and sociological (Banerji and Singh, 1985) perspectives, among others. While debate therefore remains as to the true 'drivers' of environmental change, it is clear that from the social constructivist perspective set out in Chapter 2 the activities of corporate bodies are extremely influential in this area, and thus must comprise a key component of green criminological discussions as well. As noted by Ruggiero and South (2013) in their recent discussion of the theatrical contours of green criminology and what they term 'crimes of the economy':

> Like all critical perspectives within the discipline, green criminology addresses social and political dynamics which cause collective harm and aims to investigate how such dynamics shape lawmaking and determine the very definition of what is officially identified as crime. (p.370)

With this remit in mind, it is almost impossible to consider the links between society, environmental harms and environmental crimes, and our reactions to them, without evaluating and critically discussing the position of the corporation in this dynamic.

Box 1: Bhopal – A classic study on corporate environmental harm

The major leak of highly toxic methyl isocyanate gas in December 1984 from a gas plant in Bhopal (India) owned by the Texas-based Union Carbide Corporation (acquired in 2001 by Michigan chemical giant Dow Chemicals) has a become a major rallying point for commentators and activists debating the social and legal responses to corporate environmental damage, and among green criminologists. An estimated 8,000 people reputedly died in the immediate aftermath of the disaster itself (D'Silva, 2006) although official figures put the number at 2,500 (Gupta, 2004). In addition, long-term impacts on people in the area and their children, including respiratory and neurological disorders, are still evident (Cullinan et al., 1996). A torrent civil claims is still being filed against the relevant companies (Dhavan, 1985) and attempts to bring criminal charges against the company, its directors at the time or its parent corporation(s) are also still ongoing some 20 years later, mainly in the US courts (see Earthrights International, 2014). The case has become notorious not only because of the scale of the tragedy and the apparent inability to establish criminal or civil routes of liability of the corporations involved, but because of the poor socio-economic status of many of the victims, most of whom were resident in shanty-towns in the local area. Thus, Bhopal in a sense epitomises the Marxist concern of powerful interests in society benefiting at the expense of the disenfranchised. This in fact betrays a certain anthropocentricism about most commentaries on the matter (even among green criminologists) as relatively little has been said about the long-term impact of the gas on non-human concerns and in particular water supplies in the area and the knock-on effects on the local animal population. Gupta (2004) draws on official published and wider accounts to argue that:

> More than 4000 animals died within minutes of exposure to the gas and almost 15,000 animals suffered the toxic gas effect while surviving (over three times the officially announced total).

Specifically this breaks down to:

- 790 buffaloes
- 270 Cows
- 483 Goats
- 90 Dogs
- 23 Horses

Notably even these figures are utilised by Gupta as part of a wider argument to demonstrate the potential effect on *human health* on the use pesticides in India. Thus, the role of green criminology may be to approach such issues from a more genuinely eco-centric perspective, recognising the inherent harm implied by animal deaths.

Discussions of corporate and 'white collar' crime are of course nothing new to criminologists (albeit the area remains underdeveloped) and indeed – as in past chapters – one of the main goals for this present discussion will be to examine how approaching these matters from a *green* criminological perspective might call for different methods and ways of thinking compared to a more mainstream 'criminology of corporations and the environment' perspective: albeit the lack of development of such criminology even from a 'non-green' perspective challenges its labelling as 'mainstream'. The chapter will examine in more detail the ambiguous legal/criminal status of many corporate environmentally destructive activities and begin to discuss various options for regulating such practices. It will also look at how developments in the economics literature on the corporate veil and corporate social responsibility provide important insights into the questions posed by green criminologists.

CRIMINOLOGICAL THEORY AND THE CORPORATION

The study of corporate crime and social harm, although still somewhat lagging behind in its recognition by mainstream criminology, had by the early 21st century developed a distinct criminological literature that this chapter will only be able to summarise in brief detail. Most discussions of such criminological studies begin, quite rightly, with the pioneering work of Sutherland who coined the term 'white-collar crime' and explained the criminal activities of corporations in terms of learned behaviours which in time become the 'accepted' and 'routine' way of carrying out business practices (Sutherland, 1949). In more recent times, various other theories have been put forward surrounding corporate crime. Sykes and Matza's (1957) classic 'neutralisation theory' for example has been applied to corporations to explain their use of techniques to deny responsibility, along with any injury and victimisations, caused by their activities (Piquero et al., 2005). Braithwaite (1991) has applied a form of strain theory (which holds that crimes are committed because social pressures to succeed surpass the resources available for everyone to do so without breaking the law) to the corporation arguing that corporations will employ dubious and illegal methods to maximise profits when more legitimate methods are closed to them; for example, as a result of developments in environmental regulation. In particular, many criminologists have approached corporate crime from both critical and radical perspectives that ultimately owe much to the writings of Karl Marx and Friedrich Engels. This view is particularly relevant from the perspective of environmental crime and harm because certain developments in Marxism over the years have begun to emphasise more eco-centric values. A brief overview of Marxist principles and how they have been applied to crime and criminology is set out in Box 2.

Box 2: A précis of Marxist criminology

The writings of Karl Marx and Friedrich Engels have had unquestionable influence on the development of critical criminology because fundamentally they raise important questions about the relationship between the population and the state. That said, Marx himself only tangentially applied his ideas to the question of *crime* specifically and thus the application of Marxist thought in criminological writings is still for some contentious (see Greenberg, 1993). For Marx society was to be understood by reference to *relations of production*. Essentially his observation was that a powerful and wealthy capitalist class, the 'bourgeoisie', controlled the so-called means of production. The working class (the 'proletariat') were severely disempowered by this arrangement and thus were forced to sell their labour to the bourgeoisie for survival. For Marx all other aspects of capitalist society essentially reflected this basic division and for him the maintenance and repro-duction of this status quo was endemic in its operation. Significantly for criminologists, this includes the creation of laws. For Marx, law in this society is thus designed to main-tain the position of the bourgeoisie (because only they have the power to make and influence laws). Consequently, 'crime' is understood here as a form of rebellion by the proletariat.

In many ways the advent of criminological discussions of corporate and white-collar crime somewhat undermines the basic Marxist proposition because, fundamentally, if capitalist entities such as corporations are com-mitting crimes (and sometimes to the disadvantage of *other* corporations) then crime is not simply a matter of the disempowered struggling against the empowered and the redistribution of wealth. Nevertheless, the basic propo-sition that the powerful minority might benefit at the expense of the disem-powered majority has remained an important driver of what is often now often called neo-Marxism. Thus, in arguing against the continued prolifera-tion of environmentally damaging corporate activities which are 'lawful but awful', Passas' (2005) suggested resolution clearly reflects Marxist principles:

> corporate influence on the legislative processes must be curtailed so that groups and individuals acting in the public's best interest have access to a more level playing field. (p.782)

More recently, Snider (2000) has argued that the decriminalisation and deregulation of various corporate activities – including environmentally pol-luting activates and those leading to climate change – has been prompted by the significant influence exerted by 'dominant groups' in society on the production of scientific and academic knowledge, including criminological knowledge. Indeed on this point Tombs and Whyte (2007) argue that the increased pressure of market forces on the production of academic knowl-edge (through commercial journal publications and private sector influences on universities) has inhibited criminologist writers from questioning author-ity. Simon (2000) citing Taylor (1997, 1998) expresses the point in even more stark terms:

> globally, nationally, and locally, upper-class business owners have consistently opposed cer-tain environmental regulations, approved of those that benefitted them economically, and used other as a form of social control of the lower and working classes. (p.104)

In more recent years, there have been fierce (often politically driven) debates in the literature over the extent to which Marx concerned himself with environmental questions specifically. Some commentators contend that environmental harm itself did not figure in Marx's writings and in fact he was ultimately concerned with human beings obtaining 'mastery' over nature: the very antithesis of the eco-centric view promoted by many green criminologists (Tolman, 2008). Certainly the more orthodox reading of Marx is that he was concerned largely with the labour force and its (human) workers. Other commentators sometimes referred to as 'eco-marxists' (Leff, 1993), have drawn influence from aspects of both Marx and Engels' writings that touched upon 'nature' and thus used Marxism both to explain environmental harms and to form a 'frame of reference for the fight against pollution' (Shifferd, 1972). Certainly if one examines more closely the (human) victimisation caused by environmental degradation one can see the parallels to Marxist observations. The evidence increasingly points to the fact that those most affected by the environmentally destructive practices of major corporations tend to be the poorest and most marginalised in society (and would certainly be described by Marx as the proletariat class). This will be discussed in more detail in Chapter 7. Furthermore, Saint (2008) has argued that environmental/green values are simply incompatible with the goals of capitalism:

> I began this research by outlining the rupture that exists in the idea of an environmentally friendly form of capitalism. Capitalism and the modern condition contain within them many characteristics that are incompatible with environmental protection. The hubris of humanity that exists within modernism, and the overriding desire for material wealth of capitalism, operate in a dichotomous master/slave relationship with the environment. It may be possible to have a system of capitalism that has an awareness of its impact upon the environment, but it is impossible to have a capitalist system that places that environment above wealth. (p.23)

Some criminologists have however disputed the assumption that capitalism is incompatible with more eco-centric values. Grabosky and Gant (2000) for example, writing from the Australian Institute of Criminology, argue that recent development of environmental concerns in many countries in fact represent real market opportunities for corporations and producers who might otherwise turn to secondary eco-crimes of the kind discussed in Chapter 1 to avoid environmental regulation and stay profitable. Such opportunities include the growing consumer demand for 'environmentally benign' products as well as the development of modified processes of production that consume less raw materials and 'end of pipe' pollution abatement technologies. The authors also discuss the growing preference among retailers for supplies that themselves buy and produce goods/materials in an environmentally friendly, ethical fashion and the predicted growth in the environmental services industry (including environmental monitoring, auditing, risk management and product testing).

From a capitalist perspective the above arguments sounds much more positive, but such simple solutions may in fact mask further difficulties and indeed longer-term environmentally harmful consequences. One topical example at present is the development of so-called bio-fuels, the most prominent example of which is African palm oil cultivated in Columbia (see Escobar et al., 2009). Bio-fuels are presently being touted as 'green' crops with the potential to address future energy needs in an environmentally sustainable manner (Basiron, 2007). Nevertheless, as argued by Mol (2013), the cultivation of such crops not only has negative long-term impacts for local people and their ecosystems (specifically their biodiversity), but also represents a continuation of the same process of large corporations exploiting disempowered local communities. This argument will be discussed in more detail below when we come to examine various theoretical approaches to the study of corporate environmental harm by green criminologists.

It would be impossible within the confines of this chapter to adequately cover all the varying debates surrounding the application of Marxist writings or Marxist principles to the environment (see Benton, 1996). Nor, as we have seen, is Marxism and/or the critique of capitalism the only way criminology as a whole has theorised corporate criminality, albeit Marxist principles have often been reflected in the ideas expressed by many green criminologists discussed in Chapter 4. That said, White (2011) is surely correct to point out that simply 'blaming capitalism' in fact is not of itself especially useful to the green criminological project because doing so constitutes 'little more than rhetorical shorthand for "something is wrong" rather than providing a guide to who, precisely, is doing what within the overarching parameters of global capitalism' (p.92). Ultimately this is perhaps the key shortcoming of the Marxist and the traditional critical criminological perspective in that these provide only the broad context in which environmental harms can be understood, but do not furnish criminology with the tools to analyse them in any greater detail.

CORPORATIONS AND THE CRIMINAL LAW

Sutherland's writings, while unquestionably spearheading the application of criminological principles to corporate actors and the harmful activities of the powerful, nevertheless also introduced confusion still present today between concepts of 'corporate criminality' and 'white collar' offending. Nelken (1994) in particular has highlighted the lack of clear distinctions in Sutherland's discussions between crimes committed by 'high status' people, crimes committed *for* corporations, crime committed *against* corporations and crimes which arguably have been committed by corporations themselves as independent legal entities. Such confusion has inevitably complicated still further the straightforward application of criminal law to such activities and with it the simple application of criminological theory and method.

As already noted in this book, criminal justice and criminology itself are much more regularly concerned with single offenders working for their own interests than with those working on behalf of companies, and both are still less accustomed to the notion of 'companies' committing crimes (Croall, 2001). As such, the present chapter focuses most of its attention on what might be called *organisational* crime (see Robson, 2010) allegedly committed by the companies themselves under the admittedly equivocal heading of 'corporate crime'. This is because it is here that the greatest challenges and questions for the criminal law tend to reside: in terms of fitting such liability within the confines of a traditional criminal justice model, applying standard criminological methods and assessing the appropriateness of either exercise. Consequently, it is here where the most obvious potential for a green criminology to contribute to debates might reside. As summarised by Kluin (2013):

> Organisational crime is one of the most difficult areas to study within criminology. This is due to its indivisibly and complexity, which make it even harder to investigate than common crime. (p.147)

It is also the case that environmental regulation tends to occur at the corporate level and regulatory/licensing mechanisms are directed at the corporations themselves. The other important dimension to this is that it is the large corporations who potentially have access to a level of funding which might redress extensive or widespread environmental harms (albeit in Chapter 6 we will debate the extent to which such 'redress' is possible in different situations). So, for example, following the oil spill in the Gulf of Mexico in 2010 BP agreed to plead guilty to various criminal charges and pay fines and penalties totalling over USD4 billion (Krauss and Schwartz, 2012), a sum far beyond the means of even the highest-level directors in the company.

Of course, this focus on the corporation *itself* as potentially to blame for unlawful environmental harm neglects considerable argument in the legal literature concerning the personal liability of corporate directors and/or others working for corporations in such cases. Indeed, having noted the example of the BP oil spill settlement in the United States, unusually for such cases the US Department of Justice also filed charges against *individual workers* from the Deepwater Horizon drilling rig. This example also highlights the prevailing legal problem of distinguishing the liability of *corporations* as autonomous entitles with legal personality (for legal purposes, corporations have often been recognised and treated as 'legal persons' under a doctrine known as 'corporate personhood', especially in the United States) from the actions of individuals within the corporation and the liability of company directors in particular. Generally speaking Bell and McGillivray (2008) explain that vicarious liability for criminal actions by employees tends to be vested on corporations themselves when the 'controlling mind' of that corporation was involved in the activity, whatever the 'label' being ascribed to this role in the particular case ('director', 'manager', 'CEO' and so on). Nevertheless, difficulty can occur when this 'controlling mind' is not actively involved or is otherwise very far removed from operational practices which lead to environmental crimes. So for example it is difficult in a situation like that of Bhopal in 1984 to argue that the controlling mind of Union Carbide (located in Texas) had a great deal of influence on the processes in place in the operation of their gas plant located in the state of Madhya Pradesh in India. On the other hand, Walters (2009) has contended in relation to this case that:

> it is widely known that the Union Carbide Corporation did not transport the same health and safety standards from its US operation to India, preferring to operate a cheaper and more dangerous facility. The company deliberately chose to use the lethal methyl isocyanate gas, which it stored in large containers in preference to cheaper and less toxic substances. This substance and its use by Union Carbide were repeatedly identified as dangerous to the company's management prior to the explosion, yet no actions to rectify defects and risks were taken. (p.325)

Of course, the fact the Union Carbide was *permitted* to run the plant under these conditions raises questions concerning the Indian state's complacency in the disaster, which will be discussed in more detail in the following chapter.

To some extent the rigid distinction between holding responsible 'a corporation' on the one hand and/or its directors/employees on the other for environmental harms is artificial. Treating companies as 'legal persons' is after all merely a jurisprudential fiction because companies are ultimately made up of the people who run them, this being a constituent of what is often termed the 'corporate veil' (see Anderson, 2012). Nevertheless, this distinction does bring some practical consequences and thus Bell and McGillivray (2008) offer a number of significant theoretical and practical distinctions between 'corporate' versus 'individual' environmental liability. They contend (in line with Syke and Matza (1957)) that it is often easier to classify corporate crimes as being 'morally neutral', whereas in cases of individual responsibility there is likely to be criminal intent or negligence and therefore moral blameworthiness. At the same time, the structure of large companies means that it is difficult to identify the root cause of many pollution incidents. Arguably, this has the effect of obscuring the blameworthiness of offending companies, because they seek to 'trivialize' their conduct by reference to factors outside their control. Another important dimension of the prosecution of corporate environmental offenders is the existence of the deterrence factor of bad publicity associated with the prosecution for environmental crimes, and the potential development of a 'name and shame' policy for such offenders, which is not possible for individual offenders.

Having examined the question of individual versus corporate responsibility for environmental harms, the next key issue for green criminologists is the question of whether activates fostering such harms are in fact 'crimes'. We saw arguments for and against the use of criminal law in the environmental sphere in the last chapter but specifically in relation to its use against corporations there are a number of points and perspectives we might emphasise. Notably for present purposes, Sutherland's (1949) original conception was of 'socially injurious' acts by individuals and corporations rather than officially proscribed or convicted criminal acts, which fits well with the later and broader application of social harms to criminological thought employed by many green criminologists (see Chapter 1). Just as criminal law is usually concerned with individuals and not corporations, it is also of course usually concerned with activities that are officially criminalised. In contrast however Passas (2005) makes the important point that many corporate practices that detrimentally affect the environment may be 'lawful but awful':

> By concentrating on what is officially defined as illegal or criminal, an even more serious threat to society is left out. This threat is caused by a host of company practices that

are within the letter of the law and yet, they have multiple adverse social consequences. Quite often, the main reason why these practices remain legal and respected is that these industries are able to mobilize financial and other resources in order to avoid stricter regulation. (p.773)

Others too have pointed out that the impacts of environmentally destructive corporate practices may be significant enough to be thought of as 'criminal' (applying a social constructivist approach) even if they are not officially recognised as such in the law. In a seminal criminological piece, Lynch and Stretesky (2001) analysed the question of corporate harm and violence utilising evidence from medical literature and related studies that focused on the health consequences associated with toxic waste, pesticide and dioxin exposure. In so doing, they argue that the significant health consequences associated with modern industrial production of toxic waste products 'can be thought of as "criminal" in the broadest sense since alternative, nontoxic methods of production are often available' (p.153).

As such, some authors have argued for the full use of the *criminal law* in dealing with polluting companies specifically. For example, Groombridge (1991) in describing very early work in this area by Pearce and Tombs (1990) notes that these authors 'criticise the view that the illegalities of corporations are so unique as to warrant different forms of regulation to "traditional" crime' (p.8). Groombridge compares this perspective with that of Hawkins (1990) who argues for less formal, more cooperative lines of enforcement, with greater responsibility being placed on the state. This argument raises important points to be discussed in the next chapter on state responsibility and in the following chapter where the focus will be on enforcement methods and practices. For now it is clear that such arguments reflect the observation by Mullier (2010), and noted in Chapter 2, that environmental criminal law and its application to *corporate actors* brings with it the need for a fundamental re-evaluation of the whole notion of criminal liability and to *whom* or *what* we apply this concept.

Notwithstanding the significant difficulties inherent in criminalising unlawful environmental harms caused by corporations, the criminal law in a number of jurisdictions has recently acknowledged corporate criminal liability as a concept through the introduction of various forms of 'corporate manslaughter' (manslaughter itself being a crime in several common law jurisdictions where one person has killed another, but without the necessary 'intent to kill' or cause serious bodily harm required for a murder conviction). Such a crime now exists in the United Kingdom and Hong Kong and has recently been proposed for New Zealand in the Crimes (Corporate Manslaughter) Amendment Bill (to the Crimes Act of 1961). Under this Bill:

> An organisation to which this section applies is guilty of an offence if the way in which any of its activities are managed or organised by its senior managers – (a) causes a person's death; and (b) amounts to a gross breach of a relevant duty of care owed by the organisation to the deceased. (s.5)

Of course, in relation to environmental damage the difficulty here lies in proving 'causation' to the criminal standard of proof. More generally the rise of corporate manslaughter has been criticised by those seeking a far more fundamental and widespread acknowledgement of corporate criminality both in the environmental sphere and beyond (Gobert, 2008). The restriction of such liability to cases where humans have died not only precludes more eco-centric values, it also reflects the assumption that *criminal* law must only be reserved for the most serious of cases (and that this means *human* suffering), which was discussed in Chapter 3.

GREEN CRIMINOLOGY AND THE CORPORATION: DIMENSIONS AND CHALLENGES

It is clear that the application of the green perspective to corporate harms has lagged behind even the somewhat stilted developments in the wider examination of corporate crime by criminologists introduced above. As noted by Groombridge (1991):

> Green questions need to be added to the health and safety, politico-economic and developmental questions that criminologists might ask of corporations in considering corporate crimes. All of these might combine in an eco-criminology. (p.3)

By 1997 Szasz and Meuser (1997) were still highlighting the absence of discussion concerning corporate crime within the environmental justice literature (see also Simon, 2000). South (2007) also remarked upon the failure of criminologists to examine the operation of large transnational companies, with a particular focus here on the practices of bioprospecting and biopiracy (see Chapter 2, Box 1). The remainder of this chapter therefore concentrates on how *green* criminology might contribute to the existing set of tools and theories used by criminologists in analysing corporate activities (or omissions) that lead to environmental harm. The above discussion helps demonstrate the significant challenges inherent to such an undertaking. Not only are we speaking of *corporate* perpetrators rather than the individual offenders which constitute the focus of much criminology (and criminal law) but also the harms perpetrated by their actions may fall on animals and the environment itself, which is equally beyond the scope of most mainstream criminology theory. Even criminological discussions which are less grounded in legalistic notions of 'crime' (like Sutherland's (1949) work and the work of Hillyard and Toombs (2003)) have rarely made this more eco-centric step in discussing corporate offending. It is clear however that the actions of corporations have harmful consequences well beyond the sphere of human suffering. For example, at the time of writing the British oil giant Socco International is facing mounting pressure to end oil drilling in the Virunga national park of the Democratic Republic of Congo because of the threat this poses to a rare breed of mountain gorilla resident there (Vidal, 2013). Of course, the fact that such corporations are often *international* in scope reflects broader ideas concerning the globalisation of new forms of risk (to humans, animals and the environment itself) in modernity that were argued to form a core component of green criminological thought in Chapter 2 of this book.

Various options and conceptualisations have been put forward to steer the development of green criminology in this area. South (2007) for example when discussing biopiracy in the chapter noted above draws parallels between such activities and colonial practices of theft from and denial of rights to indigenous groups, arguing that 'Today's pursuit of empire is of the corporate variety' (p.241). Mol (2013) has expanded on this idea to argue that (green) criminology needs to incorporate what she calls a 'colonial aspect' by which she means examinations of the mechanisms by which power flows through green issues or, in her words:

> a power-based approach to harm can advance understanding of the organising principles that have something to say about where harm is perpetrated; against whom and what; the nexus and shifting boundaries between crime and harm; as well as who decides on the terms of the debate. (p.255)

The above discussion and those in Chapter 1 of this book can serve to reinforces Mol's argument that 'power' is a key variable for analysis by green criminologists, and indeed this extends logically from the more traditional Marxist view of corporations outlined above. At the same time, Simon (2000) draws parallels with Sutherland's original conception of corporate crime as representing a form of differential association (whereby individuals learn criminal behaviours through interactions with each other) to argue from the green perspective:

a number of illegal and deviant acts have become institutionalized practices among certain industries that pollute, dump toxic waste, and make environmental crime victims of various global minorities. (p.103)

This view also reflects Sykes and Matza's (1957) neutralisation thesis, which holds that offending corporations 'condemn the condemners' by essentially maintaining that everyone in the industry is carrying out the same kinds of activities (notwithstanding their illegality) and thus each corporation is forced to do the same to remain competitive. One of the great potential contributions for green criminology to make in this regard lies in assessing how such neutralisation methods operate in relation to environmental damage beyond humans and to problematise this dynamic.

Partly as a result of such 'institutionalized insensitivities to right and wrong' (p.105), Simon (2000) argues that corporations committing environmental crimes frequently also commit other forms of organisational crime (while its constituent directors tend to be involved in white-collar crimes). He cites General Electric in the United States as a prime example (see case study in Box 3). This of course implies that green criminologists might well draw inspiration from more mainstream criminological writings concerning criminal careers (of individuals) and the factors which cause offenders to become either 'specialists' or 'generalists' in terms of their offending behaviours.

Box 3: General Electric: A 'Career Corporate Criminal'?

Many commentators have pointed out the long history of United States-based General Electric (one of the largest multinational conglomerations in the world) facing and being convicted of criminal activities: some of which are specifically related to the environment while others are not (see Soothill et al., 2013). The following list of criminal and potentially criminal accusations made against the company over the years (in and out of court) is adapted from GE's entry in the *Sage Encyclopaedia of White-Collar and Corporate Crime* (Simon, 2005). Particular allegations include:

- Prince fixing for electrical equipment.
- Defrauding the US Army in relation to a logistics computing contracts.
- Convictions for paying bribes to Puerto Rican officials.
- The supply of defective aeroplane parts in the United States and beyond.
- Insider trading and other questionable stock market activities.
- Bribery and mispricing in order to secure other lucrative defence contacts from the US Army.

Simon also notes that between 1990 and 2002, the US federal government launched 63 cases against GE, all of which were settled out of court for an alleged total of $982.9 million. As the author contends:

> If GE were an individual, it would be considered an habitual criminal under American law. (p.352)

GE's recorded links with environmental harms is similarly extensive and the company is recognised as one of the most polluting corporations in the United States: albeit much of this pollution is actually legal/licensed (see Political Economy Research Institute, 2003). In particular the corporation has faced long-term criticism and legal action from the State of New York over its alleged large-scale dumping of toxic waste into the Hudson River. The company was forced to initiate clean-up operations in a stretch of the river in 2002. The next year GE was issued with a Unilateral Administrative Order by the US Environmental Protection Agency forcing it to review its proposed clean-up operation at a site in Rome, Georgia, where the company had produced electrical transistors from 1952 till 1957. The EPA set out the grounds for the order as follows:

> because of concerns that GE's proposed cleanup plan may not provide for adequate protection of public health and the environment. Specifically, EPA is concerned that the proposed plan does not require a complete characterization of all source material, does not reflect an understanding of the movement of contaminants in the entire area and lacks a full examination of all cleanup alternatives. (EPA, 2003)

More recently, concern has also been expressed over GE's design of the nuclear reactors involved in the 2011 crisis at general in Japan (see pp.14 and 144 of this volume), with the same reactor design currently being used in nuclear power facilities in a number of other countries, including the United States itself (Adleman and Okada, 2013).

The above points of course raise important questions for green criminologists concerning *why* some environmentally destructive practices might become acceptable within some industries: calling to mind classic criminological and sociological discussions about why people obey the law. For Tyler (1990) most people do so most of the time because they see the law as *legitimate* rather than because they fear *punishment* if caught. Tyler (2009) has applied this perspective to the following of institutional rules and standards by employees *within* corporations by suggesting that adherence to such rules will be promoted by motivating employees to act on their own feelings of personal responsibility and ties to the organisation (loyalty) along with their own sense of morality and ethics. For corporations themselves however it is arguable that the opposite applies, and corporations will in pursuit of profit do that which they can get away with without punishment (in accordance with Braithwaite's (1991) development of strain theory discussed earlier in this chapter). Tyler and Mentovich's (2010) view on corporations themselves is that treating such 'collective entities' as people is misplaced and does not fit within standard legal mechanisms. Thus, he suggests, corporate wrongdoing should be traced back to the actual *individuals* who make decisions:

> Our results suggest that people are more capable of judging the conduct of individuals than organizations. Similarly, an identical organizational policy (in our case, gender discrimination in hiring) raised greater moral condemnation when it was executed by a person (the supervisor) rather than by the company. Therefore, if organizations personalized the policies and revealed the individuals behind their decisions, people would be more inclined and better able to morally evaluate such conduct. (p.228)

While this is undoubtedly true, the question for the green criminologists (quite aside from the normative debate over whether corporations *should* be held collectively responsible) is whether there is any benefit to be gained *from the eco-centric perspective* by pursuing the corporations as a whole for environmentally destructive activities, which has already been discussed in this chapter in terms of potential restitution of the environmental damage. In Chapter 6 we will also discuss the relative merits of pursuing corporations though criminal, civil or administrative compensation mechanisms from the perspective of human and animal victims of environmental harm. More generally, it is clear that the question of whether attention should be focused by green criminologists on the corporation or on the individuals behind the corporation will remain a key topic of debate and conjecture.

'Legitimate' and 'illegitimate' corporations?

This volume has already discussed the legal 'grey area' (at least in terms of the criminal law) into which many corporate activities that foster harm on the environment tend to fall. Green criminologists approaching the topic of major transnational coronations however will increasingly have to contend with a very different dynamic: that of 'legitimate' corporations working directly and indirectly with organised crime partners to circumvent environmental law/regulations and thus commit secondary green crimes, as well as – in all likelihood – perpetuating other, associated criminal activities (see Chapter 3). Indeed, the distinction between 'legitimate corporations' and organised crime groups is often itself somewhat nebulous. On this point Carter (1999) has commented extensively on the ascent of what he terms 'the corporate model in environmental-organised crime'. The author goes on to note:

Although the traditional form of organized crime (i.e. Mafia) appears to be on the wane, corporate forms of organized crime have already entered into the waste-trade industries to fill the void created by the extraction of their predecessors. These corporate racketeers closely mimic the old traditional form of crime they have replaced, but may prove to be even more intractable, because, as the literature on corporate crime has clearly shown, corporate entities are extremely resistant to labelling as illegitimate organizations. (p.1)

Thus, like Groombridge (1991) and South (2007), Carter criticises mainstream criminological approaches to corporate crime for ignoring the environmental element. Indeed, for him treating 'environmental-organized crime' in the same way as other (more traditional) forms of organised crime (or corporate crime) has led to a lack of change in environmental law to help tackle the problem. Carter is particularly concerned in his article with the infiltration of criminal actors within the New York City and State waste-trade industries. His conceptualisation of these criminal actors as 'within the industry' is itself telling, indicating that these are not a 'rogue element' acting beyond the 'normal' confines of waste management processes but are in fact entirely integrated and endemic within the 'legitimate' waste trade. The contracting of criminal organisations by 'legitimate' corporations for the removal, treatment, or disposition of waste in New York specifically – and in the United States more broadly (Block, 1985) – has been a recognised (if somewhat discounted) problem for many years (Szasz, 2006). The issue certainly goes beyond environmental waste and beyond corporations in the United States, prompting Simon (2000) to conclude:

In short, organized criminal syndicates have proved useful to corporate, labor and political elites for the past 50 years, sometimes for antienvironmental purposes in the pursuit of profit. (p.106)

As this book has already noted, in other areas of the burgeoning green criminology literature, the limiting of many of these studies to US cases is problematic, however the phenomena of corporate-organised crime and its links to environmental matters, particularly the transport and dumping of waste (including nuclear waste (Tomkins, 2005)) is far from restricted to the United States. Another prominent example comes from Italy, particularly in the Naples region, where Mafia groups have traditionally dominated the waste industry. As noted by Liddick (2010):

Nowhere is organised crime's involvement in the disposal of hazardous waste more evident than in Italy, where the Cosa Nostra, the Camorra, and the 'Ndrangheta [Mafia-type organised crime groups] exercise significant control over the trade.... The Camorra has dominated the garbage industry in Naples for decades, and prior to 1994, it controlled the entire waste disposal cycle. Officials believe $8.8 billion a year is earned from all environmental crimes in Italy. (p.139)

Again, what becomes clear through these examples is that simple criminological distinctions between 'criminal' and 'non-criminal' corporations will not suffice when applied to corporate polluting behaviour. To some extent we are instead talking about situations where *whole industries* are acting in a criminogenic fashion and where criminal activity, working with organised criminal groups or acting *as* organised criminal groups becomes normalised.

Piercing the 'corporate veil'

All the above points notwithstanding White (2011), in following on from his discussion of the limits of the simple capitalist critique, argues that simply 'blaming transnational corporations for everything' (p.156) is equally restrictive because this alone does nothing to establish which companies are harming the environment, how exactly they are doing so and with what justifications. Linked to this is the different question of whether the corporations (or their directors) should be the main subjects of green criminological enquiry or whether more attention should be paid to the *consuming* behaviour of individuals (especially in developed countries) which ultimately drives many of the corporate imperatives. On this point Saint (2008) criticises what he sees as a present shifting of responsibility for environmental degradation from big business to consumers and argues that national governments tend to be complicit in prompting 'solutions' to environmental problems that will not negatively affect business prospects:

> Currently, the onus of responsibility for environmental degradation weighs extraordinarily against the consumer. Fairclough writes that the problem of language and power is fundamentally a question of democracy. Those affected need to take it on board as a political issue, as feminists have around the issue of language and gender (Fairclough, in Jaworski and Coupland, 1999: 35). In this respect, I seek to offer resistance to the prevailing opinion that merely by following the rules and doing what the government says – by car pooling, sharing baths, and re-using plastic bags and bottles – the planet will be saved. (p.24)

There are interesting parallels to be drawn here with the mainstream criminological literature on crime prevention, in which many authors have argued that the state increasingly places the responsibility for preventing crime on the public particularly given the rise in so-called 'victim orientated crime prevention' (O'Malley, 1992).

White (2011) proceeds to draw on the perspective put forward by Glasbeek (2004) that the corporation as an institution was designed largely to separate the interests and *responsibilities* of its owners (shareholders) from the fictitious 'legal person' of the corporation itself. Thus, corporations are designed as 'criminogenic creatures' to remain immune from civil, administrative or legal prosecution and censure. This perspective was popularised (serving as a rallying call for those arguing against globalisation) in the 2003 documentary *The Corporation* and its accompanying commentary by Bakan (2005). Both argued that having been characterised as a 'legal person' the corporation also exhibited signs of psychopathy. As noted in the review of the film by *The Economist* magazine:

> like all psychopaths, the firm is irresponsible, because it puts others at risk to satisfy its profit-maximising goal, harming employees and customers, and damaging the environment. (The Economist, 2004: unpaginated)

It is no doubt too far to suggest that either mainstream or green criminologists must approach corporate polluters with the same determinism/free-will debates with which they have approached mental illness in human offenders (see Bean (2013) for an extensive review) but certainly such perspectives demonstrate the complexity of this subject matter and the many distinctions between this and 'regular' offending.

Given the above-mentioned complications inherent in the purposeful separation of corporations from their shareholders from a criminological perspective, White (2009) also discusses how green criminologists might draw on studies now appearing in the economics literature on the 'piercing of the corporate veil' (Anderson, 2012). In particular this literature has highlighted cases in which shareholders of big companies have rallied to hold 'their' corporations to account for polluting activates (see Prechel and Zheng, 2012). Of course this is also closely related to developing economic notions of corporate social (and environmental) responsibility. Corporate social responsibility (CSR) as a concept has developed markedly since its early appearance in the late 1960s. Generally speaking it is usually thought to constitute a form of voluntary self-regulation by corporations to achieve social goods beyond the requirements of more formal, externally imposed, regulation methods (Blowfield and Murray, 2011). Indeed, reflecting the spirit of CSR, it should be noted that some of the research carried out on the environmental policies of major corporations indicates that many companies go *beyond* the environmental regulatory requirements of their home jurisdictions: at least in terms of what they *say* they are doing in their public environmental statements (see Jose and Lee, 2007). Thus, many companies at least see the value of *appearing* to reflect more eco-centric values.

In economic terms, damage to the environment and climate change promoted by corporate activities are classic examples of what economists call 'negative externalities': where economic actors take decisions which affect other parties without their consent (Nagler, 2011). The manner in which companies respond (or are expected to respond) to negative externalities is the topic of long-running economic debate but, recently, Johnston (2012) has argued that in the globalised economy the best option is to draw on the doctrine of corporate social responsibility. For Johnston while the development of CSR is generally socially beneficial, the author notes that in reality the concern of most companies with CSR is closely aligned with their own business interests (see Carroll and Shabana, 2010). Thus, one understanding of CSR is simply that it increases shareholder value for a corporation to develop a reputation for 'doing good'. Alternatively, CSR policies can be followed on the basis of a corporation's understand that long-run prosperity depends on the well-being of its various stakeholders, including workers, suppliers and customers (Milton, 2011). In sum, therefore, 'conventional approaches to CSR always have at least one eye on the business case for voluntary action' (p.531). Johnston's argument is that because of this underlying profit motive many externalities (including environmental harms) go unresolved. The author's proposed solution is to conceive CSR in a new way, as the internalisation of externalities. Doing so, it is argued, moves corporations beyond business case justifications for particular decisions and focuses full attention on whether corporate decisions and activities are producing unacceptable social costs. As Johnston explains:

> First, CSR must be understood as corporations voluntarily taking responsibility for, or internalising, the externalities their operations create. This requires corporate decision-makers to change the frames they use so as to take account of the costs their activities create. Second, corporations must be steered towards a socially adequate identification and internalisation of those costs by the careful use of procedural, or reflexive, regulation. A reflexive regulatory approach to CSR would require corporations to meet with those who consider themselves affected in order to construct the 'facts' about the externality, and then require corporate decision-makers to internalise that externality in a manner which is acceptable to all concerned. (p.3)

Interestingly this proposed course of action is reminiscent of the work on environmental mediation discussed in chapters 3 and 7. Certainly from Johnston's perspective the role of regulation and law generally in this context is to compel and facilitate communication between the corporations and those affected by the environmentally destructive externalities. As with environmental mediation the extent to which this could encompass less anthropocentric elements is still unclear. Indeed it is uncertain whether the 'social costs' Johnston is discussing extend beyond humans. More generally, however, such debates exemplify the reality that the solution to the many difficulties of approaching corporations from the perspective of green criminology again lies in ensuring a high degree of crosspollination of ideas and concepts between traditional subject disciplines.

In sum, green criminologists need to be prepared to approach the corporation and corporate environmental harm in novel ways which acknowledge that traditional theoretical classifications of 'offending' and 'legitimate' businesses often fall down when faced with endemic and often normalised corporate environmental polluting activates. Mainstream critical criminology implies a questioning of what we term harmful and to whom or what we apply the criminal law. However, so far studies of corporations by criminologists have lacked a green element. This has meant criminology has thus far been silent on issues such as how the environment itself figures in corporations' neutralisation exercises relating to their 'offending' behaviours. Furthermore, certainly in relation to waste trafficking, we have seen evidence of whole industries demonstrating criminogenic tendencies, to the point of working with organised criminal organisation or indeed acting *as* organised criminal organisations themselves.

Again from the eco-centric perspective green criminologists have a key role to play in investigating how unlawful *polluting* activities by corporations that cause harm and injury to the wider environment and to animals may become 'normalised' within such industries. Ultimately, it has also been noted that green criminologists may need to think more like economists if they are to understand the kind of offending behaviours exhibited by organisations, and thus apply concepts like corporate social responsibility and the criminogenic nature of the 'corporate veil' to their analyses. Importantly, with corporations acting like colonisers, green criminologists need to be mindful of the underlying power relationship involved with most corporate activities and those humans and wider environments affected. Ultimately we have seen the argument that, as a result of these underlying dynamics, the corporation or even capitalism itself may not be responsible as of themselves for consequent polluting activities. Above all, such observations once again reinforce the need for a socially constructivist approach to the issues as outlined in Chapter 2.

Summary

Discussion of corporate activities has played a large part in the development of green criminology to date and is likely to continue to do so. Corporations themselves have been the subject of criminological attention since at least the late 1940s, albeit there is still much overlap and confusion in the literature between notions of 'high status' people committing crimes and the idea of corporations themselves being criminogenic. Furthermore, although the more mainstream criminological literature on corporate crime has discussed environmental pollution, it has rarely approached the issue from a more eco-centric perspective. The challenges of approaching collective legal entitles like corporations perpetrating environmentally harmful (but not necessarily unlawful) activities from a criminological angle are significant, as neither the perpetrators nor the outcomes fit neatly within standard 'crime' classifications. Indeed, even the distinctions between 'legal' and 'illegal' businesses become blurred in this area. As such, new perspectives are called for which not only approach the issue from a less anthropocentric position (which even the present green criminological literature still has a tendency to do) but also which accounts for the economic imperatives of corporations and acknowledges that as legal entities they have been *designed* to dispel liability. Thus, studies into the piercing of the corporate veil *from the criminological perspective* are vital as are thorough understandings of how environmental matters are often infused with power relations in wider society. Green criminologists must also be mindful that *whole industries* can display criminogenic tendencies in relation to environmental harms and explore how neutralisation techniques operate in relation to the environment beyond humans specifically.

Review questions

1) How have criminologists traditionally approached crimes of high-status individuals and businesses? What questions remain to be answered in this area?
2) Should corporations or the individuals behind those corporations be the main focus of green criminological enquiry?
3) What is the 'corporate veil' and how is it relevant to criminological discussions of environmental degradation perpetrated by corporations?
4) Does corporate 'neutralization' of moral blame work more effectively when no direct harm to *humans* is forthcoming?

Further reading

Jessup, E. (1999), 'Environmental Crimes and Corporate Liability: The Evolution of the Prosecution of Green Crimes by Corporate Entities', *New England Law Review*, 33: 721.
  • Very accessible overview of the key debates.

McMurry, R. and Ramsey, S. (1986), 'Environmental Crime: The Use of Criminal Sanctions in Enforcing Environmental Laws', *Loyola of Los Angeles Law Review*, 19: 1133–1169.

- An older piece with some outdated examples, but in terms of principles this is a very good discussion of the difficulties of enforcing environmental criminal law against corporations.

Passas, N. (2005), Lawful but Awful: 'Legal Corporate Crimes', *Journal of Socio-Economics*, 34(6): 771–786.

- Must reading for the student seeking detailed understanding of the means by which harmful activities remain beyond the scope of the criminal (and civil) law.

Walters, R. (2009), 'Bhopal, Corporate Crime and Harms of the Powerful', *Global Social Policy*, 9(3): 324–328.

- Another key analysis of environmental harm's grounding in powerful elite structures.

Chapter 5

The State and the Environment: Crime, Harm and Responsibility

This chapter will discuss how criminologists have addressed the concept of state crime and the connections between this and environmental harms. The chapter will also examine how corporate and state interests often coincide to facilitate environmental crime/harms and discuss a number of key examples. In the second half of the chapter we will discuss whether states themselves can be held responsible for environmental harms under international law both at home and, more controversially, in other states across national boundaries. The chapter will conclude with some discussion of where the study of state actions fits within the broader remit of green criminology.

By the end of this chapter readers will:

■ Know some of the key criminological approaches that have been applied to the state.
■ Appreciate the interactions and interdependencies between states and corporations and how these can facilitate environmental harm.
■ Understand some of the complexities of holding state actors responsible for environmental crimes and wider harms.
■ Understand the basics of international environmental law.
■ Appreciate how state actors and actions are a key topic of research for green criminologists.

The last chapter focused on 'the corporation' as an institution, essentially based on the proposition that because corporations are the organs through which power is often exercised in capitalist society (see Newell, 2013), they arguably constitute *the* key focal point for green criminological study. The case to support this position was strongly made out during the course of that chapter. Indeed, in comparing the relative political/social influence of large transnational corporations and *states* (the subject of this chapter) Rothe et al. (2009) have argued that the crimes of the former are in fact far more significant as the subject of criminological enquiry because:

> Although the problem of crimes by the state is important, we have to be cognizant that perhaps the power of states is declining and that other transnational actors like multi-national corporations are becoming more powerful and less controllable. This trend became noticeable starting in World War I. (p.5)

While there is definite truth to this position, several commentators have emphasised that corporations can only operate in the social and legal context supplied or permitted to exist by state actors (see Bowman and Kearney, 2010). Others have pointed out that the relationship between the state and the corporation, far from being a simple case of the former regulating the latter, in fact often seems to involve the two working together to their mutual benefit (Kramer et al., 2002).

The proposition that criminogenic and victimising activities/omissions of the state itself also constitute an essential area of study has always been an important component of critical criminology (Kauzlarich et al., 2001). Indeed, as we will see in a moment, several commentators have developed distinct 'criminologies of the state' to help conceptualise this dynamic. From the *green* criminological perspective then we might also be concerned with how such actions/inactions of the state (often in collusion with corporate actors) lead to environmental harm and question whether the state ultimately bears responsibility (at least partially) for such harms.

Consequently, the chapter will examine how mainstream criminology has approached the state and the concept of state-corporate crime, with a particular focus on how state actors may facilitate environmental harms. The chapter will also examine how under international law states themselves might arguably be held responsible for such harms. As in previous chapters, the primary focus here will ultimately be on how criminologists might usefully approach these issues and how doing so will require new and adapted ways of thinking about and (methodologically) researching states, criminality and social harms from a green perspective.

CRIMINOLOGIES OF THE STATE

Arguably the concept of 'state crime' has received less attention by mainstream criminologists than the criminal (or quasi-criminal) activities of corporate actors. Kauzlarich et al. (2001) for example maintained that the harmful actions of states had fallen well behind even the main vanguard of the critical criminological literature:

> The criminological study of immoral, illegal, and harmful state actions has not developed as fully as would have been expected from the explosion of research in the late 1980's to mid 1990's, which lifted the optimism about criminology's interest in understanding state malfeasance. (p.173)

There is an irony in this given that, although the concept of state offending seems at odds with standard notions of crime and criminal justice, as argued by Matthews and Kauzlarich (2007):

> The practice of states engaging in illegal and/or harmful behaviour is as old as the concept of the state itself. (p.51)

The distinction implied in this extract between 'illegal' and 'harmful' behaviour mirrors the critical criminological approach to green criminology outlined in Chapter 1. Indeed, in many ways the damaging activities perpetrated by states may constitute the archetypal 'social harms' of such interest to the critical school because it is the state itself that may ultimately decide whether its own activities are 'criminal'. Once again therefore criminologists can approach 'state crime' as a concept either from a legalistic perspective (state actors committing actual crimes recognised in national or international law) or as part of a social constructivist approach which problematises the law making process. Rothe et al. (2009) go on to argue that criminologists are in fact well placed to study such issues:

> Criminologists should be uniquely qualified to address both the parallels and differences between conventional forms of crime such as murder and rape, and such crimes carried out as part of a state endeavor. (p.9)

Indeed, as set out by Matthews and Kauzlarich (2007) from the critical perspective the question of whether state actions are 'officially' recognised as criminal is perhaps less important than the instrumental effects of those actions:

> The study of state crime, then, is not so much a question of whether harmful state practices can be defined as crimes, but rather whether there is utility in using the tools

of criminology to study them. To be sure, there are many theories within criminology that are less useful than others in helping us understand state crime. At the same time, the advances made by scholars of state crime, particularly those falling under the umbrella of critical criminology, are useful and should be continued to push the broader field forward. Critical criminologists should continue to identify and document patterns of state criminality, develop theories of state crime, and mobilize support for their control. (p.53)

In sum, therefore, the fact that a socially harmful activity is defined as 'illegal', 'criminal' or neither should not preclude the contribution of criminologists if criminological methods can add something to our understanding. The same argument would then apply to environmentally destructive activities facilitated by a state or states, regardless of whether one is prepared to accept the notion of 'state crime' as a specific legal or theoretical category.

Following on from the above discussion, several authors have made attempts to conceptualise 'state crime' and before proceeding to examine environmental harms more specifically it will be useful for the reader to be acquainted with a sample of this literature. For example, Green and Ward (2004) have argued that state criminality as a concept has two key components to it: one objective and the other subjective. The objective component is clear evidence of the violation by a state of an internationally accepted principle of human rights. Subjectively the second component is evidence of one or more social audiences (i.e. civil society within a jurisdiction or a component of that society) being negatively affected by the actions (or negligence) of the state. In terms of environmental harm this understanding, while useful, does pose a number of difficulties. Under its subjective limb, for example, we know that negative reactions to environmental degradation can only become apparent after several years, or possibly several generations, making 'clear evidence of the violation' difficult to obtain. Clearly Green and Ward are also approaching the issue from the anthropocentric perceptive, where 'social audiences' means groups of human beings rather than animals and certainly not the environment itself. While such conceptual issues could perhaps be overcome, the bigger problem still derives from the objective component because, as will be discussed in Chapter 6, it is arguable that there is no widely internationally recognised 'right' to an unpolluted environment (see Hiskes, 2008). The Green and Ward criminological understanding of state crime is therefore a telling example of why pre-existing criminological discussions cannot always be applied simply or directly to environmental harm.

Kauzlarich et al. (2003) offer their own understanding of 'state crime' that for them has four key components:

1) State crime generates harm to individuals, groups or property.
2) It is a product of action or inaction on behalf of the state or state agencies.
3) The action or inaction of the state relates directly to an assigned or implied trust/duty of said state.
4) The act in question is committed, or omitted, by a governmental agency, organisation or representative.
5) The act is committed in the self-interest of (a) the state itself or (b) the elite groups controlling the state.

The requirement that the act is in the self interest of the state or elite groups within the state resonates strongly with some of the more radical criminological discussions covered in Chapter 1 and also foreshadows the overlap and collusion of state and corporate interests in the production of green harm.

So far the criminologists who *have* examined state crime have focused their attention largely on war crimes and crimes of genocide (Maier-Katkin et al., 2009), perhaps taking their lead from the Rome Statute of the Inter-actional Criminal Court (see later in this chapter, p.119). One exception is the argument of Faust and Carlson (2011) who have labelled human rights violations in the aftermath of hurricane Katrina's devastation of New Orleans in 2005 as a state crime. Applying Green and Ward's (2004) objec-tive/subjective criteria the authors argue that firstly an objective breach of human rights was evident in the well-documented failure by the US federal and state governments to adequately prepare for and then effectively respond to the disaster. Consequently, 'with regard to the state's response to Hurri-cane Katrina, much of the suffering, deprivation, and loss of human life could have been prevented' (p.37). The authors then draw on data from surveys of Katrina evacuees and public opinion surveys that, in line with the subjective component of Green and Ward's framework of state crime,

> Katrina victims reacted most negatively to the actions of the federal government in the aftermath of Katrina, followed by the state, and were somewhat less negative toward city government's response to the aftereffects of the storm. Taken together, these results provide strong evidence in support of the Katrina case as one of state crime. (p.48)

This characterisation of the state's action/inactions following a hurricane as crime supports the argument made in Chapter 1 that green criminology is capable of incorporating natural risks as well as man-made risks (as per Giddens, 1990). Thus, the authors argue 'human agency is involved in producing the injury caused by [natural disasters] and/or in the response in the aftermath of [them]' (p.34).

White (2008b) has also discussed state crime in relation to the environmental and health effects of the use of depleted uranium (DU) munitions in both Gulf wars. His analysis draws on the notion of denial, which we saw discussed in Chapter 4 is also a tool used by corporations in relation to the environmental harms caused by their harmful/offending practices. For White, state denial of harmful or criminal activities as a result of utilising depleted uranium munitions has taken a number of forms:

- Outright denial of the harmful effects of depleted uranium munitions.
- Denial by comparison of least risk. That is, the argument that the possible (but uncertain) harmful effects of DU is acceptable compared with the risks of combat.
- Denial by refusal to pass on testing technology. In particular after the second Gulf war The International Atomic Energy Agency refused to allow Iraq to import radiology equipment needed to carry out research on the effects of DU among the Iraqi population, on the grounds that it could be used to develop nuclear weapons.
- Denial by exemption. This is the observation that the US military appear to be exempt from the same level of oversight as other producers of toxic waste.
- Denial by silencing of expertise and dismissal of experts.
- Denial by shifting of responsibility and blame. In particular the British Ministry of defence when asked about the problem of people living in and returning to affected regions, reputably responded that this was a problem for the UN High Commissioner for Refugees to solve.

Approaching the issue from a different direction, Kauzlarich et al. (2001) have attempted to develop a so-called victimology of the state. The authors' typology effectively groups 'state crime' into four classifications. Firstly, 'Domestic-International Governmental Crime' occurs within a state's geographic jurisdiction against international law or human rights. Secondly, 'International-International Governmental Crime' occurs outside a state's geographic jurisdiction against international law or human rights. 'Domestic-Domestic Governmental Crime' occurs within a state's geographic jurisdiction against domestic criminal, regulatory or procedural laws or codes and, finally, 'International-Domestic Governmental Crime' occurs outside a state's geographic jurisdiction against domestic criminal, regulatory or procedural laws or codes. The authors place environmental derogation under the category of Domestic-Domestic Governmental Crime, although it is possible to take issue with this given that actions by one state might well lead to environmental derogation in another state, possibly making this International-Domestic Governmental Crime. Specifics aside, Kauzlarich et al.'s typology nevertheless provides a rare insight into the complexities inherent in the notion of being victimised by a state, which will be discussed in greater depth in Chapter 7.

STATE-CORPORATE CRIME

As already noted in this volume, one of the longest-running debates in green criminology since its inception has revolved around the study of how states and corporations effectively work together to produce environmental harms. State-corporate crime is defined by Kramer and Michalowski (1993) as:

> Illegal or socially injurious actions that occur when one or more institution of political governance pursue a goal in direct cooperation with one or more institutions of economic production and distribution. (p.174)

Gaarder (2013) goes on to emphasise how corporations rely on states to reduce costs through lower taxes and, importantly, less expensive environmental regulation. Governments in turn rely on corporations to produce goods, deliver services, generate employment and provide tax revenues. State-corporate crime is distinguished from state crime itself or corporate crime by such public–private partnerships. In relation to the environment White (2013a) explains how this ultimately leads to the creation of more environmental harm in the following terms:

> the close alliances between economic elites and political leaders, in terms of shared ideology and contributions to campaigns and interchangeable personnel, manifest themselves in governmental platforms that can entrench an anti-environmental agenda. (p.255)

Further distinctions have been drawn in the literature between state *initiated* and state *facilitated* corporate crime (Aulette and Michalowski, 1993). In the case of the former, corporations employed by the government engage in organisational deviance at the direction of or with the tacit approval of the government. The latter category occurs when government regulatory institutions fail to restrain deviant business activities either because of direct collusion between businesses and governments or because they adhere to shared goals whose attainment would be hampered by aggressive regulation (Smandych and Kueneman, 2009).

From a green criminological perspective, Lynch et al. (2010) have remarked on the complex interaction between state and corporate liability following what they call the 'politicalization of global warming'. Citing in particular the administration of George W. Bush in the United States as facilitating corporate polluting practices and ultimately facilitating acceleration in climate change the authors argue:

> With respect to the findings, our study of global warming as a state-corporate crime highlights the extensive intersections between corporate interests and state actions during the G.W. Bush Administration. Demonstrating these extensive connections is, we would argue, the foundation for any study of state-corporate crime. (p.232)

The US government has also frequently received criticism for its very close and long-term dealing with chemical giant Dow, which is highlighted in Box 1. Kramer et al. (2002) have similarly argued that the state is often complicit in the crimes of large, economically powerful corporations based within their territory:

> State-corporate crimes are illegal or socially injurious actions that result from a mutually reinforcing interaction between (1) policies and/or practices in pursuit of the goals of one or more institutions of political governance and (2) policies and/or practices in pursuit of the goals of one or more institutions of economic production and distribution. (p.271)

Furthermore, in reference to the Bhopal Gas leak in India in 1984 (see p.84), Groombridge (1991) (citing the previous work of Pearce and Tombs (1990)) makes the following point concerning the liability of the *Indian state* for the disaster:

> They (Pearce and Tombs, 1990) open their arguments with a quote which suggests that the Indian State may have negligently licensed Union Carbide to operate a plant at Bhopal by relying on an inadequate staffed and inexpert inspectorate. They make no further reference to the quote which, out of context, may be open to a number of interpretations. It might be presumed that they intend us to understand that Bhopal may not have happened if the Indian State could afford to employ more and better inspectors and followed the policies they advocate. (p.8)

Box 1: Case study: The US government and Dow Chemicals

One of the most frequently repeated suggestions of state-corporate crime with a specific environmentally destructive component is that of the alleged collusion between the US government and the Dow Chemical Company. As summarised by Katz (2010):

> Since WW II, Dow Chemical Corporation and the US government have developed and maintained a long-term, mutually rewarding, symbiotic relationship in order to accumulate political and economic hegemony under the guise of national security and international developmental assistance resulting in transnational corporations not being held accountable for numerous environmental crimes. (p.305)

Particular attention has been paid to Dow's production and the US deployment of so-called Agent Orange and Napalm B as part of its chemical warfare programme (operation Ranch Hand) in the Vietnam war between 1961 and 1971 (see Hyoung-Ah et al., 2003). A considerable body of research has suggested that both civilians and armed personnel from both sides of the conflict who were exposed to these materials suffered long-term health impacts, as have their children. More recent research has also identified 'dioxin reservoirs' in the soil and water of the areas worst affected by Agent Orange during the conflict. Indeed, in findings which emphasise the interconnectedness of eco-centric and anthropocentric concerns in this area Dwernychuck et al. (2002) note:

> We confirm the apparent food chain transfer of TCDD [2,3,7,8-tetrachlorodibenzo-p-dioxin, a toxic component of Agent Orange] from contaminated soil to cultured fish pond sediments to fish and duck tissues, then to humans as measured in whole blood and breast milk. We theorize that the Aluoi Valley is a microcosm of southern Vietnam, where numerous reservoirs of TCDD exist in the soil of former military installations south of the former demilitarized zone. Large quantities of Agent Orange were stored at many sites, used in ground and aerial applications, and spilled. TCDD, through various forms of soil disturbance, can be mobilized from these reservoirs after decades below the surface, and subsequently, introduced into the human food chain. (p.1)

Both the US government and Dow have consistently played down the extent of any alleged effects of Operation Ranch Hand on humans or the wider environment. In particular Dow denies the link between Agent Orange and US veterans' illnesses (Dow, 2012: unpaginated). Katz (2010) also emphasises that the Indian government (along with the US government) has worked closely with Dow for economic benefits, even after Dow acquired the Union Carbide Company in 2001 (the ultimate owner and operator of the Bhopal gas works):

> In 1994 an arrest warrant was issued for the former CEO of Union Carbide, Warren Anderson, but the Indian government failed to secure extradition perhaps because to

do so would make the investment climate too hostile to transnational corporations. This became even more obvious when in January, 2007 Indian government officials began making plans for a new Dow investment in India – to the disappointment of the survivors of Bhopal. (p.303)

More recently, in addition to states' interaction with Dow, the International Olympic Committee has also received criticisms for accepting the company (along with General Electric, see Chapter 4) as an official partner (see Lowell, 2012).

Another prevailing example of state cooperation (and arguably collusion) with transnational corporations leading to major environmental harm is the situation on the Nigerian Delta, where since 1950 Oil exploitations – notably by Royal Dutch Shell – have had dramatic effects on the local environment, its human and animal populations, and in particular the indigenous Ogoni people (see Lindén and Pålsson, 2013). The Nigerian state's complicity with such harms – specifically the military government of General Sani Abacha – was brought to international attention when prominent Ogoni environmental activist and playwright Ken Saro-Wiwa was executed following his conviction for inciting the murder of four Ogoni chiefs (see Saro-Wiwa, 1992; Dillon, 2012). The charges were widely viewed as false and the trial dismissed as fixed by the authorities (Dillon, 2012). Saro-Wiwa's family have since mounted legal actions against Shell for alleged human rights abuses in the region.

The fact that the Nigerian government has vigorously supported the position of the oil companies for many years has had significant knock-on effects for the whole justice system in Nigeria. Thus, Ebeku (2003) discusses concerns that, well into the new century, Nigerian judges were succumbing to government pressure to deny compensation or restitution to individual victims or to communities bringing cases against the oil companies for the massive environmental harms caused by the industry on the Nigerian Delta. In short, it is argued, the judges were prioritising the country's economic reliance on the oil industry over the protection and restitution of the environment. The significance of the differing attitudes taken by judiciaries across different jurisdictions to environmental governance has also been highlighted by Kotzé and Patterson (2009).

The role of the government of Nigeria in perpetuating environmental harm was the subject of a major legal action taken to the African Commission on Human Rights and Peoples Rights in 1996. The Commission is the key quasi-judicial body in Africa tasked with prompting human rights and interpreting the interpreting the African Charter on Human and Peoples' Rights, including receiving individual complaints of violations. It is does not have the power to impose sanctions on states that breach the Charter but its opinions can be persuasive in effecting legal change.

The present case concerned complaints made against the Nigerian government by two NGOs (The Social and Economic Rights Action Centre (SERAC), based in Nigeria and the Centre for Economic and Social Rights (CESR), based in New York) that it had 'condoned and facilitated' gross environmental damage caused by State Oil companies and Royal Dutch Shell, leading to 'environmental degradation and health problems resulting from the contamination of the environment among the Ogoni People' (para.2). The decision from the Commission in this case goes on to lay out the harms and health impacts in particular on local communities:

> The resulting contamination of water, soil and air has had serious short and long- term health impacts, including skin infections, gastrointestinal and respiratory ailments, and increased risk of cancers, and neurological and reproductive problems. (para.2)

The full Human Rights implication of this case will be discussed in Chapter 6. The ruling however in itself represents a milestone in the cause of holding state actors responsible for their dealings with corporations and thereby permitting long-term environmental harms and the associated social, economic and health impacts on a given population, non-human animals and the environment itself (see Chapter 7 for more details on such impacts).

The final example of alleged state-corporate crime to be examined here will be the corporate exploitation of tar/oil sands in Alberta, Canada. This has been commented on by Smandych and Kuenman (2009) who argue:

> the Canadian government has been remiss in its duties to provide energy security and a long-term sustainable Canadian energy policy for future generations of Canadians by not extracting appropriate levels of compensation from oil companies through negotiating adequate royalty fees. (p.106)

'Oil' or 'Tar sands' (Smandych and Kuenman (2009) prefer the latter description because they argue the former constitutes a strategy by which the issue has been made to sound 'less dirty' by state and corporate actors) are in fact bituminous sands containing large deposits of bitumen that can be processed into exportable petroleum. The Canadian state of Alberta has the largest deposits of this resource on the planet and Canada is presently the only country with large-scale industrialised exploitation programmes. These have been ongoing since 1967. Production from the Oil/Tar sands has however increased dramatically in the last ten years as the world's supply of oil dwindles and prices continue to rise. The environmental impacts of the extraction and refining process have frequently been the subject of intense criticism from environmental groups (Woynillowicz and Severson-Baker, 2009). In particular this process requires vast amounts of water to separate the oil from the sand. In addition the procedure releases noxious gases and carbon dioxide. Smandych and Kuenman (2009) contend that the level of misinformation provided by successive Canadian governments essentially downplaying the environmental impacts of tar sand extraction amounts to 'greenwashing' and that:

> the Alberta tar sands developments stands out as a case of state-corporate environmental crime because of the extent to which it involves consciously planned and executed campaigns aimed at deceiving the public about the actual harms and risks posed by the aggressive expansion of the tar sands. (p.57)

Charges of greenwashing (misrepresenting or downplaying the environmental impacts of a given activity, or presenting oneself in a more favourable eco-friendly light than is justified) have frequently been levied at large corporations and governments by various authors (see Athanasiou, 1996; Laufer, 2003) and while the term itself has certain normative implication which perhaps do not belong in the objective study of environmental harm (although see chapters 1 and 2 for debates about the merits of objectivism in green criminology) this again raises the underlying theme that the identification of harms and the presentation of 'objective' scientific evidence must themselves be the subject of scrutiny and critique by green criminologists. Smandych and Kuenman (2010) go on to argue that both the Canadian Federal Government and the Alberta state government have manipulated environmental regulation to benefit the corporations extracting the oil from the sands, and that regulation of this industry has been purposely lax: acting as an 'enabler' of the industry rather than a 'watchdog': suggesting the state-facilitated form of corporate crime discussed above.

Importantly, the situation is not just a case of Canada exploiting its own resources. In fact Smandych and Kuenman (2009) argue that Canada has effectively ceded its 'national energy sovereignty' to the United States. This has occurred via the signing of Free Trade agreements between the two countries that essentially prevent Canada and Alberta from placing restrictions on the amount of petroleum products exported to the United States (without cutting their own consumption of the resource proportionally). Canada has thus become a major (and compulsory) supplier of energy to the United States, and in particular the US military. The underlying political motives behind these agreements and their long-term effects are the source of considerable debate in political and international legal literature which this chapter lacks space to delve into in great detail. What this does illustrate however is the political and legal background to many environmental harms, which of course once again cements the need for an interdisciplinary approach to green criminology and within this the very necessary inclusion of political sciences.

In a recent contribution Gaarder (2013) has argued that ultimately state-corporate actors work together both to hide the extent of environmental harm caused by their actions and deny responsibility for this by directing any responsibility towards already marginalised groups in society (see Chapter 7) with little political voice while attempting to direct the harm itself onto animals, who have no political constituency. At the same time, the author argues that such state-corporate actors further deny responsibility by representing environmental harm as the responsibility of individual offenders. In fact, however, the author contends:

> The majority of green harm is a result of corporate-political relationships in pursuit of profit, not just a few individuals making harmful choices. (p.170)

In sum, therefore, while it is indeed arguable that *corporations* rather than *states* are the true drivers of global environmental harm, the impact of state interests and collusion with such corporations (based on economic, political and other drivers) cannot be underestimated by green criminologists. In the light of such arguments, it seems vital to establish to what extent international law facilitates states being held accountable for environmentally destructive actions. This chapter now turns its attention to this issue.

LIABILITY OF STATES FOR ENVIRONMENTAL HARMS UNDER INTERNATIONAL LAW

The concept of holding entire states to account for environmental harm (or indeed for any harmful action) is fundamentally problematic both in terms of establishing such responsibility (or liability) in principle and also in terms of identifying a regime under which states could be 'tried'. To assist the reader a prefixed summary of the sources of international (environmental and other) law is provided in Box 2.

Box 2: Sources of international (environmental) law

Traditionally the sources of international law are listed in accordance with Article 38(1)(a–d) of the Statute of the International Court of Justice:

1. The Court, whose function is to decide in accordance with international law such disputes as are submitted to it, shall apply:

    a. international conventions, whether general or particular, establishing rules expressly recognized by the contesting states;
    b. international custom, as evidence of a general practice accepted as law;
    c. the general principles of law recognized by civilized nations;
    d. subject to the provisions of Article 59, judicial decisions and the teachings of the most highly qualified publicists of the various nations, as subsidiary means for the determination of rules of law.

2. This provision shall not prejudice the power of the Court to decide a case *ex aequo et bono*, if the parties agree thereto.

Although an apparently simple list, the interpretation of these sources (and what counts as a source of international law) has fuelled much of international legal scholarship. So, while usually the term 'Convention' is often used to denote a treaty between states which those states intended to create legally binding obligations, it is clear that states also often reach agreements between themselves which are not intended to be binding and therefore operate largely as 'soft law' (see p.224 below). Key examples we will explore below are so-called Declarations in international environmental law. Equally the debates about when a state practice has entered the lexicon of 'customary international law' (essentially through wide, although not necessarily universal adaptation: see glossary) is a matter of continued debate in many areas (see Boyle, 2006). We will see in the remainder of this chapter that accepting environmental principles as international 'law' has been a fraught process that is still the topic of great conjecture.

Thus we will see later in this chapter how the mechanisms of the International Criminal Court are sometimes argued to be adaptable to address environmental crimes/harm. Nevertheless, Article 25 of the Rome Statute (the treaty establishing the Court) makes it clear that the jurisdiction of the Court is to try individuals, not states. Indeed Article 27 further stipulates (reversing any official immunities) that individuals are still to be tried *as individuals* regardless of their official capacity and, in particular, their capacity as a 'Head of State or Government, a member of a Government or parliament, an elected representative or a government official'. Of course, the gradual expansion of international environmental law means that different states are now bound by all kinds of varying obligations concerning the environment. In terms of substantive legal instruments concerning environmental degradation, Redgwell (2014) offers a comprehensive overview of the areas in which international law has made significant strides. These areas include: protection of the marine environment; protection of the atmosphere; nuclear risks; other hazardous substances and activities; the conservation of nature and the conservation of marine living resources. The specific example of climate change will be discussed in detail below. The difficulty however is rather that state responsibility for 'environmental harm' *as a broad concept* is considerably less development either in the academic literature or as a principle of international law.

In the absence of any overarching (treaty-based) legal or judicial mechanisms, attempts to identify the responsibilities of states concerning environmentally polluting activities as a whole have generally been based around broad principles argued by some to have become implicit in customary international law.

For example, Principle 21 of the 1972 UN Declaration on the Human Environment (known as the Stockholm Declaration) imposes upon states the obligation to ensure that activities within their jurisdiction or control do not cause transboundary harm. This standard was also contained in Principle 2 of the 1992 Rio Declaration on Environment and Development. These are both non-binding instruments (i.e. they were not in principle intended to place hard legal obligations on the states which signed up to them), although there is a body of supporting evidence to suggest that the no-harm principle at least has entered into the corpus of customary international law (Sands and Peel, 2012). This line of argument traces back to a seminal judgement made against Canada in 1931 by the Mixed Arbitral Tribunal (an arbitration body constituted through a Convention between the United States and Canada) in the Trail Smelter Arbitration concerning cross-border air and water pollution. In this case the arbitrator of the Tribunal postured that:

> 'A State owes at all times the duty to protect other states against injurious acts by individuals within its jurisdiction'. In addition, the International Court of Justice in the Corfu Channel Case has pronounced that a state is under an obligation not to 'knowingly allow its territory to be used for acts contrary to the rights of other states'. (para.22)

This famous case of smoke from a Canadian smelter in British Columbia negatively impacting on forests and crops across the border in Washington State highlights one of the key reasons state liability is a significant issue for green criminologists: environmental harm often spills beyond national borders and thus the activities of one state may harm the environment (humans, animals, water, air, etc.) of another. It is this transnational element that requires the attention of international law, at least while the prevailing view remains that international law can only be used by and against states rather than individuals, or even corporations. In other words, while international law remains a system designed 'by states, for states' (see Alston and Brown, 1993) it is with *state* actors that we must establish liability in cross-border cases.

As noted by Redgwell (2014) the no-harm principle itself is limited in that it constitutes only a negative obligation on states not to allow their territories to be used for activities that cause harm to the environments of other states, or the global commons. This falls far short of a positive obligation to protect the environment. There is also no real or substantial attempt in any of these pronouncements to recognise the harm caused to individuals within states and certainly not specific non-human impacts. 'Harm' in this context seems to mean harm against another *state*. Chapter 7 will discuss the implications of this position for the human and non-human individual victims of environmental harm *within* states.

Beyond the 'no-harm' proposition, Redgwell has labeled other general principles which have been applied to environmental degradation attributable to the actions or inactions of states as 'even more controversial' in terms of their status as customary law (Redgwell, 2014: p.695). One prominent example is the so-called precautionary principle (see glossary), this being the belief that society should seek to avoid environmental damage through forward planning and blocking the flow of potentially damaging activities despite an absence of full scientific certainty on the matter. The principle is found under the Rio Declaration and has the advantage that it is able to operate despite scientific uncertainties as to the causes of some environmental degradation, in particular climate change. That said, being adopted more in Europe than the United States, again there seems to be a lack of universal application for this to be recognised as customary international law (Monaghan et al., 2012). In addition, from an evidential perspective, if there is no scientifically proven relationship between specific acts/omissions of states and the harms caused to victims this would make it very difficult to establish specific responsibility (certainly in a criminal context) or to ground compensation claims on this basis.

Other general principles which have been applied to environmental degradation include that of *sic utere tuo, ut alienum non laedas* or 'use your own property in such a way that you do not injure others', which was incorporated into Principle 21 of the Stockholm Declaration in 1972, and the principle of sustainable development, which is stated in Principle 3 of the Rio Declaration as:

> The right to development must be fulfilled so as to equitably meet developmental and environmental needs of present and future generations

While this pronouncement does incorporate the individual (human) element, it does so only in the forward-reaching, collective sense of humankind and intergenerational justice (see p.164), rather than acknowledging human agency in the here and now. Again 'generations' here clearly means human generations. In this respect the so called 'polluter pays' economic principle seems to have greater potential for attributing to the state some degree of responsibility for the harms caused to humans, animals and the eco-system by pollution. The thrust of this principle is that the wrongdoer (polluter) is under the obligation to make good the damage caused. The principle has already become widely accepted as a means of ensuring corporations pay for the cost of pollution and domestic control (Tobey and Smets, 1996), and is of particular interest in the context of the present discussion because it tends to encompass the public interest (i.e. the needs of a state's (human) *population* rather than those of the states themselves), as in Principle 16 of the Rio Declaration:

> National Authorities should endeavor to promote the internalization of environmental costs and the use of economic instruments, taking into account the approach that the polluter should in principle bear the cost of pollution with due regard to the public interest and without distorting international trade and development

The difficulty though is that the 'polluter pays' principle has so far not been applied to nation states as responsible parties for pollution (Tobey and Smets, 1996). This is in contrast to the no-harm principle that, while aimed at member states, does not concern itself with the harm caused to individuals, but rather to other states. In both cases then the established (or alleged) principles fail to join the nation state as a responsible party with the individual human or animal victims who are harmed.

To summarise the above section, some 70 years after the Trail Smelter Arbitration provided such high hopes for those seeking to assert the responsibility of states for environmental harm, including climate change, the difficulties of establishing such responsibility are still great. That said, successfully holding a state to account for environmental harms is not unprecedented. On this point we have already noted the Ogoniland decision discussed above. In addition, we might also mention the United Nations Compensation Commission (UNCC), established in the wake of the 1990–1999 Iraq war (Wyatt, 2010). Of particular relevance to this discussion is the fact that a *state* (Iraq) was held accountable through this process for wartime environmental atrocities (mainly the setting alight of oil wells during Iraq's withdrawal from Kuwait) and their aftermath. As such, according to UN Security Council resolution 687 of 3rd May 1991 Iraq was:

> liable under international law for any direct loss, damage, including environmental damage and the depletion of natural resources, or injury to foreign Governments, nationals and corporations, as a result of Iraq's unlawful invasion and occupation of Kuwait. (para.16)

Wyatt (2010) describes how the Panel of Commission for environmental claims

> drew on tests for causation elaborated in the context of peacetime environmental damage to determine what constituted a direct cause, taking a very liberal approach to 'direct causation' in one particular case where the Commissioners held that, even where there were intervening events, a direct causal link could be established so long as those events did not break the chain of causation. (p.621)

The example illustrates a point made in Chapter 3 that administrative systems are able to avoid the difficulties faced by both criminal and civil courts in demonstrating causation in such cases.

While progress has been made both in terms of substantive treaty-based international law and in terms of general principles in the international legal community, it is generally still difficult to argue that most such rules have been accepted as universal principles of international law. The no-harm principle may be an exception, although the 'harm' conceived here clearly suggest harm caused to states rather than to individual/specific humans, animals or eco-systems within states. Again, it is notable that this returns us to the critical criminological debate on what exactly constitutes 'harm'. Of course, in legal terms, establishing state responsibility for climate change is only a start. Once an obligation has been established in principle there is the need to demonstrate conclusively that a state has breached that obligation and then causation would need to be established between the actions or inactions of a state and the subsequent environmental harm caused to individuals, animals and/or the environment itself (possibly in another state). The example of climate change illustrates the difficulty of achieving this in practice.

State responsibility for climate change

Debate concerning state responsibility for climate change has been especially fraught with difficulties as the literature in international environmental law has developed, and thus will serve as an illuminating example of some of the legalistic difficulties discussed above in holding states accountable for environmental harms. Up until relatively recently holding states accountable for climate change itself has been low on the international agenda but as the practical and physical effects of this change are becoming more and more apparent a number of commentators have begun addressing this issue (Weisslitz, 2002; Verheyen, 2005). One especially stark example is that of the position of the Maldives, highlighted in Box 3.

Box 3: The Maldives: The front line of environmental harm?

The Republic of the Maldives consists of 26 atolls in the Indian Ocean with a total population of around 400,000 people. It is the world's lowest country averaging just 1.5 metres above sea level. As such, the Maldives has found itself in recent years on the front line of the climate change debate because, many argue, the country is extremely vulnerable to predicted rises in sea levels (Brown et al., 1997). Estimates of how long it will take for the whole country to be submerged vary but are often expressed in terms of less than 20 years (Jarvis, 2012). Thus, it has been argued that the Maldives are presently facing significant risk to their homes, economy and traditional ways of life. On a less anthropocentric note, the area is also host to a complex coral reef marine ecosystem supporting hundreds of unique sea-dwelling species. Small changes in temperature and depth of water can have very significant impacts on the reefs (Mohamed, 2012). The problem is thought to be so pressing by the Maldives government that its cabinet held a meeting underwater in 2009 to highlight the issue (The Telegraph, 2009). Of particular relevance to the present chapter, these discussions have reflected at length on whether corporate entities or even foreign states might be held responsible (criminally or otherwise) under international law for the damage that has been done to the islanders' traditional fishery culture (Davis, 2005). It should be stressed that this is not a unanimously held view, and indeed Mörner et al. (2004) have marshalled evidence to dispute the notion of rises in sea level, generally in the world and surrounding the Maldives in particular. The fact that such debate exists is again revealing of a situation in which apparently 'objective' evidence is still open to interpretation. The example of the Maldives is also pertinent not only for its possible front line status, but the fact that as a small, largely non-industrialised, country with an economy based on fishing and tourism, it is recognised as one of the smallest contributors to climate change as a phenomena. Consequently, the Maldives also represents a global example of the risks/impacts of environmental harm being distributed unequally around the world (from the global powerful to the global less powerful). This issue will be returned to again in Chapter 7.

The key response of the international community to the problem of climate change is the 1992 Framework Convention on Climate Change, which embodies binding obligations for states to take action to mitigate its adverse effects. The 1997 Kyoto Protocol to the Framework Convention sets legally enforceable emissions targets for countries. In international law a convention's 'protocols' are separate legally binding agreements between states intended to supplement the agreements made in the main treaty, a state may however of course become a signatory to a treaty without ratifying its protocols. In this case the Convention itself contained no binding emission limits. Some commentators have also suggested that the Kyoto Protocol might embody obligations *erga omnes* (see Higgins, 1978). In theory any state (but not individuals) can seek redress in the event that such obligations are breached, although there is little evidence that such an obligation relating to climate change has been accepted, as a principle or as a custom, into the corpus of international law.

The above paragraph notwithstanding, Kyoto is not universally applicable given that, significantly, the United States has stated that it will never ratify the Protocol. Therefore the United States, as the world's second biggest polluter (after China, see Economy, 2007) is not bound by any emissions reduction targets. Arguably the United States still has an obligation to limit its emissions of carbon and greenhouse gases because it remains a party to the FCCC and, under Article 18 of the Vienna Convention on the Law of Treaties, a party to a treaty is under an obligation not to do anything that would defeat the object and purpose of a treaty.

Perhaps the more significant impact of the US failure to ratify Kyoto is the implications this has for customary international law. That is to say, it becomes somewhat unconvincing to argue that the obligations contained in the FCCC and in Kyoto constitute the required generality of practice when one of the world's biggest polluters has rejected them. Moreover, the climate change omission targets within the Kyoto Protocol are based on a principle of shared but different responsibilities between countries. As such, while no party to the Protocol is entirely excused responsibility for climate change, developing countries – more than half of the world's nations – do not face the same level of omissions targets, including major emitters like China (now the world's biggest polluter) and India. As such, although the harm and victimisations caused by climate change and environmentally destructive activities in general is morally recognised by most states, such obligations are not in themselves customary international law.

Significantly for the present discussion, neither of the above instruments includes provisions expressly aimed at specific humans, animals or environments harmed by climate change. The FCCC acknowledges in its preamble that climate change is 'a common concern of humankind' and in Article 1(1) adopts a definition of the 'adverse effects of climate change' as follows:

> 'Adverse effects of climate change' means changes in the physical environment or biota resulting from climate change which have significant deleterious effects on the composition, resilience or productivity of natural and managed ecosystems or on the operation of socio-economic systems or on human health and welfare.

Notably this does include reference to damage to the environment in its own right (although not specifically to animals). In a more anthropocentric vein Article 4(1)(f) of the Framework Convention requires parties to minimise the adverse impacts of climate change 'on public health'. Article 3(1) also speaks of protecting the climate system 'for the benefit of present and future generations of humankind', reflecting again the notion of intergenerational justice to be discussed in more detail in Chapter 6. Notably all of these references are collective, rather than specific to particular groups of citizens, or individual animals or environments affected by climate change. This of course very much reflects the state-centred paradigm in international environmental law, as in international law in general.

EXAMINING STATE CRIME?

In the last chapter we noted the argument that corporations rather than states or individuals should most logically form the principal focus of a green criminology. While there is still much to recommend this position, for two reasons this chapter suggests the role of the state must still form a key part of green criminological enquiry. Firstly, and perhaps most importantly, it seems that the actions of major transnational coronations can only be understood in the context of the state-facilitated setting in which they find themselves. Indeed we have seen it is often difficult to draw firm distinctions between the actions of 'corporations' on the one hand and of the states which are mutually dependent on each other. Secondly, it remains the case that by its nature environmental harm can stretch beyond national borders, which ultimately means finding ways to apply international law to the question of environmental responsibility. International law remains at present a system designed by states for states and thus the responsibility of state actors in this sense remains a vital concern. Indeed, on this point White (2013a) comments:

> The nature of the state as a site for, and facilitator of, transnational environmental crimes and harms certainly warrants further explicit consideration by green criminologists. (p.258)

As noted at the beginning of this chapter, there is no fundamental reason why criminologists should be incapable of applying their theories to the state, although the development of the critical approach has been stilted in this area for many years. Linked to this however is the notion of states breaching 'rights' and, inevitably, so far in the international law literature this has meant 'human rights'. The question of 'rights' to a green and unpolluted environment, along with the notion of animal rights will be discussed in more detail in Chapter 6.

Summary

Although there has been some research and writing on 'criminologies of the state' generally speaking this is an under-developed area of criminological discussion, even within the critical school. Indeed one incidental effect of the advent of green criminology has been to reinvigorate such debates. Although major transnational corporations often in practice have more political power than some states, it must be recognised that corporations still have to work within the legal and regulatory context provided *by* states. As such the interaction between states and corporations, and their interdependencies, is an important topic of discussion for green criminologists because, as we have seen, these interactions have often been conceived as producing state-corporate crime. Bhopal, the Nigerian Delta and the Canadian Oil/Tar sand are all cases in point. Having established the need to address the state in green criminology the next question is in what ways responsibility may be attributed to the state for environmental harms. We have seen that there has been much debate in the international law literature on this point, but as yet no clear consensus has been reached. Matters are particularly unclear in relation to climate change itself. It is suggested that green criminologists, working in an interdisciplinary framework, have important contributions to make to these ongoing debates. Given that environmental harm often knows no geographical, let alone political, boundaries and given that the *state* is still the principal subject of international law, the role of state actors in these debates continues to be a key issue.

Review questions

1) Utilising criminological theory, in what ways can 'the state' be said to be criminally responsible?
2) Do corporations really 'need' states given their political influence? In what ways does this relationship facilitate environmental harm?

3) The 'no-harm' principle of international law seems very well adapted to accommodate transnational environmental harm. In what ways might it be said to be limited?
4) In what ways does the issue of state responsibility for climate change raise even more complex questions that state responsibility for distinct environmentally harmful events?

Further reading

Kramer, R. (2013), 'Carbon in the Atmosphere and Power in America: Climate Change as State-corporate Crime', *Journal of Crime and Justice*, 36(2): 153–170.

Kramer, R. and Michalowski, R. (2012), 'Is Global Warming a State-Corporate Crime?'. In R. White (ed.), *Climate Change from a Criminological Perspective*, New York: Springer, 71–88.

- Taken together, these two pieces offer an extremely thorough and critical overview of the role of states and state actors in climate change.

Lynch, M., Burns, R. and Stretesky, P. (2010), 'Global Warming and State-corporate Crime: The Politicalization of Global Warming Under the Bush Administration', *Crime, Law and Social Change*, 54(3–4): 213–239.

- Another key piece expanding on the links between states and corporations.

Matthew, R. and Kauzlarich, D. (2007), 'State Crimes and State Harms: A Tale of Two Definitional Frameworks', *Crime, Law and Social Change*, 48: 42–55.

- Does not discuss the environment specifically, but offers a theoretical model for understanding state crime as a concept.

Redgwell, C. (2014), 'International Environmental Law'. In: M Evans (ed.), *International Law*, 4th Edition, Oxford: Oxford University Press, 688–726.

- A thorough introduction to international environmental law for the student wishing to learn more about the legal basis of environmental regulation.

Rothe, D., Ross, J., Mullins, C., Friedrichs, D., Michalowski, R., Barak, G., Kauzlarich, D. and Kramer, R. (2009), 'That Was Then, This Is Now, What About Tomorrow? Future Directions in State Crime Studies', *Critical Criminology*, 17: 3–13.

- A still forward-looking piece about possible future developments in the direction of state crime.

Ruggiero, V. and South, N. (2010), 'Green Criminology and Dirty-Collar Crime', *Critical Criminology*, 18: 251–262.

- Key reading for the green criminology student, examining state-corporate actions in the environmental sphere from a criminological perspective.

Chapter 6

Responding to Environmental Harm: Policing, Enforcement and Sentencing

The previous two chapters first covered corporations and then states as potential instigators of environmental crimes and broader environmental harm. Before that, in Chapter 3, I discussed the use of criminal justice as a response to such harms and compared it to civil and administrative solutions at a theoretical level. This chapter builds on the understandings of these three chapters to discuss how environmental harm might be responded to in practice given all these complexities and underlying correlations. In so doing it will address the question of how we police environmental degradation. The chapter will also explore various models of regulation and the agencies charged with regulating/preventing environmental crime. The sentencing of environmental offenders will be discussed as will the application of crime/harm prevention theory and methods in this area. In sum, the chapter will demonstrate how, given the complexities of environmental harm, implementing and enforcing whatever systems are put in place (civil, administrative or criminal), to tackle the problems caused by this issue is fraught with difficulties.

By the end of this chapter readers should:

- Appreciate the difficulties of policing the environment, especially when polluting activities are not 'illegal' per se.
- Understand various models of regulation and their respective advantages and shortcomings.
- Be in a position to critically evaluate sentencing options and mechanisms for environmental crimes.
- Appreciate how traditional criminological crime prevention ideas might apply to environmental harm, but also their limitations in this regard.

Broadly speaking this chapter sets out to discus responses to environmental harm through criminal justice and other mechanisms. Of course as of itself this is an extremely wide undertaking and thus the goal here is not to provide an all-encompassing overview of policing, regulating, prosecuting and sentencing of all environmental crimes or harms, but rather to expose the difficulties and complexities of doing so on a practical level: quite aside from the more jurisprudential and philosophical arguments we have seen in previous chapters. In their extensive discussion on methods of preventing environmental crime, Grabosky and Grant (2000) encapsulate well the intended focus of the present chapter when they note:

> It has long been recognised that the control of conventional 'street crime' requires a great deal more than police, courts, and prisons. Similarly, the effective control of environmental crime requires much more than the detection, prosecution, and punishment of polluter. (p.xiii)

Following Grabosky and Grant (2000) this chapter will be ordered around the notions of 'detecting and policing', 'enforcing' and then 'sentencing' environmental crime and/or broader environmental harm. Each section will emphasise the complexities inherent in all three propositions and thus expand upon why much more development is needed in our understanding of this area. It should be understood from the outset that given the nature of governance (that is, the governing of the environment through networks of organisations and though public–private partnerships rather than simply by the governments alone) in this field the three issues are much more interrelated than in many other criminal justice spheres: where rigid separation between police, prosecution, trial and sentencing are often considered fundamental principles of natural justice. The chapter will also discuss the question of *preventing* environmental harms and conclude with some thoughts on ways forward for green criminology in exploring such issues further.

THE 'CULTURE' OF ENFORCEMENT

Before embarking on specific discussions of policing, prosecution and sentencing in the environmental sphere, it is important to appreciate that underlying the regulation and enforcement of environmental laws and policies lies the question of occupational cultures (see below) among those tasked with doing so. In practice wider criminological study has repeatedly shown that ultimately it is such *cultural* values (rather than official policies, rules or training) that dictate how law is enforced (Paoline, 2003). For example, more mainstream criminological literature is fairly unanimous in the view that the work of police officers is directly affected not only by their formalised training but also (and probably to greater extents) by 'a patterned set of understandings that help officers to cope with and adjust to the pressures and tensions confronting the police' (Reiner, 2010: p.87). Holdaway (1983) refers to the 'ways in which ... officers construct and preserve their idea of what constitutes routine police work' (p.134). In other words, 'occupational culture' usually refers to often deeply engrained (sometimes subconscious) working practices passed between professionals in a given sphere by those professionals interacting (professionally and socially) and swapping stories, ideas and strategies. In so doing, members of that profession build up a 'cultural toolkit' (Chan, 1996) of ready-made solutions to meet specific problems.

I have previously drawn upon the notion of 'occupational cultures' in relation to actors within the domestic criminal justice system of England and Wales (barristers, solicitors, court administrators and so on) as a tool for investigating how they construct ideas of their roles within that system, and whether such roles include considerations for victims of (mainstream) crime (Hall, 2009). The importance of culture to the debates surrounding environmental harm follows from the impression afforded in chapters 1–5 that – while there is no fundamental *incompatibility* between environmental harm and criminal justice, public policymaking, or state responsibility – cultural reticence within all these areas still seems to preclude their full consideration of environmental harms, especially from a less anthropocentric perspective.

Of course, such observational are not new to mainstream criminology. Returning to the example of police culture, one of the biggest implications of such study has been the realisation that prevailing culture might render the police 'institutionally racist' even when individual officers are not actively trying to discriminate on the grounds of ethnicity (Macpherson, 1999). Commentators have also expanded upon how police cultures affect officers' dealings with women (Phillips and Bowling, 2012); victims of sexual assault and victims of domestic violence (Jordan, 2004). In the last case in particular research has demonstrated that police have previously 'no-crimed' domestic violence by declining to respond effectively (or at all) to reports of such abuse (Dobash and Dobash, 2000).

Extending the critique introduced in Chapter 1, the above consideration of occupational cultures within criminal justice system would imply that environmental harms might not only escape official notice through a refusal of powerful interest groups to recognise these as 'crime'; equally important is the fact that whatever agencies, organisations or individuals are charged with enforcing such laws or standards *recognise* such harm as an important aspect of their work. In terms of criminal justice we might therefore debate whether the non-recognition of environmental harm is part of a broader 'legal culture' shared among advocates, judges, and criminal justice personnel. In the UK courts, for example, it will be noted in this chapter that judges have often been reluctant to consider awarding restitution orders in environmental cases. In many instances it is suggested that this derives not from a conscious *refusal* by the judiciary to consider environmental harm but rather, as the UK House of Commons Environmental Audit Committee (2004) have emphasised, from a lack of *awareness* of the issues in the first place within the legal professions. In the same report the English Law Society labelled this state of affairs as 'clearly unacceptable', again indicating that the problem lay with *attitudes* among the legal professions rather than the *law* itself. The Sentencing Council for England and Wales (2014) has recently responded to such concerns by designing new guidance for judges on sentencing in environmental cases (discussed in more detail below). Culture of course is not a monolithic entity and, as studies in the police have demonstrated (see Crank, 2004) they may vary greatly at different levels of a criminal justice system (lower courts versus higher courts, different departments within a police service and so on). Cultural working practices may also be geographically based. Different working cultures also of course pervade policymaking bodies, as noted by Rock (1986) in both Canada and the United Kingdom (Rock, 1990).

A telling example of the key role played by judicial attitudes and working cultures in relation to the recognition of environmental harms is that of the Nigerian Delta where, as will be discussed in Chapter 7, judges have traditionally disregarded the position of environmental victims in favour of the economic interests of the state (Ebeku, 2003). Of course, the point extends well beyond the judiciary. We will see below that the operation and enforcement of a great deal of environmental regulation and criminal law at present depends on the working practices and cultures of enforcement agencies (Bell and McGillivray, 2008). Indeed, for those human and animals affected by environmental harm, the capacity to access *any* form of redress mechanism or support beyond the criminal justice system will in practice be heavily reliant on a *recognition* by relevant agencies of the harm they have endured. It is a situation markedly familiar to mainstream victimologists, especially when considering, for example, rape victims, victims who are not entirely 'blameless' (Christie, 1986) and indirect victims/survivors of homicide (see Rock, 1998). Of course the lingering cultural reticence in many criminal justice systems to accept the incorporation of *any* crimes victims within their working practices still needs to be tackled by green criminologists and victimologists and this will be expanded upon in detail in Chapter 7.

In terms of furthering green criminology, the above points reinforce earlier arguments in this volume in favour of a constructivist approach which examines the social recognition of environmental harm: not just on a national or international level, but at the level of *local* enforcement. Thus, while highly developed systems of laws and regulations may exist on paper in any given jurisdiction or locale, that is not to say such devices are effective, or work as they are meant to. As noted by Walters (2010) in relation to air pollution, establishing standards and rules for environmental compliance is only the first step in addressing such matters:

> There are numerous measures proposed, or being implemented, to reduce air pollution ... However, efforts to reduce emissions must be accompanied by dynamic and effective regulatory arrangements that target the big corporate polluters. (pp.319–320)

The next three sections of this chapter, on detecting and policing, regulating and sentencing environmental harms will illustrate some of the reasons why the means of achieving such 'dynamic and effective' regulatory and other legal mechanisms is central to the green criminological project.

DETECTING AND POLICING ENVIRONMENTAL HARM

Much has been written in the literature about 'policing' the environment and whether in fact this is the role of mainstream police services, regulatory agencies, NGOs or the bodies and persons being policed themselves (see Guerrero and Innes, 2013); in reality though the distinctions between these options may be less clear-cut than it first appears. Gill (2002) for example argues:

> there is no essential difference between policing and regulation ... the analysis of contemporary policing would benefit if it was seen as one part of a broader regulatory spectrum. It is the policing of 'predatory' crime by 'the usual suspects' that comes closest to the normal view of policing as law enforcement while policing and regulatory styles are closest in the area of 'enterprise' crime. But the containment of the most destructive effects of the operations of markets (legal or illegal) and firms is actually the objective of almost all policing. (p.539)

Tellingly, by 'enterprise' crimes Gill is referring to what we might understand as occupational or white-collar offending (see Chapter 5). This implies that, in terms of detecting and investigating breaches of environmental law, and certainly environmental crime, the debates discussed in Chapter 3 concerning civil or administrative versus criminal lines of enforcement are less significant. Indeed, drawing on the work of Hawkins (1998) Gill goes on to argue that just as in practice much of the traditional policing role concerns the *management* of disorder rather than law *enforcement* or 'fighting crime' per se, this is equally the case with enforcement work in relation to environmental laws:

> Enforcement work in pollution control was similar to police work in being bound up with the 'management of appearances' and that arrests would be made only in cases of 'flagrant violations', prosecution being an indication that all other methods had failed (1998: 291–6). He [Hawkins (1998)] concludes: 'What is really being sanctioned is not pollution but deliberate or negligent law-breaking and its symbolic assault on the legitimacy of the regulatory authority'. (pp.525–526)

Thus whether we are discussing police officers or the enforcement officials of regulators or other environment agencies, Carter (1998) argues that proactive enforcement strategies are needed as opposed to the more reactive strategies he feels dominate most environmental initiatives (in this case in the United States). As an alternative, Carter argues that police officers need to adopt more proactive strategies:

> Law enforcement officers should carefully document their observations by making detailed written records of what they see, hear and smell. Photographing or videotaping suspicious operations or incidence is even better. The officers should patrol their communities with an increased awareness of the various methods used by environmental criminals. Frequent contact with community members leads to were poor and cooperation and will increase the chance of environment environmental crime initiative will succeed. (p.181)

Carter also stresses that police officers need to be trained on the dangers of environmentally harmful practices to avoid risks to themselves and thus a core of scientific expertise within the police service needs to be instilled within police working culture. The problem is also evident in the United States, where Brisman (2006) has noted the risks taken by law enforcement officers while investigating methamphetamine labs. Such officers often have little knowledge of the potential human and environmental harms caused by such operations.

Another point emphasised by Carter (1998) is the need for policing of environmental harm to be approached from a multi-agency standpoint. Again this ties in with the observation that the polic*ing* of the environment is not necessarily only done (or indeed best achieved) by *police officers* alone. Tomkins for example discusses case studies from a range of different environmental law enforcement organisation and agencies at regional, national and international levels, which he gathers under the heading 'police services/institutions'. Of course even in relation to more traditional crimes the so-called multi-agency approach to policing and crime prevention – whereby the responsibility for addressing crime is approached as a collective effort by a number of different organisations – has become widely utilised in many jurisdictions (Harvie and Manzi, 2011). Inherent advantages to the multi-agency approach are said to include increased efficiency and effectiveness (Sampson et al., 1988). It is also recognised that the causes of crime are beyond the scope of one single agency. Certainly the last two chapters have indicated this is likely to be the case for environmental harm as well. The other key advantage of the multi-agency approach is said to be that social problems no longer fall between the gaps of social institutions. Clearly policing environmental crime is a multi-agency issue requiring cooperation between different police forces and between the police and other agencies. On this point Tomkins (2005) has argued that because environmental crime can have negative impacts well outside the immediate areas where the offence has occurred, police officers from various locations and even nationalities must work together (see Box 1 for the examples of Interpol and Europol's international policing initiative concerning the environment).

Box 1: Policing the environment at the transnational level: The INTERPOL Environmental Crime Programme

The International Criminal Police Organization (INTERPOL) is the world's largest international police organisation, facilitating cooperation, exchange of information and joint operations between domestic police forces. Its dedicated Environmental Crime Programme has the following functions:

- Leading global and regional operations to dismantle the criminal networks behind environmental crime using intelligence-driven policing;
- Coordinating and develops international law enforcement best practice manuals, guides and other resources;

■ Providing environmental law enforcement agencies with access to INTERPOL services by enhancing their links with INTERPOL National Central Bureaus;

■ Working with INTERPOL's Environmental Crime Committee to shape the Programme's strategy and direction.

■ The INTERPOL Wildlife Crime Working Group, Pollution Crime Working Group and Fisheries Crime Working Group bring together criminal investigators from around the world to share information and initiate targeted projects to tackle specific areas of environmental crime (INTERPOL, 2014).

EUROPOL AND EnviCrimeNet

According to the European Police Office (Eurpol) itself, the organisation's stated aim is to 'help achieve a safer Europe for the benefit of all EU citizens by supporting law enforcement authorities through the exchange and analysis of criminal intelligence'. Although Europol has no specific mandate to address environmental crime or wider harms, it has developed various initiatives under its 'Platform for Experts' scheme, including the online resource EnviCrimeNet. EnviCrimeNet is 'a unique and international network of experts from European law enforcement and investigative competent authorities committed to fight serious environmental crime' (www.eurocrime.net) and is intended to facilitate exchange of best practice between national experts involved in combating illegal waste management using risk profiling to identify potential illegal disposal sites and protecting public officials from the hazards associated with the retrieval of illegal waste repositories.

Both these international examples thus empathise the multi-agency approach and in particular cooperation between police organisations, especially in the form of exchanging information, as a means of policing environmental harm/crime.

This raises particular challenges to green criminologists interested in this area, specifically because:

> We need to know what kinds of structures and strategies are needed to facilitate cooperation between different police services dealing with this type of crime ... police cooperation from the local to international level raises important questions about how policing organizations view other policing institutions whom they may work with when investigating environmental crime. (Tomkins, 2005: p.305)

Another significant aspect of enforcement work commented on in the literature is the degree to which enforcement officials/police actually know and understand the relevant environmental laws and regulations. Thus, one reason the police are often ineffective in this regard is likely to be that they do not have the relevant skills or training (as suggested by Carter (1998) and Brisman (2006)) to recognise when an environmental crime has occurred/is occurring. Nevertheless, even more specialist enforcement bodies can have difficulties in this regard. For example, in the context of lobster poaching in Southwest Nova Scotia in Canada McMulan and Perrier (2002) note:

> We found that regulators in the lobster fishery are uncertain of laws, puzzled by the frequency and complexity of variation orders, and convinced that the sanctions are paltry and symbolic. (p.715)

Research by the UK Environmental Law Association (2011) was similarly critical of environmental legislation in that country:

> Initial findings indicate a range of areas where environmental legislation is so complex that it is difficult to access, understand and apply. (p.52)

On the other hand, Du Rées (2001) argues that in her research (based on the enforcement of evidential criminal law in Sweden) what she calls a lack of 'regulatory acumen' among investigative agencies is not the problem, as this naturally builds up with experience. For her difficulties rather derive from the (minimal) likelihood of being sanctioned for breaking environmental rules and the lack of severity of the punishments imposed (on which see below).

In Chapter 5 it was discussed how states have increasingly tended to place responsibility for environmental harm on consumers and the population at large rather than on – in particular – corporate actors themselves. While there we saw that such moves can be criticised as constituting scapegoating and a divesting of responsibility, the multi-agency approach would support the notion that partnerships need to be brokered between corporations, police and indeed the public in general. On the last point, O'Rouke and Macey (2003) have discussed the example of so-called Bucket Brigades in the United States, whereby local community activists using inexpensive homemade equipment ('buckets') assist authorities in monitoring air omissions near industrial facilities. The authors argue that this essentially represents an extension into the environmental realm of so-called community policing, which in recent years has become a staple subject of mainstream criminological discussion of the police:

> 'Community environmental policing', through programs such as the bucket brigades, is similar to community policing in that it seeks to place external community pressure on government officials to change agency practices, consider local issues more seriously, and collaboratively address problems. (p.386)

Understood this way, community engagement in environmental policing is not so much a divesting of responsibility, but rather a call for regulators to correct regulatory shortcomings and for the police to take the issue seriously. Indeed, here one may draw parallels with how the victims (of crime) movement has facilitated serious attention being paid by police and prosecutors to certain kinds of crime which previously were often dismissed as 'minor' or beyond the 'proper' scope of criminal justice work, the most obvious of which is domestic violence (Association of Chief Police Officers, 2008). A similar point has was made by Cable and Benson (1993) as they charted the growth in local 'grass roots' environmental organisations, which they argued frequently make up for the shortcomings of official regulators (see below):

> Emerging in the 1980s, community-based grass root environmental organizations represent a new trend within the larger environmental movement...unlike well-known lobbying organizations such as the Sierra Club and the National Resources Defense Counsel these grassroots organizations focus specifically on local environmental problems are less concerned with national environmental policy and form in opposition to the problem of pollution caused by local businesses. (p.464)

In any case Carter (1998) makes the point that enforcement agencies must work with local communities who in many cases will be reporting any environmental transgressions that come to the attention of police. This again reflects mainstream policing literature in that while environmental regulators are often criticised for taking a *reactive* rather than *proactive* approach. In terms of criminal justice the police are in fact most often a reactive body and have sometimes described as a 'fire brigade' service (Reiner, 2012), except in specific areas such as child pornography (Johnson and Onwuegbuzie, 2004) and terrorism (Pickering et al., 2008). Arguably therefore one of the roles of green criminology may be to help establish whether environmental crime and environmental harm also need to be added to this list of 'proactive' policing issues.

Corporate self-policing

Another key debate in the literature concerning the policing of environmental harm concerns whether the focus should be on mechanisms that permit corporations to police *themselves*. The most widely discussed example of such a system is that initiated in 1995 by the US Environmental Protection Agency. The EPA's so-called Audit Policy essentially guarantees significantly lower penalties and reduced inspections for companies who voluntarily disclose and correct breaches of environmental law within 60 days of their occurrence. The argument follows that this reduces costs and thus (from a rational choice perspective (see p.29)) increases compliance with environmental regulations and laws. Of course, from a more critical perspective some have argued that the Audit Policy is another means by which powerful corporate actors may be permitted to profit from their polluting activities essentially with the consent of an ineffective regulator representing state interests (Guerrero and Innes, 2013). It has been difficult to prove conclusively that the Audit Policy has had its intended effect although, as Stafford (2003) notes 'there is little basis to argue that the federal and state policies have decreased [environmental] compliance' (p.22).

Quantitative analysis by Stretesky (2006) attempted to establish whether companies could be compelled towards embracing self-policing mechanism by stricter use of more compulsive methods in the sector. The author's conclusion was that 'There is no evidence that inspections and enforcement increase Audit Policy use' (p.608). To put it another way, traditional methods of policing and enforcement do not increase self-policing of environmental transgressions among companies as of themselves. That said the study did demonstrate that larger companies were more likely to disclose transgressions under the Audit Policy and that this was also more likely in the case of smaller violations. Importantly, for Stretesky this demonstrates not so much that deterrence is ineffective in relation to companies, but rather that such deterrence and associated moves towards self-policing are *not* based *on the actual levels of punishment* a company and its directors observe being applied in the sector (so-called objective deterrence). This does not however mean that more *subjective* modes of deterrence – based on directors' *perceptions* of the likelihood of punishment – may not work better in the environmental sphere (see Braithwaite and Makkai, 1991).

For their part, Braithwaite and Fisse (1987) present what they argue to be essential requirements of a successful company self-regulatory system as including:

- Top management commitment to the system and backing for compliance personnel.
- Clearly defined lines of accountability within the organisation.
- Careful monitoring of the organisation's performance.
- Prompt communication of compliance problems to those responsible for rectification.
- Appropriate training and supervision by front-line supervisors.

Of course, the extent to which states prefer to adopt self-policing/regulatory frameworks for environmental harm raises much bigger questions of interest to criminologists concerning the nature of modern governance. For example, Osborne and Gaebler (1992) argued that given the natural restraints and limitations of top-down regulation, governments adopt the role of facilitator and broker, rather than that of commander. They suggest that governments 'steer' rather than 'row', and that they structure the marketplace so that naturally occurring private activity may assist in furthering public policy objectives. Thus Grabosky and Grant (2000) argue that in moves towards greater use of green self-policing:

> What we may be witnessing is not so much an abdication of government responsibility for the control of environmental crime, but rather a transformation of social control. Ironically, what we are experiencing could well entail less government regulation, resulting in the improved environmental performance of business and of individual citizens. (p.2)

Clearly environmental crime and wider harm raises considerable challenges to traditional modules of regulation and certainly traditional models of policing. Guerrero and Innes (2013) have examined both the 'privilege' afforded to self-reporters of environmental transgressions in the United States (whereby if breaches are self-reported the information cannot be used by regulators beyond the narrow confines of the self-reported violation) and offering polluters immunity from prosecutions in return for their self-policing. In sum their conclusions are that the latter is likely to increase environmental pollution but the former, depending on how it is implemented, may well serve environmental needs:

> Overall, our results suggest that providing firms with positive incentives for environmental self-auditing, by protecting their audits from use by government prosecutors, can be a valuable component of environmental law enforcement as it reduces both pollution and enforcement costs. They also suggest the need for care in the design of self-auditing inducements and argue against blanket privilege and immunity protections and instead in favor of more targeted and limited protections. (pp.28–29)

With much debate now being had by mainstream criminologists and other commentators in the social sciences on the nature of government, governance and concepts such as corporate self- and community-policing, it is clear that this will remain fertile ground for green criminologists as well.

ENFORCING ENVIRONMENTAL LAW AND REGULATIONS

Many of the points raised in the previous sections overlap and flow into the question of (in criminal justice language) the bringing of prosecutions against those causing unlawful environmental harm. Indeed, historically Bell et al. (2013) note, 'there have been many overlaps between the operational and regulatory functions carried out by environmental agencies' and, furthermore, 'the operational arms of the regulatory bodies [frequently] caused the greatest breaches of environmental laws' (p.285). Aside from the question of policing both Du Rées (2001) and Bell and McGillivray (2008) argue that the problems inherent in many criminal justice systems' approach to environmental crime really begin at the stage of *prosecution*. While Du Rées puts greater emphasis on the frequent failings of criminal laws or regulations to adequately set the boundaries for the operation of regulatory agencies, both authors effectively agree that the difficulty lies with the working practices of those agencies, rather than fundamental incompatibilities between environmental concerns and criminal justice. Bell and McGillivray (2008) also make the point (discussed earlier in this chapter) that, for a great deal of environmental regulation at present, enforcement depends very much on the working practices and cultures of enforcement agencies. It is also subject to the complexities inherent in a high degree of *informal* resolution, which in some cases might amount to regulatory capture, to be discussed in the next paragraph (Dal Bó, 2006).

Regulatory capture and related concepts lie at the heart of many of the criticisms of environmental regulation regimes and associated legal regimes. Essentially such capture is said to occur when, in the words of Shapiro (2012b):

> regulated entities have substantial influence over policymaking. In the second derivation, it is an accusation that the agency has failed to serve the public interest. (p.103)

As such, Shapiro (2012a) has argued that the 2010 BP Oil Spill in the Gulf of Mexico, for example, was facilitated to a significant extent by the regulatory capture of the US Mineral Mining Service (now the Bureau of Ocean Energy Management) principally because:

> We now know that the oil industry largely drove policy decisions in the agency. At the same time, there can be little doubt that the result did not serve the public interest, having resulted in the death of eleven workers and the worst environmental disaster in the United States. (p.103)

The extent of the regulatory capture in the BP/MMS case was highlighted in a report from the US Department of the Interior (2010) that subsequently became widely publicised in the press. The report highlighted the significant pressures the oil drilling industry was able to exercise over MMS and its inspectors to reduce the number of inspections and minimise the reporting of violations and that:

> inspectors expressed the need for more effective leadership in daily operations and for greater management support when faced with pressure from industry. (p.15)

In Japan, regulatory capture has also been blamed for the Fukushima nuclear disaster in 2011 (see Box 2). Simon (2000) argues that in the United States the Environmental Protection Agency has long since shown signs of capture by the waste industry and that 'given its past [criminal] activities, it was inevitable that the waste industry would corrupt the EPA, and that is exactly what has happened' (p.111). Of course much has been written more generally about regulatory capture, with some economists predicting that it is inevitable in most regulatory situations. This is because those with the highest stake in promoting regulatory arrangements that benefit themselves have a definite political voice (e.g. major polluting corporations) whereas those who benefit from stricter regulations (the majority of the public) are more diverse and thus not able to mount the same political pressures. Needless to say we might add from the eco-centric perspective that 'nature' and non-human animals are unable to mount pressure at all in most cases. Furthermore, because regulation of any complex industry requires specialist knowledge and expertise in that industry, in practice over time the regulators and regulated become the same people. As contended by Simon (2000):

> Today there are 20 high-ranking former EPA administrators that have left the agency and become millionaire waste-industry executives, giving rise to charges of a revolving door between the EPA and the hazardous waste management industry. (p.112)

Herein of course lies one possible advantage of criminalisation over regulation, in that courts and the criminal justice system as a whole are arguably less likely to be 'captured' than lay regulators. That said, cases like that on the Nigerian Delta and the influence exerted on judges indicate this cannot be guaranteed. The same might be said for the pervasive influence of mafia organisations on the waste industry in Italy and the United States (see Chapter 4). The other point concerning criminalisation in this context is of course that, in line with the cultural arguments noted earlier, it will still be down to state prosecutors (or possibly other bodies) to elect to bring such criminal cases to court. The bringing of more cases might be facilitated if strict liability principles (see p.36 for an explanation of this legal term) are applied in either the criminal or administrative sphere. Indeed, the strict liability approach to environmental harms might be said to promote the public interest goal inherent in environmental legislation, making prosecutions easier to achieve and thus act as a deterrent to other polluters (but see Stretesky (2006) discussed above). Strict liability in this context also conforms to the polluter pays principle discussed in Chapter 5. Indeed, Bell et al. (2013) point out that in practice when environmental harm *is* criminalised many of the offences are ones of strict liability, subject to the possible defences of acting with statutory consent, emergency situations, exercising due diligence or 'reasonable excuse'.

In their wider discussion of environmental criminal law, Bell et al. (2013) have drawn on the 'enforcement pyramid' posited by Ayres and Braithwaite (1997) to describe enforcement tactics of many jurisdictions in relation to environmental 'crime'. Essentially this pyramid puts 'persuasion' at its base as the most commonly used mechanism of environmental law enforcement. The diagram then works up the pyramid from persuasion to warning letters, enforcement notices, criminal penalties, suspension of operations licences and, at the apex (least utilised), revocation of license. Revocation is deemed the most serious penalty under this model because revocation of a company's license to operate is in fact far more damaging than, for example, a relatively small fine imposed by a criminal court. The pyramid represents a model of so-called responsive regulation whereby different enforcement options are made available and the enforcement officer chooses the least significant one that will achieve an overriding goal of *compliance* (rather than *punishment*).

Box 2: The regulatory capture of the Japanese Nuclear and Industrial Safety Agency?

Controversy concerning the Japanese Nuclear and Industrial Safety Agency (NISA) revolves around its approving on February 2011 of ten further years of use for the oldest (of 6) nuclear reactors at the Fukushima Daiichi nuclear power plant. This was despite having received warnings as the safety of continuing to use of the reactor, which had reached the end of its designated period of operation and was scheduled for decommission. In the light of the Fukushima nuclear disaster of March that year – dubbed by many the 'worst nuclear accident since Chernobyl' (Pandey, 2014) – NISA's decision and the processes behind it have come under severe scrutiny. The result of such scrutiny points to severe inefficiencies and ineffectiveness in the operation of the regulator and weak oversight of its operations. Particularly strong connections have been identified between NISA and the Tokyo Electric Power Company (TEPCO). Furthermore Wang and Chen (2012) argue that the transfer of personnel from the regulator to the nuclear industry and vice versa means corporate interests are routinely prioritised. As the authors surmise:

> With such incestuous relationships between the nuclear regulators and nuclear utilities being regulated in place, inspections have been superficial. (p.2611)

Interestingly from the perspective of green criminology, Wang and Chen go on to provide a sociological explanation for the high degree of regulatory capture seen in Japan's nuclear sector and beyond. For them the frequent movement of industry managers into high-level regulatory jobs and of government personnel into executive positions in industry reflects Japanese society and in particular its Confucian adherence to strict social hierarchies. Indeed the practice of high-level government bureaucrats retiring to highly lucrative private sector positions is culturally incorporated within traditional Japanese society and is known as 'Amakudari', meaning 'descent from heaven':

> As a Confucian country, rigid social hierarchy has remained popular in Japan, although it has achieved industrialization, urbanization and modernization. Confucianism leads bureaucrats to see themselves as samurai and the business as serfs. And business voluntarily looks to government for guidance. This culture allowed the Japan's government to strongly influence business. (p.2612)

This has brought about a situation in which there exists 'an illegal revolving door between many branches of the Japanese government and corporations has become a widespread practice' (2615). Indeed, NISA is in fact part of the Japanese Ministry of Economic, Trade and Industry, which has a mandate to *encourage* the development of the nuclear industry. The example illustrates not only the complexity of regulation even beyond the criminal justice sphere, but also again highlights the points made in chapters 4 and 5 concerning the close interrelation in many contexts between government and business interests in a given state.

Aside from the imposition of regulation by external bodies (a so-called sanctioning approach) or the 'mixed' approach implied by more responsive regulation models like that of Ayres and Braithwaite (1995) discussed above, others have argued that corporations in particular must to be permitted to engage with regulators on a more cooperative level, progressing towards models of self-regulation. We have already noted one model of self-regulation (and self-policing) in the US Audit Policy discussed above, where we saw it brought many potential advantages in theory, although it was difficult to demonstrate their operation in reality. Walters (2010) has gone further to criticise the self-regulation approach taken to air pollution control in the United Kingdom. In this case, although the system has been praised for its definitive and multi-level system of permitting the release of air-polluting agents, Walters emphasises that 'installations are entrusted with the responsibility to self-regulate and manage the conditions of their designated permit' (p.311). In practice he notes that (predominantly financial) penalties imposed under this system for violations have been minor compared to the profits of the corporations involved:

> air pollution control in the UK, which has been praised as a flagship model, remains based on trust, partnership and operator self-regulation. The involvement of operator appointed scientific expertise to assess and process permits raises serious questions that challenge the regime's ability to make impartial judgments. The existing regulatory regime of air pollution in the UK lacks neutrality. It is a process that remains biased towards the economic imperatives of free trade over and above the centrality of environmental protection. (p.320)

Again the key implication of this discussion is that both the decision as to how to enforce environmental law and the structure of the legal and regulatory regime put in place to achieve this raises complex and multi faceted issue for green criminology. Such questions combine fairly traditional criminological factors like occupational cultures, regulation and 'law in action' with a host of sociological, economic and political issues. Again the need for an interdisciplinary approach is clear.

RESPONDING TO, CENSURING AND SENTENCING ENVIRONMENTAL TRANSGRESSIONS

Discussion of how regulatory or legal agencies actually respond in proven cases of environmental transgression or harm has already been touched upon in the above discussion, emphasising once again the interrelationship between policing, enforcement and punishment/redress in relation to environmental harm. Generally speaking much of the literature on punishment and other mechanisms of censure for causing illegal environmental harm emphasise the point that such punishments that are imposed are frequently minimal, especially when compared to the profits of large international corporations who are the main polluters. Thus we have just noted Walters' (2010) contention that:

> The penalties imposed for operator's breaching permits are minor in comparison to corporate profits. The more severe penalties are rarely imposed. Thus, the system of

regulation and control is not based on deterrence but on incentive and partnership. Moreover, the existing regime must inculcate greater independence and public visibility. (p.320)

Such concerns have also been reflected in the United Kingdom by the House of Commons Environmental Audit Committee (2004) when it reported:

> We are concerned that the general level at which fines are imposed neither reflects the gravity of environmental crimes, nor deters or punishes adequately those who commit them. This is clearly unsatisfactory. (para.16)

Of course in discussing regulators' (and society as a whole's) response to environmental harm we are raising very old criminological debates about the purposes of any such responses. Are we setting out to *punish* transgressors? Restore damage to the environment? Deter future transgressions both on the part of the same operator (specific deterrence) or by other operators (general deterrence)? As The House of Commons Committee also noted in relation to financial penalties, minimal levels of fines will have a direct effect on whether some of these sentencing outcomes can be achieved:

> Courts – and prosecutors – need to bear in mind that unless the polluter pays substantially more than the sum he profits by from his crime there will be no real deterrent or punishment value to the sentence given. (para.21)

In the criminal justice system the Committee recommended the training of specialised teams of dedicated judges and magistrates who would become well versed in the sentencing of environmental offenders. One option explored by Walters and Westerhuis (2013) is that specialist criminal courts may be developed to this end just as recent years (certainly in the United Kingdom) have seen specialist courts develop to tackle domestic violence and drug related crime. More recently the England and Wales Sentencing Council has developed new guidelines for the imposition of fines in environmental crime cases (Sentencing Council, 2014). This example will serve as a useful representation of the complexities inherent in this sentencing exercise. In a model that closely resembles that suggested by Mandiberg and Faure (2009) the guidelines set out a system for determining fine levels based on two key factors: the degree of environmental (and related) harm caused and the level of culpability of the polluter. Under this system the most serious form of 'Category 1' harm is described as:

■ Polluting material of a dangerous nature, for example, hazardous chemicals or sharp objects.

- Substantial adverse effect or damage to land, air or water quality, amenity value, property.
- Polluting material was noxious, widespread or pervasive with long-lasting effects on animal health, human health or flora. Substantial costs incurred through clean-up, site restoration or animal rehabilitation.
- Substantial interference with or prevention of other lawful activities due to offence.

Similar lists of progressively less seriousness effects are then given for Category 2, 3 and 4 harm. In line with the modern concentration on *risk* as well as *actual* occurrence of environmental harm the system also encompasses potential harms. Thus Category 2 harm includes 'the risk of Category 1 harm', Category 3 includes the risk of Category 2 and similarly Category 4 includes the risk of Category 3. Once the level of harm has been categorised offenders are judged by their level of culpability ranging from deliberate actions following through to recklessness; negligence or little or no culpability (the latter being relevant given that many of these crimes are strict liability offences). The guidelines then marry the category to the culpability to produce tables of associated 'starting points' for sentencers in determining fine levels. The guide provide three such tables for small, medium and large firms and then provides lists of mitigating and aggravating factors which could raise or lower the initial determination.

The goal of the guidelines is predominantly to improve consistency of sentencing in environmental cases, which had been very haphazard. Of course, with any guidelines there is the risk of reducing discretion to the point that cases must be 'fitted' within rigid categories, which given the complex and differing situation in which environmental transgressions can occur may not always be desirable.

For O'Hear (2004) such questions of sentencing are vital, as for him the role of the *sentencer* in environmental matters, given the uncertainties at enforcement and prosecution stage discussed in the last section, is paramount:

> Specifically, defenders of the current regime rely on prosecutorial discretion to protect the 'morally innocent' from criminal sanctions for low-level environmental violations. Critics, however, find prosecutors less trustworthy. Both sides have missed the potential for another actor in the criminal justice system, the sentencing judge, to protect low-culpability defendants from harsh sanctions. (p.487)

As noted previously however *criminal* sanctions are actually well down the hierarchy of responses to environmental transgression in many jurisdictions in terms of amount utilised. In Chapter 3 I discussed the general trend as being a move away from criminal enforcement towards civil enforcement. To this end, the UK Environment Agency in 2010 was given a host of new civil enforcement powers described by the Agency in the following terms:

> Civil Sanctions provide us with new ways to protect the environment. They focus on investment in environmental clean-up rather than paying fines. Civil sanctions do not replace any of our current enforcement tools. They provide us with a more flexible range so that we can choose the most appropriate enforcement action when an offence occurs. We will still prosecute serious offenders, but we will be able to use alternative sanctions with legitimate businesses who are trying to do the right thing. They will be able to put right the damage they have done and local communities will see a direct improvement in the environment as a result. (2014a, unpaginated)

Interesting this statement has definite eco-centric overtones and certainly implies that restoring the environment itself may be prioritised over punishing offenders. It also espouses one of the key benefits associated with civil sanctions in the form of flexibility. The sanctions available are presented in Figure 6.1.

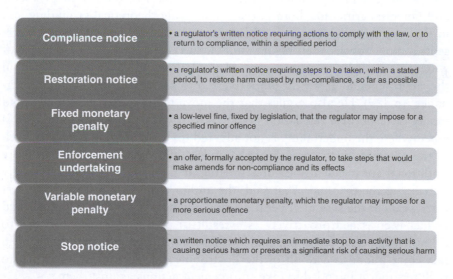

Figure 6.1   Regime of civil sanctions available to the UK Environment Agency

Possibly the most controversial of these measures is the enforcement undertaking. Given the above discussion on regulatory capture the argument would be that these effectively allow environmental polluters to quickly come to arrangements with the Agency to avoid further sanction: raising important question as to how easily this can be achieved. That said, arguably enforcement undertakings above all other measures reflect the benefits of flexibility and tailoring responses to particular situations. The underlying legislation (the Regulatory Enforcement and Sanctions Act 2008) does in fact require (in s.50(3)) that the agreements must have certain aims, namely:

1) To secure that the offence does not continue or recur.
2) To secure that the environmental position is, so far as possible, restored to what it was before the offence was committed.
3) The action must be to the benefit of any persons affected by the offence.
4) Where restoration of the harm caused by the offence is not possible, the action must secure equivalent benefit or improvement of the environment.
5) The undertaking must specify the time in which the agreed action must take place.

Pederson (2013) has reviewed the introduction of enforcement undertakings and while generally arguing in their favour notes a number of problems and potential criticisms, both in their underlying theoretical grounding and in the way they appear to have been applied. The system effectively represents a move towards self-regulation, which Pedersen views as indicative of wider trends 'away from state-centred regulation and governance', which in the environmental area is at times referred to as 'new environmental governance' (p.329). He also argues that the move takes us beyond the pyramid model of responsive regulation noted above (Ayres and Braithwaite, 1995) albeit where the undertaking is not adhered to, we likely find ourselves back in the pyramid, as the breach of the undertaking becomes subject to more traditional enforcement measures starting at the lower echelons, gradually moving up the pyramid. That said, the author notes that in fact in the first three years of the system's operation only a handful of the undertakings had in fact been issued proactively as a result of polluters coming forward to acknowledge their environmental transgressions. The vast majority had in fact come about as a result of the Environment Agency itself indicating to polluters that it intended to take enforcement actions against them.

Pedersen's primary concern is with the inclusion of charitable donations in many of the enforcement undertakings seen so far. Ostensibly the idea here is that the environment can be restored partly through giving money to charities with environmental remits. In practice however Pedersen argues it is unclear whether the Agency or the polluters are choosing which charities are to benefit. As such:

> An associated accountability problem with the strong emphasis on donations to environmental organisations is that it seemingly favours organisations which, for some reason or another, are already known to the offender and the Agency, potentially at the exclusion of other worthy causes. Naturally, the offender is free to make charitable donations as part of its day-to-day business operations but the problem with a donation forming part of an undertaking is that it serves a regulatory purpose and is carried out in the place of a criminal sanction. (p.334)

More specifically, Pedersen's concern is that such donations may in fact be disguising 'rent-seeking activity' on the part of offending corporations or individuals. In other words the argument is that by contributing to the charities corporations gain social capital (and perhaps tax breaks) and so gain wealth without creating wealth. Thus, while the author accepts that the system may assist in instilling environmental protection values in offenders (as seems to be the case with environmental impact assessments (Holder, 2004)) there is presently a lack of overarching scrutiny of this system.

Criminologists clearly have much to offer in any debate concerning the impact of various responses to environmental offending or more general environmental harm. In particular the factors that serve to deter both corporations and individuals from offending have long been the subject of widespread criminological discussion. What is less apparent in traditional criminology is of course is where the environment itself or non-human animals sit within this dynamic. We have seen hints above that new sentencing regimes are exploring ways to incorporate more eco-centric concerns and this is clearly an important direction for a *green* criminology to pursue further.

PREVENTING ENVIRONMENTAL HARM

This chapter is not specifically focused on the issue of *preventing* environmental harm (see Brickey, 1996) but a brief review of the key debates on this subject will be provided as clearly there is considerable overlap between this issue and the above discussions. In particular, notions of 'preventing crime' borrowed from mainstream criminology are in fact closely aligned to the notion of managing environmental *risk* first introduced in Chapter 1. Interestingly the *prevention* of crime did not become a staple topic of mainstream criminology until relatively late in the development of the wider criminological literature and indeed this development is still largely restricted to the last 30 years. This chapter has already touched upon attempts to deter future environmental offending which, certainly among corporate actors, are often largely based around the assumption of a rational choice exercise and the application of cost-benefit analysis by such polluters or would-be polluters (see Paternoster and Simpson, 1996). Much of the writing so far on the prevention of environmental crimes or wider environmental harms has revolved around the elimination of perceived inefficiencies in the flows of information between regulators and regulated actors and – as hinted earlier – a widespread lack of understanding of legal and regulatory arrangements by both. Thus the argument goes that:

> Non-compliance with environmental laws often flows from the belief that the laws in question are unnecessary or unreasonable. Basic information about legal requirements and the reasons why they exist can lower resistance to regulation and make it easier for an individual or a company to do the right thing. (Grabosky and Grant, 2000: p.6)

The distribution of information between regulating agencies and police services is of course the driving philosophy behind many international cooperative mechanisms set up to tackle the spread of environmental harm. INTERPOL's stated successes in this regard are highlighted in Box 3. That said the example of INTERPOL should be approached with caution given a waning by Stretesky and Knight (2013) who argue that that while international non-government organisation (INGOS) have taken a 'major role' in the enforcement of environmental law and the prevention of environmental harm, they also represent global inequalities between rich and poor in their choice of where to direct their activities. This is because the headquarters of such organisations are almost always based in wealthy states and thus, the authors argue, their activities inevitably reflect the views and priorities of powerful elites on a global scale.

Box 3: INTERPOL's recent stated operational successes (adapted from INTERPOL, 2014)

Operation Cage (2012) – against the illegal trade and exploitation of birds and their products. More than 8,700 birds and animals, including reptiles, mammals and insects were seized and nearly 4,000 people arrested in an operation across 32 countries.

Operation Enigma, Phase I (2012) – to combat the illegal trade of electronic waste (or e-waste). The operation resulted in the seizure of more than 240 tons of electronic equipment and electrical goods and the launch of criminal investigations against some 40 companies.

Operation Lead (2012) – INTERPOL's first international operation targeting large-scale illegal logging and forest crimes. The operation resulted in 194 arrests and the seizure of timber worth USD 8 million and some 150 vehicles across Latin America.

Operation Libra (2012) – against the illegal poaching and trade in pangolins. The operation involved investigations and enforcement actions across Indonesia, Laos, Malaysia, Thailand and Vietnam and led to the arrest of more than 40 individuals, with some 200 additional cases opened for investigation.

Operation Prey (2012) – targeting the illegal trade in Asian big cats and wildlife products. The operation was conducted across 10 countries and collectively led to the seizure of 40 live tigers and big cat skins, along with other protected wildlife and flora products.

Operation Worthy (2012) – combating the illegal trade in elephant ivory and rhinoceros horn in 14 African countries. Seizures included nearly two tons of contraband elephant ivory, more than 20 kg of rhinoceros horn, various other wildlife products, and more than 30 illegal firearms.

Grabosky and Grant (2000) also emphasise in their list of proposed strategies for the improvement of environmental performance the provision of information about environmental risks, responsibilities and opportunities. Carter (1998) notes the need for such flows of information to come *from* corporations as well as *to* them. The UK House of Commons Environmental Audit Committee (2004) also acknowledged the importance of information flows for criminal enforcement in particular at all stages of the criminal justice process:

> Information is key to fighting crime, and all those dealing with environmental offences, whether they be sentencers, prosecutors, investigators, or those dealing with clean-up or with prevention, require a good corpus of information on which to build effective strategies. We look to the Government, in co-operation with other engaged bodies, to examine practical means to set up a comprehensive database of environmental crime to improve information in this area. (para.38)

Both Carter (1998) and Grabosky and Grant (2000) also call for further moves towards what has been described above as self-regulation or cooperation-based regulation, which increasingly appears to be the trend in the United Kingdom and arguably in some parts of the United States. Carter's call for partnerships to be built between regulators, police and corporations mirrors the multi-agency approach to crime prevention (as well as policing, noted above) that has received much discussion by mainstream criminologists (see p.136).

More generally White (2013b) and South (1998) have remarked on the lack of application thus far of crime prevention theories from mainstream criminology to either environmental crime or wider environmental harms. For Grabosky and Grant (2000) this is a key oversight because successfully *controlling* environmental crime in the first place avoids the significant challenges associated with establishing workable and robust legal or regulatory mechanisms around this problem. Thus the authors call for:

> a more expansive conception of environmental crime control which would harness a wide variety of institutions and influences in furtherance of improved environmental performance. When functioning properly, these institutions can significantly reduce the necessity for environmental enforcement. (p.v)

The under-theorisation of crime prevention methods in the environmental sphere is particularly apparent in the case of wildlife offences, as noted by Nurse (2013b):

> Wildlife resources are not closely monitored by criminal justice agents. Nor are they the subject of intensive crime prevention or target hardening initiatives employed to protect other valuable commodities. (p.131)

It should be noted that Nurse's use of the language of commodification in relation to wildlife 'resources' is purposely anthropocentric in this extract as the issue is being discussed in the context of a debate concerning a model of offending behaviour in which offenders seek to gain financial benefits from offending activities. In emphasising so-called target hardening (the prevention of crime through increased physical security) in this extract the author is in fact pointing to methods of situational crime prevention, whereby crime is prevented through minimising the criminal opportunities arising from the routines of everyday life. The perspective is closely linked with rational choice theory (see p.36) and routine activities theory (assuming crime occurs as a result of the structure of everyday life). Wellsmith (2010) has offered an extended discussion on the possible application of situational crime prevention methods to reduce the illicit trade and ultimate extinction of endangered species of animals and plants. So, to give three examples, she suggests increased use of CCTV and satellite imagery to prevent illegal fishing, the use of pilot-less drones to prevent elephant poaching and to hide endangered flora within other (non-invasive) crops.

Nurse (2013a) notes that in the United Kingdom situational monitoring initiates by NGOS, police and local community volunteers have had some success in preventing the stealing of birds' eggs for private collections. At the same time however Nurse injects a hint of caution about the assumption that offenders committing wildlife crimes are motivated or driven to do so by the same drivers as other types of offenders. The wider point is thus that the simple transplantation of tried-and-tested situational crime prevention techniques into the environmental sphere is unlikely to meet with complete success. So, in the case of poaching birds eggs, far from being a rational choice, or even an economically driven endeavour, Nurse points out that 'Egg collecting has been likened to a form of kleptomania or obsessive-compulsive disorder; offenders are driven to commit their crimes and are even addicted to the adventure of doing so' (p.138). Although a very specific example, this once again implies that green criminology as a whole needs to set out with different assumptions about crime and offenders than more traditional criminological endeavours. Furthermore, Wellsmith (2010) notes that situational crime prevention techniques may not always be compatible with green criminology's focus on *harm* rather than crime if in fact such techniques mean other environmental harm is caused even while the specifically targeted activity or crime in question is reduced (a phenomena criminologists call 'displacement'). So for example if poachers are dissuaded by situational methods from harvesting elephant tusks but adapt to poaching rhinoceros horns, there is little to recommend this from a species justice perspective.

Arguing from the perspective of victims of environmental harm (both human and non human) Bisschop and Vande Walle (2013) have argued that restorative justice options based on victim-orientated and community orientated crime prevention schemes may be adaptable to prevent environmental harm. In particular they highlight local community initiatives in Ghana concerning the harmful affects of e-waste, a considerable problem for the country. Their work emphasises how community groups draw attention to these problems and also incorporate 'naming and shaming' methods to prevent future harm. We saw in Chapter 3 how Mares (2010) has similarly advocated a 'shaming' approach be taken to preventing environmental harm, noting:

This article argues that formal mechanisms of social control are unlikely to succeed in bringing about behavioral change. Instead, I argue that more informal processes of shaming and status rewards are likely to be more successful. (p.291)

The possibilities of restorative justice options being applied to environmental harm/crime has already been discussed in Chapter 3 and will be returned to in Chapter 7. In particular these authors emphasise that such options '[pay] attention to future harm without neutralising or denying the harm inflicted' (p.44). Verry et al. (2005) have also advocated the use of restorative options in environmental cases:

> Clearly, restorative justice is not a route through which offenders, particularly repeat offenders, can minimise penalties. Rather, it appears to be a promising new way of dealing with environmental offences that can create positive outcomes and minimise prosecution costs, creating a win-win-win solution for the environment, offender, and prosecuting body. (p.8)

Ultimately the lack of detailed research applying crime prevention theories of various shades from mainstream criminological discussion to the issue of environmental harm mean at present much of the above is inevitably guesswork. Key work for green criminologists therefore lies in assessing how green crime and green harms can be prevented and what changes to existing crime prevention methods might be needed to achieve this.

RESPONDING TO ENVIRONMENTAL HARM: CHALLENGES TO GREEN CRIMINOLOGY

In sum the above discussions highlight the diverse issues and debates inherent in the notion of mounting official or less official responses to environmental harm at the national or international level, either through the criminal justice process or though other mechanisms. What is clear is that tried and tested theories concerning policing, prosecution, sentencing and prevention need to be reanalysed from a green perspective if they are to be effectively applied to environmental harm. Notably much of the literature on environmental regulation at present is focused on the United States and, to a lesser extent, the United Kingdom. The example of the Fukushima nuclear power plant and the possible regulatory failing of the nuclear industry in Japan (highlighted above in Box 2) emphasises that for a truly international green criminology this will be insufficient. In a list of successful examples of environmental law enforcement initiatives the Environmental Investigation Agency (2007) highlights good practice in this area as necessarily including regional cooperation among different agencies, local partnerships, national coordination of initiatives, specialised intelligence and the presence of political will in the government to effectively oversee the operations of the regulator. It is therefore clear that, particularly in relation to environmental regulations, the way things are perceived and done *on the ground* may be more important than the 'law in books'. As such, green criminology needs to encompass a focus on the social, political and economic context of environmental law, crimes and regulatory or administrative mechanisms: as well as the socially constructed views of those tasked with enforcing them.

Summary

Responding to environmental harm or more specific environmental crimes is a complex, multifaceted issue: where questions concerning policing, regulation, enforcement, sentencing and prevention all overlap. In all cases green criminologists must be mindful of the very real differences between regulation and laws in theory and how they operate in practice, and how these become refracted though the occupational cultures of those tasked with applying any system. It is clear that the effective policing of environmental harm cannot be achieved by 'the police' alone in any criminal justice system, but must instead encompass a multi-agency partnership which may include those being policed or regulated. Many forms of regulation exist and while the general trend appears to be towards more self-regulation and a cooperative approach, history has taught us that the underlying power relations and political issues bound up with environmental harm mean constant vigilance and oversight is needed to ensure such mechanisms are robust, fair and effective. Responding to or otherwise sentencing proven breaches of environmental law or regulatory regimes itself raise fundamental questions about what the sentencing exercise can and should be setting out to achieve, and as yet green criminological research has many questions still to answer in this regard. Similarly the prevention of environmental harm, or even environmental crime, is still a vastly under-researched area badly in need of attention from criminologists working from a more eco-centric perspective.

Review questions

1) What agencies/organisation or other contributors might be involved in a multi-agency policing initiative on environmental crime?
2) Why is regulating environmentally harmful activities much more about ideas in practice rather than ideas on paper?
3) Why has regulatory capture proven a particular pervasive issue in attempts to respond to environmental harms?
4) How can traditional notions of crime prevention espoused by criminologists be adapted to the environmental sphere?

Further reading

Stafford, S. (2003), *Does Self-Policing Help the Environment? EPA's Audit Policy and Hazardous Waste Compliance*, Williamsburg: William & Mary College.
- Very useful evaluation of the role of police in environmental enforcement.

Flournoy, A., Andreen, W., Bratspies, R., Doremus, H., Flatt, V., Glicksman, R., and Mintz, J. (2010), *Regulatory blowout: How regulatory failures made the BP disaster possible, and how the system can be fixed to avoid a recurrence*, Centre for Progressive Reform White Paper No.1007. Washington, DC: Centre for Progressive Reform.

- Thorough discussion from the perspective of regulation rather than criminalisation.

Cable, S. and Benson, M. (1993), 'Acting Locally: Environmental Injustice and the Emergence of Grass-Roots Environmental Organizations', *Social Problems*, 40(4): 464–477.

- Examines the role of non-state actors and the third sector in environmental enforcement.

Lemieux, A. (2014), Situational Crime Prevention of Poaching: An International Perspective. Crime Science Series. Abingdon: Routledge.

- Interesting application of more traditional crime prevention techniques from the criminological arena to an environmental issue.

Lemkin, J. (1996), 'Deterring Environmental Crime through Flexible Sentencing: A Proposal for the New Organizational Environmental Sentencing Guidelines', *California Law Review*, 84: 307–341.

- Offers discussion of the question of what should be done following conviction/enforcement of environmental laws/regulations.

Chapter 7

Environmental Victimisation

Victimological literature increasingly recognises that some groups have been left behind the main vanguard of the so-called victims movement. Among these still neglected groups are those victimised by actions of the state, corporate victims, the corporate and individual victims of white-collar crime and those harmed by the adverse effects of pollution and climate change. As such, this chapter turn to focus on environmental victims specifically to examine how we conceptualise 'environmental victimisation' to human and non-human animals and to the environment itself. The chapter will discuss the unequal impact of environmental crimes and harms between different human populations, countries and species. In the second half of the chapter I will discuss various mechanisms and ideas for offering redress to environmental victims and conclude with some thoughts on the future of a 'green victimology'.

By the end of this chapter readers will:

- Understand how environmental victimisation fits within broader notions of victimisation and victimological study and also the limits of this.
- Appreciate the difficulties in conceptualising 'environmental victimisation', especially from a more eco-centric perspective.
- Know some of the key legal measures that have been taken at the international level concerning environmental victimisation.
- Be in a position to argue the relative merits and demerits of various systems intended to offer compensation, restitution and/or redress for environmental harms falling on humans and non-humans.

This chapter will focus attention on human beings, animals and environments that are subject to the environmental crimes and wider environmental harms discussed in previous chapters. I have previously written about this topic from a more anthropocentric perspective, contending that the impacts of (human) environmental victimisation can be conceptualised under the banners of harm to health, economic harm, social harm and harm to security (Hall, 2013). These harms were reflected in Chapter 2 in a discussion of the social changes precipitated by environmental transformation and how these might bring criminogenic outcomes. This present chapter will offer further comment on the impacts of environmental harm at a local, national and international level. In particular it will emphasise the unequal manner in which this harm falls on various populations and environments. Moreover, it will examine the position of human and non-human victims of such harm in various legal and administrative processes with a specific focus on systems of compensation and restitution. Throughout, the goal will be to incorporate the eco-centric perspective, acknowledging that while much of the focus in the literature has been on the *human* costs of environmental crime, in fact it is almost possible to distinguish such harms from less anthropocentric impacts on non-human animals and the environment itself. Indeed it will be argued that a key role of green criminology and/or victimology is to draw attention to this.

VICTIMOLOGY AND VICTIMS OF ENVIRONMENTAL HARM

Victimology has been referred to as variously as a 'subdiscipline'; the 'younger sister of criminology' (Tilburg Law School, 2013) and 'a rather ugly neologism' (Newburn, 1988). As with criminology, almost all the work carried out by victimologists on the impact of victimisation, its causes and the way societies respond to it has focused on human victims and, more specifically, human victims of officially recognised criminal offences. As such the critical critique levied at criminology for focusing too narrowly on official notions of criminality can be applied equally to victimology. Indeed, for McBarnet (1983), victimologists themselves are partly to blame for the stifling of the critical project. By concentrating their attention predominantly on traditional notions of victimhood (with particular emphasis on rape victims) the author argues that researchers have played into the hands of governments wishing to derive political capital from victims and from punitive criminal justice responses.

This state of affairs is somewhat ironic given that the victims' movement in the United States was originally driven by a diverse group of advocates utilising broad notions of victimisation. These ranged from feminists and mental health practitioners, to survivors of war and atrocities such as the Nazi concentration camps (Young, 1997) as well as victims of the apartheid regime in South Africa (Garkawe, 2004) and, significantly for present purposes, victims of natural disasters (Cressey, 1986; Spalek, 2006). In other words, as conceived in its early days, victimology concerned itself with much more than victims of crime, including victims of abuse of power by the state and victims of what Giddens (1990) would call natural risks.

Even among the critical school of victimology, victims of environmental harms have been overlooked in the literature: although the first call for the development of what was then termed 'environmental victimology' came as early as 1996 in an article by Christopher Williams. Williams (1996) begins by addressing environmental victimisation and notes the 'obvious need for social justices to parallel formal legal processes' (p.200). Williams calls for a move away from prevailing concepts of 'environmental justice' (see Chapter 7) which he criticises both for its subjectiveness and because for him this is overly swayed by activism. In Chapter 1 I presented counter-arguments that in methodological terms these characteristics were not necessarily undesirable for the development of green criminology as a whole.

It is clear that further development of victimological study in this area has been slow to progress from this point, even as green criminology as a whole has gathered pace. Skinnider (2011) empathises the need for such specific research given the difficulties of applying broad-brush victim reforms to environmental harm:

> The characteristic of the collective nature of this kind of victimization needs to be understood, particularly with its implications for victims to seek assistance, support and redress which have predominately developed for traditional crimes involving individual victims. (p.26)

Notwithstanding such arguments, there are isolated exceptions to the general proposition that something 'more', or at least 'different', is needed for environmental victims over and above that which is already being provided for victims of crime: the most significant of which being the application of the US Crime Victims' Rights Act 2004 (CVRA) to victims of environmental crime, discussed in Box 1.

Box 1: Environmental victims under the US Crime Victims Rights Act

Heralded as a major breakthrough by proponents of a more judiciable form of victims' rights, (Doyle, 2008) the 2004 Crime Victims Rights Act (CVRA) introduced the concept of victims' rights into the US penal code for the first time. The first application of the CVRA to victims of *environmental* crime followed the explosion of a BP Oil Refinery in Texas in 2005. In this case the US Fifth Circuit court ruled that the government had violated victims' rights under the CVRA by failing to consult with those locals affected by the explosion (mostly in the form of personal injury and property damage) in the agreement of a plea bargain with BP (Starr et al., 2008). This was despite the fact that the number of victims stretched into the hundreds and the CVRA neither includes nor, on a standard reading, conceives harm caused by environmental damage. More recently in the case of *W.R. Grace & Co.*, the named company was prosecuted under environmental legislation for 'knowingly endangering' the residents of Libby, Montana, by exposing them to asbestos through mining activities. The federal judge in the case had ruled that 34 prospective victims of these activities (local residents) did not fall under the definition of victim within the CVRA and as such excluded them from the trial proceedings. At appeal, *In Re Parker; U.S. v U.S. District Court* and *W.R. Grace & Co.* the United States Ninth Circuit Court of Appeals reversed this ruling, thus suggesting that prospective victims of environmental harm are indeed included within the ambit of rights provided under the 2004 Act. The case is interesting not only for the specific result, but as a demonstration of the breadth of the term 'victim' and gives weight to the contention that it includes (or should include) environmental crimes even where there is no specific mention of this category of harms within the rights-enabling legal instrument.

The victimological literature on environmental harms has remained scarce until quite recently. Thus when South and Beirne (2006) compiled one of the first collections of writing on green criminology in 2006, Williams' (1996) work was still the only piece specifically focused on the victims of environmental crimes. This collection also contained a section entitled 'Rights, Victim and Regulation' which included another important intervening contribution from Lynch and Stretesky (2001) on toxic crimes and what they called 'corporate victimization'. In this paper the authors present evidence of the significant health effects (mainly to humans) of corporate practices (specifically the production of pesticides) leading them to conclude that relevant corporations 'show a blatant disregard for the effects of their products and by-products on human and animal populations' (p.165).

Following South and Beirne's (2006) edited collection progress towards understanding environmental crime/harm from a victimological perspective continued to stall. Thus in White's (2009) reader on environmental crime, three years later, the only chapter dedicated to victimisation was another reprint of Williams' (1996) paper. A further edited collection from White (2010) has no specific chapter on victimisation, although South (2010) reflects upon the unequal impact of climate change on various groups of (usually poor) victims, and the possibility that some 'environmental rights' are being breached. This discussion contradicts one of Williams' views that the impacts of environmental harm are more evenly spread between rich and poor. White (2011) has more recently dedicated a chapter to environmental victims in which he emphasises the socio-cultural context of understanding and responding to environmental harm:

> Ultimately the construction of [environmental] victimhood is a social process involving dimensions of time and space, behaviours involving acts and omissions, and social features pertaining to powers and collectivises. (p.122)

Again this would suggest that a social constructivist approach should be adopted by green criminologists and green victimologists. More recently, Spencer and Fitzgerald (2013) have offered fresh insight into environmental victims by essentially taking the argument beyond its (predominantly, they argue) Marxist roots to apply more poststructuralists thinking. In particular they apply Felix Guattari's (2008) critique of what he called integrated world capitalism to the question of corporate environmental offending and subsequent victimisation: using the 2010 BP Oil spill in the Gulf of Mexico as a case study. Thus, the authors argue, this victimisation event can be understood in terms of environmental, social and mental ecologies. In so doing, the authors expose the complex and multifaceted nature of such victimisation itself both in human terms and in terms of the environment and non-human animals. Another recent chapter by Bisschop and Vande Walle (2013) discusses (human) victims of illicit e-waste transportation practices and in particular calls for involvement of local stakeholders in addressing these problems in line with concepts of environmental justice.

DEFINING ENVIRONMENTAL 'VICTIMS'

For Williams (1996) 'environmental victims' are:

> those of past, present, or future generations who are injured as a consequence of change to the chemical, physical, microbiological, or psychosocial environment, brought about by deliberate or reckless, individual or collective, human act or omission. (p.35)

This definition embodies intergenerational justice (Hiskes, 2008) and, importantly for Williams, is grounded on the notion of 'injury' rather than 'harm'. Williams' argument is that this is a useful starting point if the goal is to develop functioning legal systems around environmental victimisation, especially in criminal justice, as the concept is more objective and measurable. As well as restricting such victimisation to legally proscribed activities, this is also of course an entirely anthropocentric definition. In a seminal contribution to the victimological literature Nils Christie (1986) famously argued that the victims movement, and in particular the attention paid by policymakers to victims of crime, was in fact limited in focus to those victims displaying 'ideal' characteristics. Such characteristics included being weak, being a stranger to a 'big and bad offender', carrying out an innocent activity and cooperating with the authorities. Such was the anthropocentric bias of academic study in this area though that even Christie did not specially problematise the fact that the ideal victim is of course also human.

In Chapter 2 I noted Hans Boutellier's (2000) conception of the 'victimalization of morality' as a theoretical basis for the shift in attention from crimes to harms. The same shift is evident in the victimological literature and indeed in national and international documents related to victims (see Hall, 2009). While Boutellier's notion is therefore also anthropocentric, there is no reason why the focus on harm – 'the suffering of others' – cannot equally apply to a greater understanding of the suffering of other *species* and indeed harm to the environment itself. Certainly on this point there is arguably greater public awareness of the damage being done to the non-human components of the environment than at any time in the recent past (Molloy, 2011). The plight of *certain* animals (see below) also attracts much more media attention, with some instrumental impact on social attitudes. For example, media coverage of food production practices is thought to influence demand for some meats in the United States (Tonsor and Olynk, 2010).

The above points notwithstanding, given the lack of research conducted on the impacts of environmental harm on humans and (especially) on non-human animals, it is impossible to paint a full picture of these impacts. Particularly concerning is the lack of research in this area which asks (human) environmental victims *themselves* about their experiences and support needs. In the modern context, with the focus now being on so-called evidence-based policymaking (see Lawrence, 2006), this lack of direct consultation with environmental victims is concerning. Hall and Shapland (2013) have suggested that this is because more direct consultation would mean confronting what victims themselves say and think, rather than 'using' them as exemplars of damaged people in line with Garland's (2001) view of 'the culture of control'. Of course, in this sense environmental victims are threats not only to lawyers and the state, but also to environmental activist groups wishing to attack states if (for example) it turns out that they desire only respectful treatment, information, understanding and an apology as opposed to more retributive outcomes.

What is clear from the literature is that the impacts of environmental victimisation are extremely varied and wide-ranging, which is a key reason that states find it difficult to implement proscribed or firm procedures of regulation and restitution. In this book we have already noted examples including the destruction of local economies (Helm and Hepburn, 2009); serious impacts on the way of life of individuals and communities; comprised viability of some plants (MacLeod et al., 2010); and eradication of non-human animals. Certainly the health impacts to *humans* at least of various legal and illegal environmentally destructive practices are becoming more understood. The regularity with which we are presented with alarming statistics concerning the impact on human health of environmental pollution reflects the significance of the challenges faced by the world's legal and administrative systems, and by green criminologists hoping to understand these patterns of social change. In the United Kingdom alone the Department of Health (1998) estimated that at least 24,000 deaths are attributable to air pollution each year. Globally, the World Health Organization (2008) has estimated around two million premature deaths annually.

Mortality rates of course only represent a very small proportion of all human health impacts brought about by air pollution. Indeed the World Health Organization's 2,000 working group on the Quantification of the Health Effects of Exposure to Air Pollution identified premature deaths as the least numerically significant of a whole continuum of health effects. These included such diverse impacts as cardiovascular hospital admissions, chronic change in physiologic function and lower birth rates (WHO, 2008). As we broaden the scope of the discussion beyond air pollution, Patz et al. (2000) reported that the long-term consequences of climate change will bring about adverse impacts on public health via a diverse range of consequences including heat-related illnesses and deaths, extreme weather events, water and food-borne disease and vector and rodent-borne diseases. Similar predictions have more recently been discussed by Agnew (2012) and Brisman (2013).

Ruggiero and South (2010b) cite numerous cases of death and illness brought about in areas exposed to hazardous waste materials, including the so-called cancer villages of China, where residents' increased susceptibility to several classifications of tumours has been directly attributed to their exposure to cadmium and mercury released through the recycling of e-waste (Watts, 2010: p.21). In Italy, Martuzzi et al. (2009) have identified a statistically significant increase in cancer mortality and congenital anomalies in Campania, a region subject to intense environmental pressure due to uncontrolled and illegal practices of industrial waste dumping (see Chapter 4). More recently, the United Nations Environment Programme has reported that the environmental restoration of Ogoniland in Nigeria (see Chapter 5) could prove to be the world's most wide-ranging and long-term oil clean-up exercise ever undertaken. The data for the report include over 5,000 medical records and the conclusion drawn reveal that 'at least 10 Ogoni communities where drinking water is contaminated with high levels of hydrocarbons, public health is seriously threatened' (UNEP, 2011).

Of course, the above examples do not incorporate the impacts on humans, and certainly not on non-human animals, of distinct man-made environmental 'disaster events' like the Deepwater Horizon Oil Spill. The human health implications of this event – including both physical and mental health implications – are now the subject of a rapidly escalating scientific literature (Lee and Blanchard, 2010; Yun et al., 2010). Another example is the negative long-term health impacts of the 1984 Bhopal gas leak, including respiratory and neurological disorders (Cullinan et al., 1996). In Chapter 4 it was noted that the negative impact on animal life has also been significant in the Bhopal region. While disasters such as these have received a great deal of media attention and a level of notoriety, the crucial point is that these more visible examples of environmental victimisation are inevitably a tiny minority of all those suffering health complains as a result of environmental harms; certainly when one considers the effects beyond the human population (Agnew, 2013).

THE UNEQUAL IMPACT OF ENVIRONMENTAL HARM

Researchers are increasingly coming to understand that the effects of environmental harm at all levels do not fall equally on all parts of the world or indeed on all groups of humans or animals within a country. From the eco-centric perspective we can also see that animal and plant life is often seen as an 'acceptable' cost of industrial and commercial practices. Certainly the impacts upon animals are deprioritised, even in much green criminological writing. Beirne (2007) has commented on this disregard for the harm befalling animals and plants by reference to the language used (even by environmentalists) to render non-humans 'the other'. This includes more obvious examples of referring to humans as 'human beings' whereas non-human animals are simply 'animals', to the more subtle phraseologies that 'hinge on animals' master status as the property of humans' (p.63). Beirne here gives the example of the terms 'fisheries', 'laboratory animals', 'pets' and 'race horses'. Nurse (2013a) takes a slightly more positive view, drawn from Arluke and Sanders (1996), in arguing that social views on animal harm change over time and, as such, reflects again the social constructivist perspective espoused earlier in this volume, as the author notes:

> Such attitudes change over time so that animal harm may become an issue of core importance in public policy when the public demands that it should be, or is considered to be a fringe issue at other times (Arluke and Sanders, 1996). (p.65)

At the same time, however, Nurse also expresses the view that 'Public policy on animal harm is predominantly concerned either with animal protection or welfarism rather than animal harm as an aspect of criminal justice' (p.126). Thus, from a criminological perspective, the victimisation of non-human animals as well as the environment itself is not being recognised in the same manner as human victimisation, that is, worthy of the 'criminal' label.

For their part, Beirne and South (2007) argue that if society is going to concern itself with *some* environmental harms, then the impact on non-human animal cannot be separated from this endeavour:

> Animals of course live in environments, and their own well-being – physical, emotional, psychological – is absolutely and intimately linked to the health and good standing of their environments. (pp.xiii–xiv)

This implies that whenever we are talking about harm to the environment we are necessarily talking about victimisation of non-human animals. In these terms the continued anthropocentric bias of victimology, and certainly green victimology, seem unjustifiable.

The suggestion that the costs of environmental harm are borne disproportionately by non-human animals and the environment itself – being classed as 'expendable' (see Opotow, 1993) or at least of less concern compared with more anthropocentric issues – is an important argument of the eco-centric approach. Even from the more anthropocentric perspective, however, while we may argue that the victimisation of 'humans' as a whole tends to be treated more seriously in the literature and by policymakers, it is also becoming clear that not *all* humans are *equally* subject to environmental harm. Indeed while in his early contribution Williams (1996) called the assumption of the powerless as environmental victims and the powerful as environmental victimisers 'a stereotyped view that omits the victimisation of those with power and wealth' (p.201), the overriding evidence now points to endemic inequality in the distribution of the environmental harms discussed in this book.

Certainly the *geographically* unequal impact of environmental degradation is well recognised by the international legal order, with the preamble to the 1992 UN Framework Convention on Climate Change (FCCC) acknowledging the particular vulnerability of 'low-lying and other small island countries, countries with low-lying coastal, arid and semi-arid areas or areas liable to floods, drought and desertification, and developing countries with fragile mountainous ecosystems'. This was also accepted in the Outcome Document deriving from the 2012 UN Rio+20 Conference on Sustainable Development. Of course, as already discussed in this chapter, it is important that this focus on the inequalities of environmental harm fostered by physical geography do not distract us from the more complex – social, economic and cultural – aspects of environmental victimisation. Examples like that of the (alleged) sinking of the Maldives therefore reflect the further important observation that in terms of victimisation as a result of climate change, it is the *poorest*, most disadvantaged countries, groups and species within countries tending to suffer most. As acknowledged by the International Association for the Study of Insurance Economics (2009):

> unmitigated climate change may have significant adverse effects on the long-term development of the world economy, ranging from water shortages for food production to an increased severity of tropical windstorms. Developing countries are particularly vulnerable, facing the risk of social disorder and mass migration. (p.108)

Thus, the impacts of environmental degradation tend to weigh most heavily on the poorest developing countries as well as the poorest people within those countries. Mendelsohn et al.'s (2006) analysis of statistical data/prediction on climate change puts the matter succinctly:

> Overall, the poor [countries] will suffer the bulk of the damages from climate change, whereas the richest countries will likely benefit. (p.173)

The authors' contention that rich countries may benefit from climate change is based on the observation that they are 'located in the mid to high latitudes and are currently cool' (p.162) thus warmer temperatures may actually be closer to optimum for crop production. Indeed, Deschênes and Greenstone (2007) suggest an increase in annual profits from agricultural land of $1.3 billion in the United States as a direct result of climate change over the next decade. Such observations/estimations are however contestable, especially if one expands the scope of the discussion beyond crop production. White (2011) for example notes how 'countries of the West are now beginning to experience climate-related disasters' (p.25).

Beyond climate change, the unequal distribution of environmental harm has been commented on by South (2010), who sees this as reflecting wider tendencies towards 'social exclusion', which have long been a topic of research and discussion in mainstream criminology as well (Byrne, 1999). In relation to environmental victimisation, Lee (2009) has summarised the situation in the following anthropocentric terms:

> Poor people are usually excluded from the environmental decision- making process, and once a policy is made, they are usually powerless to change it. (pp.3–4)

For South (2010), the depletion of resources caused by environmental derogation can only exasperate the existing social division between the well off and the poor. Certainly the contention that environmental degradation leads to increased division on grounds of ethnicity is well supported in the literature, to the extent that it has been called 'environmental racism' (Spencer et al., 2011). Economic theories as to why exposure to environmental harms apparently varies by race include 'pure discrimination by polluters or politicians in sitting decisions; differences in willingness to pay for environmental amenities linked to income or education levels; and variations in the propensity of communities to engage in collective action to oppose the location of potential polluters' (Hamilton, 1995: p.1). Over the years considerable evidence has development linking sites of environmental degradation (especially the dumping of toxic materials) and black communities within the United States. Similar results have been replicated at the international level (Alston and Brown, 1993). Boer et al. (1997) confirm that, statistically, the appearance of discrimination in the location of hazardous waste treatment, storage and disposal facilities (TSDF) proximate to areas where ethnic minorities live in Los Angeles is not explained by alternative, non-racial factors.

The argument that environmental harm also disproportionately falls on *women* is of course the main contention of the feminist critique, as discussed in Chapter 1. There are numerous studies that support this gendered interpretation of environmental victimisation. Wachholz (2007) has summarised these effects as being linked to gendered division of labour in many developing countries, where women are disproportionately responsible for subsistence farm labour, child care, care of the sick and infirm and the gathering of household bio-fuels and water. Essentially, the effects of environmental degradation on traditional farming industries, water supply and health increases the workload of these women 'reducing their opportunities for personal and social development' (p.169), exasperating the poverty women the world over disproportionately find themselves subjected to. As the author summarises:

> The IPCC has warned that climate change is likely to actuate gaps between the world's rich and poor, and women are already amongst the poorest. (Wachholz, 2007: p.171)

This reality has also been acknowledged by the UN Development Programme (2010) in its advancement of UN Millennium Development Goal 3, to promote gender equality and empower women:

> Climate change, including increased severity and frequency of extreme events, puts women and girls especially at risk of loss of life and livelihoods, exploitation, and further marginalization. Inequitable access to food, shelter, and medicines also increases gender impacts post-disaster. (p.2)

The Rio+20 Outcome Document noted above similarly has paragraphs on 'Gender equality and the empowerment of women', with particular focus on women 'in rural areas and local communities and among indigenous peoples and ethnic minorities' (Paragraph 238). One major concern about the impact of environmental degradation, and climate change in particular, on women is the possible link to violence. Essentially this is due to the fact that violence against women tends to increase in the aftermath of natural disasters. On this point, Wachholz (2007) compiles evidence of an increase in such violence following hurricanes, floods and droughts (see also Brody et al., 2008).

So far we have noted that, as a result of structural and social inequalities and perspectives, the impacts of environmental harm tend to fall/are allowed to fall on animals and the environment itself rather than on humans and that among humans the more disempowered and marginalised groups (at the national and international level) seem to bare the brunt of this. In fact however it is also worth emphasising the point that for non-human victims of environmental harm not all animals (for example) are equally affected by environmental pollution. In a revelling commentary Nurse (2013a) contends:

Informal rules, embedded in specific practices and nuances might dictate, for example, that in some inner-city police areas most animal harm (except possibly wildlife crime and the trade in endangered species) is seen as being a low priority for police investigation whereas in rural areas (such as Scotland where rarer birds such as the golden eagle and the osprey are seen as being part of Scotland's heritage or heritage or those parts of the United States where California condors or bald eagles hold special cultural significance) considerable police and criminal justice resources may be directed at those offenders who seek to exploit wildlife resources. (p.201)

From this we can draw the conclusion that from an anthropocentric perspective not all animals are equally without worth to all humans, although notably the worth they do have is once again based entirely on human prejudices and social/cultural labelling. The observation also highlights that geographical location impacts upon the degree of victimisation suffered by different species, a point we have seen is equally true of human victims. It is thus unsurprising that the inequality of impacts of environmental harm operates not just between different social and economic groups within jurisdictions, but also between jurisdictions as a whole. Following on from this point, it can be argued that the true extent of inequality endemic to environmental victimisation lies not in the differential impacts on rich versus poor, or as dictated by geographical phenomena, but rather in the ability of the rich to shift such harms *to* the poorer countries. In a process which Stebbins (1993) dubs 'garbage imperialism' industrialised nations are increasingly exporting unwanted waste materials to third-word and developing nations. Indeed, the United Nations General Assembly, in its Millennium Declaration of 2000, alludes to this same point in stating:

> Most US e-waste simply is disposed of in landfills or is incinerated, but a considerable portion of it is gathered for recycling and is exported to developing nations for remanufacture or refurbishment. (Stebbins, 1993: p.546)

The key difficulty with this approach however is that many recycling facilities in developing nations, however, are not equipped to handle e-waste, and much of it is not processed but is instead dumped in local villages near people and water sources. The transfer of waste from rich nations to poor nations is not just a question of the former taking advantage of looser regulatory regimes in the latter, but rather the trade in such waste may actually become an industrial and economic necessity for developing countries (Critharis, 1990).

Waste materials may not be the only exported environmental harms from the global rich to the global poor. Walters (2006) has described 'the ways that powerful governments and corporations seek to dominate global food markets whilst exploiting, pressuring and threatening vulnerable countries' (p.1). In particular, he discusses the political, economic and even spiritual pressure exerted by the United States on Zambia in the effort to convince the African nation to import its genetically modified crops. The long-term implications of such crops for human health and bio-diversity are of course still the topic of heated debate, as noted in Chapter 2 (see Malarkey, 2003).

Green criminologists might well be in a position to develop this notion of 'garbage imperialism' to cover the fostering of environmental harm away from humans and on to non-human animals and the ecosystem. In any case, it is this transnational element to the question of environmental victimisation that again demands the consideration not only of national legal remedies, but also of remedies provided by the international legal order. It is clear from the above paragraphs that this is a highly complex multifaceted problem which combines very practical consequences with economic and socially dependant variables. As always in such cases, developing a legal or administrative system that adequately encompasses all these elements is a significant task to which green criminology and victimology are well placed to contribute.

RESPONDING TO ENVIRONMENTAL VICTIMISATION: COMPENSATION, RESTITUTION AND REDRESS

Previous chapters have introduced arguments concerning the use of civil, criminal or administrative systems to respond to environmental harm, and above we have discussed the victims of such harm. As yet however we have not reflected on what form of 'redress' (in a broad sense) might be appropriate for such victims following any of these processes. The picture here is in fact very complex because environmental harm, as we have seen, may be addressed through national or international systems that are criminal, administrative or civil. Indeed, in principle at least there is scope for *human* victims at least to approach all of these sources for restitution and compensation. For the purpose of this section the term 'compensation' will generally be used (unless otherwise stated) to refer to monies paid to victims of environmental harm by states from public funds. This will be contrasted to 'restitution', which will normally come from perpetrators of environmental harm (whether individuals or corporations) following conviction in a criminal court. I will refer to both terms (along with civil damages and restorative resolutions) collectively as 'redress' but it should be noted that in the wider literature all these terms can be used interchangeably, and in markedly different ways.

Recently there have been a number of international developments prompting states to foster system of redress for environmental victims. Indeed, a recent draft of a potential UN Convention on Justice and Support for Victims of Crime and Abuse of Power put forward by a consortium of the World Society of Victimology, the International Victimology Institute of Tilburg University (INTERVICT) and the Tokiwa International Victimology Institute (TIVI) contained the following provision:

> In cases of environmental crime, States Parties shall legislate to include restitution to restore the environment, reconstruction of the infrastructure, replacement of community facilities and reimbursement of the expenses of relocation, whenever such harm results in the dislocation of the community. (Article 10)

The difficulty of incorporating appreciation for harmful effects on humans and non-human animals in public international law and international criminal law is well recognised in the literature (Thirlway, 2010; Redgwell, 2014). A further important issue is whether redress mechanisms should cover only the identifiable physical and economic costs of presently affected individuals and groups, whether provision should be made to restore the damaged ecosystem to its previous state, thus reflecting a more eco-centric agenda, and whether further provisions should be made for future generations of humans and non-human animals affected by present environmental degradation.

Nevertheless, Skinnider (2011) has discussed how the UN Commission on Crime Prevention and Criminal Justice in fact adopted a resolution on environmental crime as early as 1994 in which Member States were called to:

> consider in the framework of the constitution and the basic principles of the legal system, the rights of identifiable victims, victim assistance, facilitation of redress and monetary compensation, by removing legal barriers such as standing to sue, participation in proceedings and actions by citizens, including class action suits and citizen suits. (OSOC Resolution 1994/15 (25 July 1994))

Similarly, Principle 6(2) of the International Law Commission's (2006) response to the issue of compensating victims of environmental harm states:

> Victims of transboundary damage should have access to remedies in the State of origin that are no less prompt, adequate and effective than those available to victims that suffer damage, from the same incident, within the territory of that State.

'Victims' within the draft principles include 'any natural or legal person or State that suffers damage'. 'Damage' in the above definition is said to include loss of life, personal injury and financial costs attributed to environmental harm. Notably this is anthropocentric (and in particular casts environmental damage purely in terms of its economic impact) but the above principle is interesting in that it expressly foresees victims from one country being able to acquire redress from other countries, something that is presently very problematic under international law.

A more 'hard law' example can be seen in the 1989 Basel Convention on the Control of Transboundary Movements of Hazardous Wastes and their Disposal, specifically its Protocol on Liability and Compensation for Damage Resulting from Transboundary Movements of Hazardous Wastes and their Disposal. Although this instrument does not make states directly liable to provide such compensations, the protocol does mention in its preamble the obligation of states to 'develop international and national legal instruments regarding liability and compensation for the victims of pollution and other environmental damage' and as such compels states to 'provide for a comprehensive regime for liability and for adequate and prompt compensation for damage resulting from the transboundary movement of hazardous wastes and other wastes and their disposal including illegal traffic in those wastes' (Article 1).

A number of authors have commented on the application of redress mechanisms in cases of environmental victimisation, although almost none of this literature considers the environment itself or any redress aimed at non-human animals. Lee (2009) for example has championed a holistic, welfare approach to environmental harms, rather than concentrating purely on financial compensation or restitution. As an alternative to simple, blanket, monetary compensation, Lee puts significant weight on the provision of long-term, tailored support and restoration packages in individual communities. Given that 'different localities inherit different cultural norms and characteristics' (p.29), Lee also emphasises the vital role of local government in developing and facilitating the delivery of such packages. Further indications that at least some human victims of environmental degradation need much more than simple monetary recompense can be found in a case study by Wheatley (1997), concerning the significant cultural impacts on Canadian aboriginal peoples following mercury poisoning of their traditional lands:

> Even after compensation was paid social problems persisted, especially in Whitedog, where solvents are smuggled into the community and 4 suicides were reported in the spring of 1995. (p.78)

This raises key questions as to whether compensation or restitution schemes should focus on the short-term needs of individuals affected by environmental harm, or the longer-term needs of the community as a whole, along with the needs of future generations of potential (cultural, economic and physical) victims of such harm. The importance of non-monetary restitution is further supported by the more established victimological literature, which consistently holds that payments from offenders themselves carry greater symbolic value to victims of crime than monies allocated from taxation (Shapland, 2003).

In England and Wales, court-based restitution for successfully prosecuted environmental crimes has not been widely utilised. On this point, the House of Commons Environmental Audit Committee (2004) received evidence from the Environmental Industries Commission suggesting: 'this may be because of uncertainty in applying the concept to environmental offences)' (p.63). Bell et al. (2013) argue that the explanation for the underutilisation of restitution orders (actually called 'compensation orders' in that jurisdiction) in cases of environmental crime in England and Wales lays mainly with the existence of many statutory powers of clean-up and cost recovery available to regulatory agencies in defined situations (for example, s.59 of the Environmental Protection Act 1990 and s.161A of the Water Resources Act 1991). In addition, the authors argue, under s.131 of the 2000 Act restitution orders are restricted to a maximum of £5,000, a sum that in fact may often be insufficient to fully restore victims or their environment to their previous state (see Chapter 2), if indeed any sum of money can achieve this. A further problem in some jurisdictions, notably Canada, is that restitution orders are restricted to certain offences, which do not include environmental crime (see Canadian Department of Justice, 2012).

Skinnider (2011) has commented on the difficulty of applying restitution orders in cases of 'mass' or 'community' environmental victimisation, although also suggests a number of solutions including:

(i)   an order for restoration of any harm to the environment caused by the commission of the offence;
(ii) payment of the costs and expenses incurred by a public authority in restoring any harm to the environment;
(iii) costs for carrying out a specified project for the restoration or enhancement of the environment in a public place or for the public benefit;
(iv) payment of a specified amount to an environmental trust or a specified environmental organization for the purpose of a specified project for the restoration. (p.55)

Of course, a more fundamental difficulty with relying on restitution orders as the principal form of redress for environmental harm is that achieving criminal convictions in such cases is very difficult. Of course, as an alternative many states now offer a state-based compensation scheme for victims of crime which, importantly for these purpose, usually do not require a conviction to be achieved. Notwithstanding this, however, the overriding impression given by the available reviews of state-based criminal compensation mechanisms in operation in most developed nations is that they are aimed at very restricted groups of ideal (individual) victims and at stereotypical notions of suffering, both of which, as we've seen in previous chapters, tend to exclude environmental victims (see New Zealand Law Commission, 2008; Irish Criminal Injuries Compensation Tribunal, 2009; Hall, 2010).

If restitution under the criminal law or state-based compensation schemes are unable to offer significant redress to human or non-human victims of environmental crime, or certainly wider environmental harms, we might consider the possibility of pursuing civil law suits either on behalf of human victims or – as discussed by (Favre, 2004) – on behalf of the environmental or non-human animals, plants and also on. Civil law suits in fact represent the default 'traditional' mechanism of victims acquiring restitution payments (damages) from polluters whose actions have lead them to suffer environmental harm (McEldowney and McEldowney, 2011). Despite this pedigree however, generally speaking the tone of the recent literature in this area is very disparaging of so-called toxic torts (a 'tort' in law being a civil wrong against which action can be taken in the civil court) (Goldberg and Zipersky, 2011) as a means of adequately redressing environmental victimisation.

Lin (2005) recognises that tortious remedies do bring at least two advantages over administrative compensation systems. In the first instance, this is because the public agencies, which administer such schemes, may be more vulnerable to regulatory capture than the judiciary or the executive. Secondly, it is argued, remedies in tort are based on fuller information about the precise impacts of the alleged environmental harm, whereas administrative mechanisms may not have access to such detailed information. Of course, claims in tort are not the only civil remedies available. In some jurisdictions the state has legislated for specific causes of civil action in cases of environmental pollution. One example from Canada is the Alberta Environmental Protection and Enhancement Act 2000, which creates a civil cause of action for any victims suffering loss or damage as a result of conduct constituting an offence for which the defendant was convicted under the Act. Victims can thus recover 'an amount equal to the loss or damage proved to have been suffered' (s.219).

The above notwithstanding, civil actions also present considerable difficulties for environmental victims, Skinnider (2011) summarises these in the following terms:

> Limitations for such remedies include where the perpetrator is not in the same jurisdiction as the victim; where the perpetrator is not readily identifiable; evidentiary burden of proof; and costs of litigation. (p.74)

As such, tort action must still establish culpability on the part of specified respondents, which given the nature of polluting activity is likely to be problematic in many cases. Furthermore, and significantly, civil cases cost considerable amounts of money for which, in most jurisdictions, there is little to no public funding. This means the cost of such actions must be borne by victims or victims' groups (Castle, 1996). This again emphasises the significance of the above observation that, at least in human terms, environmental victims tend to represent the less financially stable elements of society. Examples such as the economically impoverished and displaced peoples of the Nigerian Delta and those affected by the Bhopal gas leak are testament to the failure of civil law suits to adequately compensate these peoples many years after the events (Van Tassel, 2011).

One potentially very important advantage of civil litigation as a means of securing compensation and restitution for environmental victims is the class action process available in many jurisdictions, which might allow a large group of victims to sue polluters collectively (Johnson, 2004). Clearly this offers an important advantage over both the generally individualistic criminal justice system and the administrative compensation systems discussed below, because it accounts for the element of 'mass victimisation' that is often present in environmental cases. Nevertheless, class actions too have been criticised from the perspective of environmental harm, principally because 'these legal rules were not designed with environmental actions specifically in mind and have been noted to be notoriously difficult to get certified in environmental cases' (Skinnider, 2011: p.75). In addition, Lin (2005) has noted the alleged misuse of the class action system in a number of (US) cases of environmental damage to 'enrich attorneys rather than benefit plaintiffs [i.e. those bringing the actions]' (p.1516). Given the difficulties inherent in providing redress for environmental harm through either civil damages or criminal restitution, many have argued that the advent of administrative compensation schemes offer numerous advantages over either systems, this will be discussed in the next section.

Administrative compensation schemes: A solution to environmental redress?

O'Hear (2004) has argued that administrative compensation systems (either state funded or funded by polluting agents) for environmental damage carry numerous advantages over both civil and criminal court procedures. His main argument is that such schemes can operate under a more comprehensive set of pre-defined rules. Lin (2005) adds to this argument by noting the benefits of such schemes' use of standardised schedules of damages. This is certainly the case under most *criminal* compensation schemes, although a criticism of this is that while it offers greater certainty it also allows for very little adaptation of the rules to specific situations. Given the broad range of environmental harms discussed throughout this book, and the general gaps in our knowledge concerning these effects, an over-rigid system may not serve some victims of environmental harm particularly well.

Following on from the last point, O'Hear argues that more diverse forms of environmental harms (in this case impairment of 'characteristics of the landscape' and disruption or impairment of lifestyles of indigenous communities) have 'traditionally not received nearly as sophisticated consideration in the legal system as have others' (p.162). O'Hare supports his argument with a further comment from Bowman (2002), in which the latter argues that such compensation schemes that have been implemented around the world in response to environmental degradation:

> have not really involved recognition of harm to the environment at all, but have been concerned with the infringement of established human interests relating to the person or property caused through the medium of the environment. (pp.12–13)

This demonstrates that administrative compensation schemes are often concerned with individual human claimants rather than restoration of the environment. On a more affirmative note, however, such schemes are usually designed to cater for large groups of victims (see Box 2), one of the rationales being that approaching such mass victimisation in this manner is more efficient (in terms of time and costs) than multiple civil tortious cases going through the courts for a protracted period, as occurred (and is still occurring) after the 1984 Bhopal disaster. Indeed, Lin (2005) has argued that a key advantage of administrative compensation schemes in cases of environmental harm is that they have the potential to compensate those who are *not yet* affected by environmental damage but are at a significant risk of becoming so. Lin's argument is grounded on his notion of a 'risk-based' compensation system for victims or potential victims) of environmental harm, whereby claimants are made awards based on their scientifically verifiable increased risk to environmental harm as a result of polluting activities.

Farber (2007) too has argued along similar lines that the problem of establishing full (or even partial) causation in cases of environmental crime can be avoided by offering victims what he calls 'proportional recovery':

> Thus, if there is, for example, a sixty percent chance that a victim's injury was caused by exposure to the toxic chemical, the victim would receive compensation for sixty percent of her loss. (pp.1637–1638)

In cases where different groups of victims have different chances of becoming subject to environmental harm, O'Hear too advocates the risk-based approach. This again avoids the difficulty of proving causation in the criminal (or indeed, the civil) courts.

For Lin (2005) the advantages of administrative compensation systems over civil courts are clear. He argues that administrative systems typically employ specialised or expert decision-makers who can conduct their own studies and consider a broad range of information. He also suggest that administrative systems can also provide more continuous oversight and distribute compensation more fairly among a class of victims, while also being more politically accountable than the judicial system. Lin's notion of a risk-based, administrative compensation system for victims of environmental harm is encouraging, although he does place considerable faith in the ability of modern science to assess risk accurately. This may be overly generous given the continuous development in knowledge of environmentally induced harms along with the still considerable gaps in that knowledge. Furthermore, we have already seen that the presentation and interpretation of apparently 'objective' scientific date is itself heavily influenced by value judgements. To give one pertinent example, Cross (1989) has highlighted the difficulties in drawing verifiable conclusions in relation to environmentally induced cancers. In addition of course it might be argued that administrative systems such as this lack the symbolic recognition afforded to victims by a ruling in a criminal, or even a civil, court.

Box 2: An example of an administrative compensation scheme

One of the most recent high-profile administrative compensation systems related specifically to environmental victimisation is the $20 billion fund constituted through talks between BP and the US government following the 2010 Deepwater Horizon Oil Spill in the Gulf of Mexico. The fund is financed by BP and administered by an 'Independent Claims Facility' that, controversially, is managed by an employee of BP (2010). Consequently, this is perhaps better thought of as an administrative restitution scheme which can pay monies to businesses, state departments and, significantly for present purposes, individuals demonstrating 'legitimate claims including natural resource damages and state and local response costs' (BP, 2010). Given the worldwide interest in the case it might be speculated that the speed and efficiency with which the United States and BP brokered the deal may reflect the kind of political underpinnings to the scheme predicted by Elias (1983) and Harland (1978). The continued high degree of controversy and interest in the workings of the scheme by the US media in particular has maintained the disaster as a political issue. While overall the scheme is a positive step in the direction of addressing the needs of environmental victims more broadly, some commentators have used it to exemplify the disparity between the treatment of environmental victims in such particularly newsworthy cases compared to provisions for such victims more broadly at the national and international level, Van Tassell argues (2011):

> The Gulf of Mexico oil spill and British Petroleum's quick efforts to pay for clean-up and compensation for victims may lead many people to falsely conclude that national and international laws operate effectively to make the polluter pay for harm. In truth, clean-up and compensation is rarely accomplished so efficiently, and laws operate to insulate polluters when they disaster occurs in poorer countries. (unpaginated)

Nevertheless, administrative compensation schemes also have their share of weaknesses. One key question is *what* precisely they should be compensating. Many such schemes have been limited to offering compensation for specific health impacts and medical expenses. From our discussion in Chapter 1 however we know that this is a very anthropocentric approach, and it may be argued that such schemes should provide something towards remedying the environment itself. In Chapter 3 it was noted that such payments were made available following a *criminal* procedure in the Alaskan Exxon case. This does however raise the further question as to whether such schemes should apply compensation for past *or future* harms. If the schemes are limited to the former then this rules out any appreciation of intergenerational justice or very long-term impacts which do not present themselves for many years. This is a core reason for Lin's (2005) focus on risk in his model of an administrative compensation scheme. The counter-argument, however, is that such schemes rely on our scientific knowledge being capable of predicting accurately how people/places/communities will be affected in the future by environmental degradation today. The rapidly developing nature of such scientific evidence suggests such assurance may be misplaced. Nevertheless, Farber (2007) notes that the longer such systems wait to award compensation the less likely it will be that victims will actually see it.

Despite their potential advantages, the fact remains in reality that most administrative compensation schemes appear to be largely ad hoc, or focused on very specific forms of environmental harm. The criticism is that while highly visible, relatively lucrative compensation schemes are available for major one-off polluting events in developed jurisdictions (where the ability exists to put pressure on large multinational corporations), this does little to address the more general absence of such compensation or restitution mechanisms internationally for more endemic, but perhaps less media-friendly, examples of environmental victimisation. This disparity also reflects the inequality of impact of environmental harm between rich and poor nations discussed above.

Restorative justice as a means of redress

In light of the quickly developing discussions surrounding restorative justice in wider criminology and victimology, such mechanisms are likely to prove an important topic of further research for green criminologists as well. In this instance by 'restorative options' I refer to the procedure put in place to facilitate compensation or restitution as being 'restorative' (as opposed to more traditional forms of adversarial or inquisitorial, formal, justice) rather than the 'restorative' impact of such payments themselves. Space is lacking here to go into the growing application of restorative justice in a number of jurisdictions, and its impact upon victims (usually of more traditional crimes), although generally speaking pilot restorative justice schemes for adult offender, in England and Wales and elsewhere, seem to confirm that when victims of crime do become involved in restorative processes they draw benefits from doing so, as does the restorative enterprise itself (Shapland et al., 2006; Shapland et al., 2011).

Information concerning the application of restorative processes to cases of environmental harm is mainly anecdotal in nature. There is however a small but growing literature on what has been variously termed 'environmental mediation' and 'environmental alternative dispute resolution' (ADR) (see Edwards, 1985 and p.17 of this volume). As with 'mediation' as applied to restorative justice options, the term is variously defined, although one concise definition is provided by Amy (1983):

> Put most simply, environmental mediation is a process in which representatives of environmental groups, business groups and government agencies sit down together with a neutral mediator to negotiate a binding solution to a particular environmental dispute. (p.1)

Of course, this definition actually excludes environmental victims, which in itself is quite telling. In fact, victims themselves feature relatively little in this literature, with much of the discussion revolving around the role of 'environmentalists' or 'environmental groups' the extent to which such groups represent real victims of environmental harm is a moot point. Furthermore, one of the few studies to examine environmental ADR empirically, as well as to discuss the position of the victims directly (Matsumoto, 2011), suggests that when environmental victims engage representation, or collectively group together in an effort to increase bargaining power, this in fact complicates the process to the extent that it becomes more cumbersome:

> Far from the conventional expectation that representation hastens the resolution of environmental disputes, our empirical results suggests ADR becomes less effective when many agents are involved. (p.665)

Generally speaking the key advantages of mediation or alternative dispute resolution in environmental cases is said to considerably lower costs compared to civil or criminal justice resolutions, as well as shorter timescales (see Mernitz, 1980) although in fact very little detailed empirical evaluation has been done to test these claims. One expectation is that of Sipe (2007) who demonstrates via quantitative analysis that environmental mediation does produce a statistically significant increase in settlement rates, when compared to civil law actions, but no difference in compliance rates with these agreements. Again it is notable that Sipe's analysis fails to mention the victims of environmental harm directly.

Much of the literature concerning environmental mediation is based in the United States, which of course is a disadvantage given that it is underdeveloped nations and their people who tend to fall victim to environmental harm. Nevertheless, in one of the first test cases, Gerald Cormick and Jane McCarthy of the University of Washington's Environmental Mediation

Project were appointed by the governor of Washington State to serve as mediators in a dispute among environmentalists, farmers, developers and public officials over the damming of the Snoqualmie River. According to Shmueli and Kaufman (2006), 'the resulting agreement illustrated one of mediation's main assets – its capacity to generate creative solutions that satisfy the interests of all parties involved' (p.17). Certainly the adaptability of mediation and other restorative options is a big plus, especially given the long-standing criticisms of mainstream victimology that policies aimed at victim tend to assume specific victim characteristics and needs. As noted by Shmueli and Kaufman (2006):

> Each environmental conflict has a unique cast of characters, a history unlike any other except in broad strokes, a singular pattern of resources, interrelationships among parties, a special set of issues and a unique set of moves that defies simple classification and comparison. (p.20)

Furthermore, Matsumoto (2011) notes that mediation is a fitting solution for a situation in which, as in many environmental pollution disputes, 'the polluter and its victims are located near each other and will remain in place and maintain an on-going relationship after their dispute is resolved' (p.660).

Positive features notwithstanding, environmental mediation does nevertheless also bring difficulties, not least of which is the fact that 'those who have the time and resources to participate in a mediation process are not necessarily representative of the interest groups affected by the decisions issuing from this process' (Shmueli and Kaufman, 2006: p.21). This might be especially true given the economic and social standing of many victims of environmental harm discussed above, and returns us to the argument that 'environmentalists' or 'environmental groups' may not be representing the interests or needs of real environmental victims (whether human or non-human).

Amy (1983) has further discussed the opinion expressed in some quarters of environmentalism that mediation in fact panders to the benefit of big industry and the polluters themselves. Thus, the author contends, most environmental mediation actually takes place in a context of palatable political bias, power imbalance and the illusion of voluntariness. For example, Dryzek and Hunter (1987) have suggested that in the aftermath of the Indian Bhopal disaster, Union Carbide was in fact very keen to engage in attempts by Environmental Mediation International to establish a good compensation scheme rather than going down more legalistic routes. Of course, this is a rather pessimistic interpretation of the motives of corporations wishing to enter into environmental mediation. An alternative suggestion is that mediation and alternative dispute resolution is in fact the usual manner in which corporations resolve conflicts with each other, and thus it may simply be the route with which they are most familiar.

Overall, the cause of environmental mediation is at present severely held back by a lack of quite basic empirical data concerning the nature of the settlements (including much information about the compensation agreements reached), the processes used and the effectiveness/enforcement of these agreements. Without such information, it is very difficult to test the more alarmist claims of power imbalances and so on. It is also problematic that the majority of information we have comes only from developed countries, which, as noted previously, simply do not bear the brunt of environmental victimisation. Even within these countries environmental victims will tend to be especially marginalised groups, lacking power and social capital. The concern then is that such groups lack the power to meaningfully influence a mediation exercise when the other side of the table one has large multinational corporations, and perhaps their own state. In such instances it is suggested that such victims may well need the guarantees and protections (and the enforcement power) of formalised justice systems (whether criminal or civil). There is also a further complication in that the existing literature on environmental mediation, when it mentions victims' difficulties at all, fails to consider the possibility of multiple groups of victims with competing interests sitting around the table. That said, a recent mock-ecocide trial experiment staged at the Supreme Court of the United Kingdom has indicated the suitability of restorative justice as means of sentencing offenders for environmental crime. On this point Rivers (2012) notes:

> The experiment proved that there is real potential for using restorative justice in conjunction with ecocide. It enables dialogue, understanding, healing and creativity to emerge. It is about making whole again rather reinforcing separation and fragmentation through punishment of perpetrators and exclusion from the process of victims. (p.18)

Another experiment with environmental mediation and a mock ecocide trial was hosted at the University of Essex in 2012. Significantly, this involved representatives acting for nature (birds, wild spaces, etc.) in a restorative justice forum with actors representing oil and industry polluters, indicating the possibility that less anthropocentric interests could be injected within systems of redress for environmental harm. Clearly such development represents yet another important line of enquiry and will pose more challenges to green victimologists. The future potential for further development of the restorative approach, particularly in regard to case disposal, is therefore clear.

WAYS FORWARD FOR GREEN VICTIMOLOGY

The absence of detailed discussion and research into the victimisation aspects of environmental harm is a large oversight in the development of wider green criminology so far, although one which is now starting to be corrected. Nevertheless, it is clear that – as in the relationship between green criminology and more mainstream criminology – existing victimological writing and theory does have much to contribute to the question of environmental victimisation. As in other areas discussed in this book, the whole issue of non-human victimisation is markedly lacking in the literature so far but even in terms of human victims there remains an almost total absence of empirical research for which *these* victims have been directly questioned on what they would hope to take away from a justice systems (of any kind) when that system endeavours to respond to environmentally destructive activities perpetrated by individuals, corporations or states. Victimisation, whether human or non-human, is arguably at the heart of environmental concerns and, as such, there is a case that green victimology has a significant role to play as much more than the 'little sister' of green criminology.

Summary

The construction of 'environmental victimisation' is a deeply integrative social process. Much as victims of more mainstream criminal behaviour were ignored by criminologists for many years, so too have the victims of environmental harm tended to receive significantly less attention in the green criminological literature so far. This is particularly the case with non-human animal victims, despite the fact that harms vested upon them are almost impossible to separate from wider environmental harms experienced by humans directly or the ecosystem as a whole. What is clear is that there are systemic inequalities in relation to both the human and animal population bearing the brunt of environmental victimisation at a local, national and international level.

Clearly states are being increasingly prompted to respond in some way to the problems faced by environmental victims, although how they do so is variable. In terms of offering redress to human environmental victims both criminal restitution and civil lawsuits have generally proved ineffective. Administrative compensation schemes may offer more benefits to environmental victims (and perhaps the environment itself) in the longer term, but at present their application has been limited to the very specific and often mediatised cases of environmental damage, as well as to 'ideal' notions of victimisation. Restorative justice may offer a partial solution and also has the potential to incorporate a less anthropocentric perspective, but at present this is untested. In sum it is clear that much more research is needed into the question of victimisation, drawing on victimological and other studies as well as – in the case of humans – drawing opinions and perspectives from those harmed and finding ways to incorporate the perspective of non-humans in pursuance of a true eco-centric approach to environmental harm.

Review questions

1) In what sense could victims of environmental harm be classed as either 'ideal' or 'non-ideal' victims?
2) Are 'victims of environmental harm' different from victims of more 'mainstream' criminal harm? If so, how?
3) Why do victims of environmental harm find it difficult to claim redress for their suffering?
4) Despite the anthropocentric tone of the literature, are humans in fact the least numerate and perhaps least serious victims of environmental harm?

Further reading

Cardwell, P., French, D. and Hall, M. (2011), 'Tackling Environmental Crime in the European Union: The Case of the Missing Victim?', *Environmental Liability*, 19(2): 35–44.

- Focuses on the EU's incorporation of victims of crime in its more recent legislation and question the extent to which this applies to environmental victims.

Skinnider, E. (2011), *Victims of Environmental Crime – Mapping the Issues*, Vancouver: The International Centre for Criminal Law Reform and Criminal Justice Policy.

- Key reading for any student interested in the question of environmental victimisation, very through overview of all the relevant issues.

Walters, R. (2006), 'Crime, Bio-agriculture and the Exploitation of Hunger', *British Journal of Criminology*, 46(1): 26–45.

- As well as the wider impacts of bio-agriculture, this is an important piece for those interested in the cultural impact of environmental harm in some communities.

Wheatley, M. (1997), 'Social and Cultural Impacts of Mercury Pollution on Aboriginal Peoples in Canada', *Water, Air & Soil Pollution*, 97: 85–90.

- Another key discussion of less 'tangible' environmental impacts.

Chapter 8

Exploring Environmental Rights

Previous chapters in this book have discussed some of the difficulties inherent in responding to environmental harm, environmental crime and environmental victimisation through traditional national and international criminal justice systems. We have also seen the difficulties of applying civil law, regulatory and administrative systems to this area. In this chapter we will examine a further alternative that is fast gaining support in the green criminological literature: the application of human and non-human rights to environmental issues. The chapter will discuss how the notion of 'rights' has been applied to the environment and to those affected by environmental harm, critically assessing this application from an eco-centric perspective. Discussion and examples will follow covering the development of a distinct 'right to a green environment' as well as the application of other (mainly *human*) rights to environmental issues. The chapter will also discuss the role of human and non-human victims of environmental harm in the justice processes set up to defend or guarantee such rights. Ultimately it will be shown that the 'environmental rights' perspective has great potential to address some of the shortcomings seen in other approaches taken to environmental harm discussed in this book, albeit the development of such rights is still at a very early stage in most parts of the world and at the international level. Ultimately the further development of such rights will likely prove another important component of green criminology.

By the end of this chapter readers will:

■ Appreciate the difficulties and advantages of combining 'animal rights' and 'environmentalist' perspectives.
■ Be aware of the steps that have been taken towards establishing an internationally recognised 'right' to an unpolluted environment.
■ Understand the notion of 'greening' human (and non-human) rights and appreciate the difficulties of expanding human rights in this area.
■ Appreciate the difficulties of incorporating victims of environmental harm as 'participants' in criminal and other justice mechanisms designed to facilitate 'environmental rights'.
■ Be familiar with several of the major arguments for and against such rights.

In this chapter we will extend our discussion of environmental victimisation, which began in Chapter 8, to examine the application of so-called environmental rights to humans and non-humans affected by environmental crimes and broader environmental harms. In previous chapters we have discussed the various theoretical and practical difficulties which arise when attempting to fit environmental harm within the traditional framework of criminal justice, as well as pointing out the complexities and barriers to applying civil law, administrative sanctions and regulations to this issue at the national and international level.

In recent years, many international environmental lawyers, when faced with the above dilemmas, have turned to the notion of human rights – including so-called environmental rights – as a means of attributing responsibility to states and other parties for environmental harms. Beirne and colleagues (2009) have described this developing focus on rights as 'perhaps the most significant shift in the focus of international law' (p.269). In this chapter it is suggested that such moves also provide considerable impetus to the cause of green criminology and victimology and to the acknowledgement of victimisation by the state in relation to environmental harms.

The above developments notwithstanding, for international environmental lawyers the application of human rights to instances of environmental degradation and environmental harm remains distinctly underdeveloped. This reflects the continued state-orientated nature of international law that, as noted earlier in this book (see p.121), is often still conceived as a system built 'by states, for states'. From a green perspective, a further level of complexity lies in establishing whether any such environmental rights are in fact purely *human* rights or whether they extend to encompass less anthropocentric concerns. Linked to this is the question of how the environmental rights of individual humans or human communities should be weighed against damage (or potential damage) to the wider environment, the ecosystem, non-human animals and so on (White, 2008a). Consequently, approaching this issue from a green perspective inevitably invites some discussion of animal rights as a concept and of 'nature' itself as a harmed party. Indeed, recently such debates have attracted worldwide (if sometimes derisive) media attention with the proposed introduction of a Declaration of Rights for Cetaceans. This example is further discussed in Box 1 below.

In addition to the above questions, many authors have pointed out that 'rights' of any kind are only effective when backed by effectual and robust enforcement mechanisms (Jackson, 2004). Consequently, when we are discussing 'rights' in this context we are in fact raising two distinct issues.

Box 1: Do whales and dolphins have rights?

Although the extension of environmental rights to non-humans is often still considered an anomalous notion, public awareness of conservationists' arguments to this end is growing. In one thought-provoking example, the outcome of a conference that took place in Helsinki in May 2010 on Cetacean Rights: Fostering Moral and Legal Change received widespread intentional media attention when the group of 'experts in philosophy, conservation and animal behaviour' called for the recognition of a 'non-human persons' status for dolphins, whales and porpoises via a Declaration of Rights for Cetaceans (Hue and Anton, 2011). The text of the draft document sets out a number of rights including cetaceans' right 'to the protection of their natural environment' and to be free from 'disruption of their culture' (cetaceanrights.org, 2014). Although the 'Declaration' is (at present) only a thought-exercise, it does illustrate the kinds of questions a genuinely eco-centric (or at least less anthropocentric) approach to 'environmental rights' might foster.

On the one hand the primary question might be whether or not there exists a right for humans or animals to enjoy or reside within an unpolluted environment. A subsequent issue however would be the extent to which such rights are given effect through the *participation* of these rights-bearers in environmental decision-making. This is the 'environmental justice' perspective first set out in Chapter 1. Drawing on broader victimological literature, such debates might extend in this case to examining what role (if any) is played by human or non-human environmental victims in any justice system set up to tackle illegal environmental harm and/or offer redress for breaches of environmental rights.

The remainder of this chapter will proceed as follows. First the notion of 'rights' as a concept applying beyond human beings in the environmental sphere will be discussed. This will necessitate a brief overview of animal rights perspectives and, in particular, a discussion of the sometimes uneasy relationship between the animal rights movement and environmentalism. The chapter will then explore the development of a 'right' to an unpolluted environment in several parts of the world. Following this the discussion will be broadened to examine other more established categories of (mainly human) rights and how these have been applied to the environment. Finally, the chapter will discuss the concept of participation by environmental victims (both human and no-human) within criminal and other mechanisms of justice, restoration or redress, on the national and international level. The chapter will conclude with some key observations concerning the future of environmental rights' as a concept and its place as an important object of green criminological study.

GREEN CRIMINOLOGY AND NON-HUMAN 'RIGHTS'

There is a vast quantity of philosophical and sociological literature in which the notion of 'animal rights' is discussed and debated. It is not the purpose of the present section to offer an extensive review of this field (for a much fuller account see Varner, 2002). Nevertheless, if we are to examine the idea of a right to an unpolluted environment from a truly green criminological perspective we will need at least some background in animal rights discourse and its relationship with environmentalism. In approaching animal rights one preliminary issue to emphasise is that, while often 'the environment' and 'non-human animals' are amalgamated into a single issue in green criminological writings, in fact there are arguably wide conceptual differences between the development of the animal rights, or, for some, 'animal abuse' (Varner, 2002) movement on the one hand and 'environmentalism' on the other. As noted by Beirne (2007), while the two areas ostensibly have much in common:

> The task of finding in the area of animal abuse common ground between environmentally- (or ecologically-) based green criminology and an animal-centered animal rights theory, worthwhile as it might be, is not altogether a straightforward one. (p.56)

Beirne goes on to classify animal rights and animal abuse perspectives into three broad groups: always acknowledging that this represents a vast oversimplification of what is actually a very diverse movement (on which, see Munro, 2012). The first of the three perspectives Beirne emphasises is the utilitarian argument – which gives animals rights on the basis that they are 'sentient beings who can suffer and feel pain' (p.67) and thus in keeping with the utilitarian philosophy of maximising pleasure while minimising pain, humans should not inflict pain upon them. This is contrasted to the 'animals as moral patients' argument whereby animals are conceived as the 'subjects-of-a-life' and, while they are not capable of 'doing right or wrong' themselves, in moral terms they are equivalent to human infants, the mentally ill and young children by reason of their ability to suffer. Thus, it is argued, failing to respect the rights of non-human 'moral patients' while preserving the lives and avoiding harm to human moral patients would be arbitrary and thus unjust. Thirdly, Beirne discusses the feminist perspective of animal rights, which holds that the failure of both the utilitarian and moral patients understanding of this concept is their dismissal of purportedly 'un-masculine' traits of sentimentality and emotional attachment to animals. This 'effectively equates "sentimental" and "emotional" with "irrational" and all three traits with "less than male" and "female"' (p.71). In contrast, it is argued that from a feminist perspective such traits are perfectly acceptable as moral justifications for the recognition of animal rights.

It is clear that there is much in the above summary which links animal rights arguments to the development of green criminology as discussed in previous chapters. Certainly if it is 'harm' we are discussing rather than 'crime', the utilitarian and moral patients arguments offer clear reasons why 'harm to animals' is as significant as 'harm to humans'. We have also seen in previous chapters that feminism has already played a significant role in the development of more environmentally based approaches to criminology and thus there are many parallels to be drawn. That said, and as also discussed by Beirne (2007), the above philosophies of animal rights do not neatly map onto the eco-centric concern with non-living aspects of the environment such as the oceans, atmosphere and so on. Nor indeed would the above perspectives clearly cover flora and thus issues like biopiracy, genetic modification, diversification of crops and so on, unless they are defined as capable of 'suffering'.

Of the three animal rights perspectives outlined by Beirne the feminist perspective is probably most adaptable to unite these argument with the green perspective, and we have already seen examples of so-called ecofeminist discourse in this book (see p.52). That said, from the rights perspective ecofeminism tends to be more concerned with the manner in which the disregard for nature reflects male hegemony and female supplication in wider society, and thus is less concerned with ascribing 'rights' to nature per se. In sum, while out of convenience this chapter, like may green criminological texts, will approach the 'rights' question in a way that unifies both non-human animals and the environment itself, it is important to acknowledge that these two issues are arguably – from a conceptual and philosophical perspective – raising quite different questions, especially in relation to the idea of a 'right' to an unpolluted environment, to which this chapter now turns its attention.

A 'RIGHT' TO AN UNPOLLUTED ENVIRONMENT?

At first glance, a simple solution to many of the environmental issues discussed in this book, and certainly in relation to many forms of environmental victimisations discussed in Chapter 7, might be the development/recognition of a 'right to an unpolluted environment'. Such a right could then be invoked by (human) victims when they feel it had been violated by other individuals, corporate entities or states themselves. The transnational nature of much environmental harm makes the 'rights' solution seem particularly attractive because, if such rights were recognised at an international level, in theory this avoids the complexities of different domestic justice systems with different legal approaches to environmental harms interacting, with victims from one country (feeling the effects of environmental harm) taking action in another country (where that harm originated) and so on. In line with the above discussions, for non-humans, such a concept could even be extended to animals, and perhaps to the environment itself, although already in such cases we encounter difficult questions regarding how non-humans could 'bring' such an action and who would represent them.

In any case, while considerable progress has been made in more recent years towards the assimilation of *human* rights within the green agenda, and indeed within the scope of national and international environmental law, there have also been significant challenges to what in both cases is undoubtedly a novel application of the rights concept. Furthermore, given the grounding of these arguments in *human* rights instruments, very little of this work has taken a more eco-centric stance. Indeed, contrary to the ideal situation described above, even *human* rights traditionally have not been conceived as extraterritorial in nature (D'Amato, 1982). As such, no right to a healthy or clean environment has yet been widely recognised by the international legal order (Redgwell, 2014) although there are examples of such a right – at least for humans – at a more regional level.

One such example can be found in Article 11 of the American Convention on Human Rights and its Protocol of San Salvador (see p.36 for an explanation of 'convention' and 'protocol'), which reads:

1. 'Everyone shall have the right to live in a healthy environment and to have access to basic public services.
2. The States Parties shall promote the protection, preservation, and improvement of the environment.'

Notably, this places a positive obligation on states in relation to environmental protection and improvement, as opposed to merely requiring them to refrain from destructive activities. Such positive obligations are significant when one considers that states generally do not accept responsibility for other kinds of harm (especially criminal harms) to humans or non-humans on the basis that they have a positive duty to 'protect' them. This is commonly reflected in the rationales given for state-funded compensation systems for crime victims, most of which make it very clear that the money is paid from the public purse not out of recognition that the state has failed in some protective duty, but rather on welfare, communitarian or other grounds (see Miers, 1991). By contrast such a right as described in Article 11 of the American Convention might imply that a state is directly responsible if through a failure to promote and improve the environment, and certainly if its actions lead to hazardous pollution, humans (assuming 'everyone' is so restricted) are caused environmental harms. 'Environment' is given no specific definition in the document although clearly the implication here is that a duty exists beyond simply protecting humans from the effects of environmental harm, which is a significant break from more anthropocentric traditions.

In a different localised context, the 1981 African Charter on Human and People's Rights (see p.116) states in Article 24 that:

> All peoples shall have the right to a general satisfactory environment favourable to their development.

This article has achieved special prominence within the international legal scholarship on human and environmental rights following its interpretation by the African Commission on Human Rights and Peoples Rights in the 1996 *Ogoniland* decision as follows:

> The right to a general satisfactory environment, as guaranteed under Article 24 of the African Charter or the right to a healthy environment, as it is widely known therefore imposes clear obligations upon a government. It requires the State to take reasonable and other measures to prevent pollution and ecological degradation, to promote conservation, and to secure an ecologically sustainable development and use of natural resources. (available at http://www1.umn.edu/humanrts/africa/comcases/155-96.html: Para. 52)

We saw in Chapter 5 how this decision went on to lay out the full harms and health impacts on local communities. The Commission further ruled that African states were obliged under the Charter to 'prevent pollution and ecological degradation, to promote conservation, and to secure ecologically sustainable development and use of natural resources' (Para. 52).

Coomans (2003) makes the point that the Commission in this case was adopting an 'obligations' approach, whereby states are required to *respect*, *protect*, *promote* and *fulfil* relevant (in this case, environmental) rights. Significantly, Coomans argues that this effectively puts civil and political rights (often called 'first generation' rights) on an equal footing with cultural, economic and social rights (often referred to as 'second generation' rights):

> The use of the typology [of obligations] implies that realization of each separate right in the African Charter may involve duties to respect, to protect, to promote and to fulfil. In other words, a State Party may not limit itself to observance of one specific obligation only. In most cases, implementation of civil and political rights as well as economic, social and cultural rights will require observance of all levels of duties: all types of obligations are interrelated and interdependent. (p.753)

While only a local judgement, conferring what can be viewed as a collective right on a community of people, Beirne et al. (2009) have called this 'a remarkable decision which goes further than any previous human-rights case in the substantive environmental obligations it places on states' (p.273). Indeed from the critical criminological perspective, if the juxtaposition within this judgement of official state (economic) interests and the rights of victims of environmental harm is significant, the fact that the impact on victims essentially won through is extraordinary. Furthermore, the ruling emphasised potential victims' rights to *information* concerning environmental hazards, appealing to the Nigerian government to begin:

> Providing information on health and environmental risks and meaningful access to regulatory and decision-making bodies to communities likely to be affected by oil operation. (pp.15–16)

At the same time, it is clear that in the Ogoniland case judgement the Commission was almost exclusively concerned with the rights of *humans* rather than the impact on animals or the environment itself. The only part of the judgement to consider non-human impacts is paragraph 9, which holds:

> The government has participated in irresponsible oil development that has poisoned much of the soil and water upon which Ogoni farming and fishing depended. In their raids on villages, Nigerian security forces have destroyed crops and killed farm animals. The security forces have created a state of terror and insecurity that has made it impossible for many Ogoni villagers to return to their fields and animals. The destruction of farmlands, rivers, crops and animals has created malnutrition and starvation among certain Ogoni Communities.

It is clear that references to soil, water and animals in this extract are all firmly related to the value derived from these as resources by humans ('crops', 'farming', 'fishing', 'farm animals').

The African and South American examples cited above are interesting and significant cases of *local* applications of what might be called rights to a clean and unpolluted environment. Other isolated examples do exist, such as the Jamaican Charter of Fundamental Rights and Freedoms (Constitutional Amendment) Act, 2011, which affords Jamaican citizens:

> the right to enjoy a healthy and productive environment free from the threat of injury or damage from environmental abuse and degradation of the ecological heritage. (s.(13)(3)(l))

The Constitution of South African has a similar provision, reflecting the 1981 African Charter discussed above. Notably, the above extract does not require environmental victims to demonstrate *actual* harm, but rather the *threat* of harm, avoiding difficult issues concerning causation.

Such a right was also suggested by the 1972 UN Conference on the Human Environment (a major turning point in the development of international environmental law, see p.120), and is reflected in Principle 1 of the resulting Stockholm Declaration. That said, the follow-up 1992 conference on Environment and Development in Rio failed to develop this suggestion any further. A right to a healthy and decent environment has also been suggested by the UN Sub-Commission on the prevention of Discrimination and Protection on the grounds that it would enhance the standing of environmental concerns when balancing conflicting rights and objectives (see Sierra Club Legal Defence Fund, 1993), although this recommendation was similarly not taken forward.

THE 'GREENING' OF EXISTING RIGHTS

The second mechanism for establishing 'environmental rights' to receive extensive discussion in the green criminological and wider literature is to ground such expectations in *existing* rights, which have already met with wider acceptance at the domestic and international levels. In other words, it is argued that more established rights could be interpreted in ways that preclude environmental victimisation. Generally speaking, there is evidence of a greater acceptance of this class of environmental rights by international organisations compared with a distinct right to a clean environment discussed in the last section.

The European Court of Human Rights (ECtHR) is the body which hears allegations from Council of Europe member states to the effect that their rights guaranteed under the European Convention on Human Rights have been breached (all Council of Europe members must become contracting parties to the Convention and thus agree to adhere to its principles, in addition all members of the European Union must be members of the Council of Europe and therefore also sign up to the Convention). In recent years the ECtHR has taken the lead in these developments from a judicial perspective. In particular there are now numerous cases in which Article 8 of the European Convention on Human Rights (the right to respect for private and family life and one's home) has been interpreted by the ECtHR as including environmental factors, generally on the understanding that localised environmental degradation restricts a person's ability to live where they choose (DeMerieux, 2001). A landmark ECtHR case on this matter is that of *Lopez Ostra*, in which the court ruled in relation to an alleged breach of Article 8 caused by the sighting of a waste disposal plant near the complainant's home:

> Naturally, severe environmental pollution may affect individuals' well-being and prevent them from enjoying their homes in such a way as to affect their private and family life adversely, without, however, seriously endangering their health. (para.51)

Furthermore, the Spanish State had, as respondent in this, case failed:

> in striking a fair balance between the interest of the town's economic well-being – that of having a waste-treatment plant – and the applicant's effective enjoyment of her right to respect for her home and her private and family life. (para.58)

Notably the ruling draws on 'balance' rhetoric: whereby any economic benefit to the state of permitting environmentally destructive activities is weighed against the likely impact on individuals and communities. The ECtHR has continued to rule in favour of breaches of Article 8 in cases of where it has considered levels of polluting activity within a state to infringe upon Article 8 rights in the cases of *Tatar v Romania* and *Olui v Croatia*. In the case of *Borysiewicz v Poland* the court set out the test to be applied in assessing the level of interference with family or home rights required to raise an issue under Article 8:

> the interference must directly affect the applicant's home, family or private life and the adverse effects of the environmental hazard must attain a certain minimum level of severity. The assessment of that minimum is relative and depends on all the circumstances of the case, such as the intensity and duration of the nuisance, and its physical or mental effects. (para.100)

The court was silent here on how such a minimum threshold could be established, and whether doing would include direct consultations with those people or communities whose rights had been interfered with. This is significant when we consider the rights of environmental victims to *participate* in the justice process, which will be discussed in greater detail below. In making this ruling the Court also emphasised 'that there is no explicit right in the Convention to a clean and quiet environment, but where an individual is directly and seriously affected by noise or other pollution, an issue may arise under Article 8 of the Convention' (para.98). This understanding was repeated in *Leon and Agnieszka Kania* v *Poland*.

Not all ECtHR case rulings on Article 8 have expanded the application of Convention rights to environmental degradation. In *Powell and Rayner* v *UK* the European Commission of Human Rights argued that a State has the obligation to *protect* (as well as *respect*) the rights under Article 8 and that excessive noise pollution would indeed constitute interference with a person's right to enjoy their home and, therefore, to a private life. The alleged breach of Convention rights came about as a result of noise emanating from low-flying planes near Heathrow Airport. The Court ruled that no such breach of Article 8 had occurred. This result raises questions as to the relative weight given to victims' rights (residents living in the vicinity of Heathrow Airport) when compared with wider economic advantages for a region or the state as a whole, especially when compared to the outcome of the African *Ogoniland* case discussed above, where state economic interests apparently ranked second to the question of environmental harm (at least so far as this impacted upon humans and communities).

The ECtHR has also considered claims for breaches of the right to life in Article 2 of the Convention as a result of environmental degradation. In particular, in *Budayeva and others* v *Russia* the court held that a failure by authorities to provide adequate warnings to the public and to put in place containment mechanisms against dangerous mudslides was a breach of Article 2. Local officials in this case had received advanced warnings of possible danger to residents in the local area from scientific experts. As summarised by Wilson (2011):

> When the government has knowledge of an imminent risk to lives or severe failures in current protections from natural disasters, the government must take all diligent measures to protect the right to life In this case, the government took essentially no steps to remedy the known risk to life from mudslides, so there seems to be a very clear violation of Article 2. This decision is notable because natural disasters are almost inherently unforeseeable, but there was enough information available about the risks such that, in this instance, the risk was still considered imminent. (p.6)

This returns us to the importance of 'risk' as a founding concept of green criminology (see Chapter 1) and also empathises that natural disasters – and in particular governments' reactions to natural disasters (natural risks) – are an important topic of concern to this subject area despite the fact that they are not 'crimes' in the traditional sense.

Beyond the ECtHR, the so-called greening of existing recognised human rights has been distinctly less developed, although in the case of *Port Hope Environmental Group* v *Canada* the UN Human Rights Committee accepted that dumping nuclear waste does raise serious right-to-life issues in relation to both present and future generations. Of course, given the focus on *human* rights there is little in these judgements to hint at a wider form of rights for non-human animals or the environment itself.

PARTICIPATION RIGHTS IN RELATION TO ENVIRONMENTAL HARM

As was alluded to already in this chapter, notions of environmental justice usually include the understanding that (ideally human and non-human) stakeholders in decisions affecting their environments are given the opportunity to participate in the decision-making process. Extending this idea to the application and enforcement of any 'environmental rights', and drawing also on the victimological literature introduced in Chapter 7, it follows that such environmental victims should also be afforded some place in whatever mechanism of justice exists to defend such rights.

In legal terms the above proposition is encapsulated in the notion of 'standing' to participate in the criminal (or other legal) process. Indeed, the International Law Commission has positively remarked that '[t]he definition of victim [of environmental harm] is thus linked to the question of standing' (ILC, 2006: p.137). The ILC also here highlights the example of France, where 'some environmental associations have been given the right to claim compensation in criminal cases involving violation of certain environmental statutes' (p.137). The further important example of the 1998 UNECE Convention on Access to Information, Public Participation in Decision-Making and Access to Justice in Environmental Matters is discussed in Box 2.

Legal standing is certainly at the heart of most of the victimological debates concerning rights for victims of more traditional crime because, in recent history, victims have lacked party status in most domestic criminal justice systems (Hall, 2010). As a consequence of this legal reality, it is the

---

Box 2: Participation for (human) environmental victims? The 1998 UNECE Convention on Access to Information, Public Participation in Decision-Making and Access to Justice in Environmental Matters

Possibly the most progressive source of legally binding environmental obligations in the corpus of international law is found in the 1998 UNECE Convention on Access to Information, Public Participation in Decision-Making and Access to Justice in Environmental Matters (often shortened to the 'Aarhus Convention'). The Convention requires governments to bring individuals who may be affected into the *decision-making* process when environmental issues are at stake. In terms of holding states to account for the harm caused by environmental degradation what is significant about the Aarhus Convention is that, almost uniquely within international law, under Article 15 it is envisioned that members of the public are able to refer possible breaches of their rights under the Convention to its Compliance Committee:

> The Meeting of the Parties shall establish, on a consensus basis, optional arrangements of a non-confrontational, non-judicial and consultative nature for reviewing compliance with the provisions of this Convention. These arrangements shall allow for appropriate public involvement and may include the option of considering communications *from members of the public* on matters related to this Convention. (emphasis added)

The key question from a (green) victimological perspective is whether these provisions under Aarhus are the equivalent of giving victims a level of discretion over what in the criminal context would be prosecution decisions (a 'procedural right'), something that has thus far been vigorously avoided in all jurisdictions, or whether it is more akin to the complaints mechanisms offered to many other types of victims the world over (a 'service' right). Most recent indications suggest there have been few applications made to the Compliance Committee. It is known that the body cannot issue binding decisions, but rather makes recommendations to the full Meeting of the Parties (Beirne et al., 2009). Thus, while the Aarhus convention offers something of a 'way in' to the international legal order for those humans affected by environmental harm, in practice this Compliance Mechanisms can be subject to the criticism that there is a lack of real compulsive power on behalf of the Compliance Committee to actually address victims' complains and ensure restitution/apologies from perpetrator states is forthcoming.

---

state that acquires the rights of individual victims, effectively forcing those affected by crimes and other social misfortunes to take a subsidiary role in proceedings. This was famously captured by Nils Christie (1977) who argued that the state effectively 'steals' conflicts from their rightful owners, namely the victim and the accused. The same could aptly be said of the victims of environmental harms, especially in relation to their exclusion from the international legal order. Indeed in this instance the victims' plight is almost entirely taken over by the state because, as already discussed in Chapter 5, under international law it is the state and not the individual which can draw on the international legal order against another state.

For DeMerieux (2001) the key benefit of affording victims of environmental harm the right to participate in any justice mechanisms intended to defend environmental rights is that this will allow for better and more effective *enforcement* of environmental laws. Of course, it is important to appreciate that a 'right to participate' covers a breadth of possibilities, ranging from the nominal to the much more substantive. In the mainstream victimological literature Edwards (2004) has labelled participation 'a comfortably pleasing platitude', which is rhetorically powerful but conceptually abstract. In his discussion, Edwards describes four possible forms of victim participation in criminal justice. The most significant casts victims in the role of *decision-makers*, such that their preferences are sought and applied by the criminal justice system. Less far-reaching would be *consultative* participation, where the system seeks out victims' preferences and takes them into account when making decisions. Edwards sees the traditional role of victims in terms of *information provision*, where victims are obliged to provide information required by the system. Finally, under *expressive* participation, victims express whatever information they wish, but with no instrumental impact; here Edwards highlights the danger of victims wrongly believing their participation will actually affect decision-making.

An early example of the consideration of participation rights for victims of environmental harm is found in the 1992 Rio Declaration on Environment and Development. Under Principle 10 of this document states are encouraged to ensure 'public awareness and participation by making information widely available'. The provision goes on to say that '(e)ffective access to judicial and administrative proceedings, including redress and remedy, shall be provided'. Under ECtHR jurisprudence such a right of participation in environmental cases has most frequently been upheld in relation to Article 6 (the right to a fair and public hearing to determine civil rights). Thus, in *Zander* v *Swedeni* the court held that a couple's inability under Swedish law to contest the granting of a licence by the government permitting a company to dump waste adjacent to their property, leading to the pollution of their drinking water (which was drawn from a nearby well) violated Article 6. Article 6 requires the infraction of a 'civil' right to be admissible, and on this question the Court ruled that the relevant right that had been affected was the right to peaceful enjoyment of one's possessions (Article 1). Analogous sentiments are found in the 2012 Rio+20 Outcome Document, which followed the United Nations Conference on Sustainable Development that year. This document, while often criticised by international environmental lawyers as having little if any legal force (Morrow, 2013), does acknowledge how 'broad public participation and access to information and judicial and administrative proceedings are essential to the promotion of sustainable development' (para.46).

In terms of victim participation, a further key initiative relating to the criminalisation of environmental harm and the participation of environmental victims in criminal justice is the 1998 Council of Europe Convention on the Protection of Environment through Criminal Law. Although this treaty has not yet entered into force (and indeed has secured little State support) it is significant as the precursor to the adoption of EU Council Directive 2008/99/EC within the European Union (see p.2). While the latter instrument almost entirely excluded those humans and non-humans affected by environmental harm, the 1998 Convention contains a significant provision relating to the participation of environmental victims in criminal justice mechanisms. Article 11 reads:

> Each Party may, at any time, in a declaration addressed to the Secretary General of the Council of Europe, declare that it will, in accordance with domestic law, grant any group, foundation or association which, according to its statutes, aims at the protection of the environment, the right to participate in criminal proceedings concerning offences established in accordance with this Convention.

This article has the potential to be groundbreaking, raising the very real possibility of opening up environmental criminal proceedings to wider participation by the victims of environmental harms themselves. In the context of EU environmental (and criminal) law the adoption of the language of 'participation' in relation to such organisations is a significant step forward, albeit the question of whether such groups envisioned in this article represent the majority of 'real' environmental victims remains moot.

Interestingly, it can be noted that Article 11 of the 1998 Convention is carefully worded to remove any sense of the *individual* victim. Nevertheless, its inclusion is an important indication of changing attitudes. No longer is the State viewed as the sole trustee of the public good: as is often still the case in international environmental law. As the explanatory report to the Convention notes:

> The main reason for allowing NGOs access to environmental proceedings is that criminal law in the environmental field protects interests of a highly collective nature, in view of

the fact that the various forms of pollution potentially affect the interest not only of single individuals, but also of groups of persons. (Council of Europe, 1998)

A further notable example of participatory rights for victims of environmental harms, albeit again concerning only the *administrative* (rather than criminal) liability of polluting operators, is that of the 2004 EU Environmental Liability Directive. That instrument includes a key role for those affected by environmental harm. Key provisions from this instrument are reproduced in Box 3.

Box 3: The 2004 EU Environmental Liability Directive

As Article 12 (entitled 'request for action') and Article 13 ('review procedures') of that Directive state:

Article 12

1. Natural or legal persons:

(a) affected or likely to be affected by environmental damage or
(b) having a sufficient interest in environmental decision making relating to the damage or, alternatively,
(c) alleging the impairment of a right, where administrative procedural law of a Member State requires this as a precondition,

shall be entitled to submit to the competent authority any observations relating to instances of environmental damage or an imminent threat of such damage of which they are aware and shall be entitled to request the competent authority to take action under this Directive.

What constitutes a 'sufficient interest' and 'impairment of a right' shall be determined by the Member States.

To this end, the interest of any non-governmental organisation promoting environmental protection and meeting any requirements under national law shall be deemed sufficient for the purpose of subparagraph (b). Such organisations shall also be deemed to have rights capable of being impaired for the purpose of subparagraph (c).

Article 13

1. The persons referred to in Article 12(1) shall have access to a court or other independent and impartial public body competent to review the procedural and substantive legality of the decisions, acts or failure to act of the competent authority under this Directive (emphasis added).

(© European Union, 1995–2014)

Notably, this instrument set out in Box 3 includes *individual* victims as well as groups and NGOs purporting to represent them. It should also be mentioned in this section that EU citizens (as individuals or represented by groups) have the right to 'petition to the European Parliament on a matter which comes within the Union's fields of activity and which affects him, her or it directly' under Article 227 of the Treaty on the Functioning of the European Union. Lenaerts and Gutiérrez-Fons (2010) have argued that this provision could be utilised by (directly harmed) citizens who feel that national legislation is conflicting with EU environmental law.

One final example of an instrument in which victims of environmental harms are granted participatory rights on an administrative level is that of the North American Agreement on Environmental Cooperation (NAAEC). Under this instrument, submissions can be made to the secretariat of the Commission for Environmental Cooperation asserting that a 'party to the agreement is failing to effectively enforce its environmental law'. If the submissions satisfy criteria specified in NAAEC, the secretariat may request a response from the party named in the submission. While such representations will usually be made by another of the parties to the agreement (these being the United States, Mexico and Canada), the agreement also stipulates at Article 22(3) that:

> a third Party that considers it has a substantial interest in the matter shall be entitled to participate in the consultations on delivery of written notice to the other Parties and to the Secretariat.

In addition, Article 29 – entitled 'Third Party Participation' – reads:

> A party that is not a disputing Party, on delivery of a written notice to the disputing Parties and to the Secretariat, shall be entitled to attend all hearings, to make written and oral submissions to the panel and to receive written submissions of the disputing Parties.

Although the NAAEC procedures is strictly administrative, it is particularly significant for present purposes in that it relates to a state's lack of enforcement of (environmental) *criminal* law. A similar provision can also be found under the Canadian Environmental Protection Act 1988, which gives citizens the right to sue authorities if environmental laws are not enforced. Girard et al. (2010) have remarked on the increasing use of this provision by environmental activists in Canada in the face of what they term 'the Conservative government's continued intransigence' (p.233) on environmental matters.

WAYS FORWARD FOR 'ENVIRONMENTAL RIGHTS'

The above, necessarily brief, discussion indicates that the concept of humans (at least) having 'rights' which relate to their natural environments has now received general acceptance both in the academic literature and by some judicial bodies. Clearly however many questions remain as to the specific nature of these 'rights', as well as their enforceability and the role of environmental victims in that enforcement. At present the most widespread developments have occurred in relation to expanding more mainstream and accepted rights to cover environmental harms. Indeed, further extension of a specific right to an unpolluted environment will require more radical amendments to existing human rights instruments or the introduction of new instruments such as the Council of Europe Convention on the Protection of Environment through Criminal Law. It is also very clear that, from a green criminological perspective, markedly absent from many of these developments is a genuine appreciation for non-human rights. The literature is especially muted on means by which *non-humans* (including non-living components of the environment) might be given representation in any legal or administrative proceedings designed to defend their rights. In the last chapter I noted the mock ecocide trial was hosted at the University of Essex in 2012, which involved representatives acting for nature (birds, wild spaces, etc.) in a restorative justice forum. Such exercises, while path-breaking, are however still at the level of intellectual thought-experiments.

Despite the above difficulties, the developments that have occurred in the application of environmental rights' so far indicate that this will continue to be an important area for green criminologists. Conceiving environmental harm in terms of breaches of rights may well prove instrumental in avoiding the difficulties associated with more traditional models of criminal, civil or administrative enforcement when applied to the environment. Effective 'rights' by their nature must be respected by individuals, corporations and states in all countries and irrespective of where the harmed party comes from or resides. As such, the further development and application of environmental rights has real potential to address many of the limitations highlighted elsewhere in this volume associated with more traditional justice mechanisms and their handling of environmental harm.

Summary

The extension of 'rights' concepts to the environment and the impacts of environmental degradation is still a novel development, but one which is increasingly influential as a potential solution to some of the shortcomings of more traditional criminal- or civil-based resolution and redress mechanisms for environmental harm. While much of the established literature and jurisprudence on this issue is focused around humans, from a philosophical/theoretical perspective the notion of applying such rights to non-human animals and perhaps the environment itself is consistent with the broader green criminological project. So far such 'environmental rights' as have been recognised by states and international bodies mainly constitute an extension of existing rights to cover environmental harm, especially Articles 2 and 8 of the ECHR. There are significant examples of distinct rights to a green environment existing in localised contexts, but these have not yet received the level of intentional acceptance required to qualify as established principles of the international legal order. The question of how both human and non-human victims interact with the mechanism of justice intended to defend any such environmental rights harks back to broader victimological questions about the role and participation of victims in justice systems. Again non-humans have generally been excluded from such questioning thus far. In sum, the question of environmental rights is an important issue for green criminologists and one still badly in need of theoretical development, particularly in relation to no-human animals and the environment itself. Nevertheless the concept has great potential to address many key green criminological problems.

Review questions

1) Why have a 'right' to a green environment? What added value (if any) does this bring when trying to practically address environmental harms?
2) Are green criminologists necessarily correct in trying to combine animal rights/animal abuse perspectives with 'environmentalism'?
3) What existing 'rights' have been applied to the environment? Can you identify other existing rights that might be adapted in this way?
4) What are the challenges to involving environmental victims in upholding their own environmental rights?

Further reading

Benton, T. (2009), 'Rights and Justice on a Shared Planet: More Rights or New Relations?', *Theoretical Criminology*, 2(2): 149–175.

- Especially useful as this piece is written from a criminological perspective.

Brisman, A. (2013), 'Environmental and Human Rights'. In Gerben Bruinsma and David Weisburd (eds.), *Encyclopedia of Criminology and Criminal Justice*, Vol.3, New York: Springer Verlag, 1344–1345.

- Thorough examination of several conceptions of 'environmental rights'.

Coomans, F. (2003), 'The Ogoni Case Before the African Commission on Human and Peoples' Rights, *International and Comparative Law Quarterly*, 52: 749–760.

- The Ogoni case is still perhaps the major development in international law concerning the possible future development of environment rights.

Gleick, P. (1998), 'The Human Right to Water', *Water Policy*, 1: 487–503.

- An older piece, but useful to demonstrate how broader environmental rights could apply to more specific issues.

Chapter 9

Exploring Green Crime and Wider Harms with Green Criminology

This final chapter will compile and evaluate key themes and methodological issues from the previous eight chapters with a view to mapping
out future directions and areas of development for green criminology
as a subject of research and a driver of policy movement. The chapter
will revisit green criminological 'theory' and methodologies (or lack of
thereof) in the light of the discussions presented in the preceding chapters. In so doing the chapter will examine how green criminology relates
to other criminological topics and to victimological concerns. I will also
comment here on the tensions which exist between approaching green
criminology from a wider 'macro' perspective at the level of states and
broad societal trends versus focusing down more specifically on distinct
examples of illegal polluting activities and on major 'disaster' events. The
chapter will also reflect further on the significant connections between
green criminology and other (often more established) areas of criminological
enquiry.

By the end of this chapter readers should:

■ Appreciate how the debates and topics raised in previous chapters can
   be drawn upon to reach broader conclusions about green criminology as
   a subject area and its potential future directions.

- Be aware of the methodological challenges and possibilities of 'doing' green criminology.
- Understand the synergies that exist between victimology and green criminology.
- Appreciate the clear links between green criminology and more traditional criminological approaches in terms of methods and theory.

GREEN CRIMINOLOGY THEMES AND 'THEORY'?

In Chapter 1 of this volume I noted the recent view of White (2013a) that 'there is no green criminology *theory* as such' (p.22) and that 'those who are doing green criminology define it in ways that best suit their own conception of what it is they are doing' (p.17). This is both a useful but at the same time challenging perspective. On the positive side this view broadens rather than restricts the boundaries of the subject: it is inclusive and thus encouraging for the development of multidisciplinary links in the study of environmental harm. It also helps to dispel conceptions of green criminology as 'fringe' or as an eccentric subtopic pursued by a dedicated minority of impassioned criminological researchers. Instead the implication is that green criminology may in fact be integral to what other researchers are doing in wider criminology and beyond it (I will expand more on the 'mainstreaming' of green criminology below). At the same time however such a broad understanding of green criminology, certainly in labelling terms, risks presenting the developing field as impossibly fragmented. Of course, White's point is not that green criminologists do not *utilise* theory to drive their hypotheses or support their cases, but rather that identifying consistent theoretical and methodological positions uniting *all* green criminologists is presently impossible, and perhaps undesirable. Although on this last point Agnew (2011) has written on the desirability of a 'united' criminology, Brisman (2013) criticises this view both in terms of its characterisation of criminology as fragmented in the first place and on whether such diversity is necessarily as prejudicial to the cause of criminology as Agnew believes.

The previous chapters bear out these observations, where we have seen arguments throughout based on an eclectic mixture of criminological positions including rational choice theory (Chapter 6); neutralisation (Chapter 5); routine activities theory (Chapter 6); and strain theory (Chapter 5) to name but a few. At the same time, however, during the course of this book one can identify certain recurring themes, if not fully developed 'theories', which seem to have driven much of the green criminological debate thus far. These themes are highly interconnected and include power relations and inequalities; the identification, management and distribution of risk; a more eco-centric perspective; and what I will call the cultures of regulation. It may be useful at this point to briefly review each theme and how it has been reflected in the previous chapters.

Power relations and inequalities

Power inequalities in society, both at the national and international levels, have been close to the heart of many of the debates presented and assessed within this volume. We saw conceptualisations of power inequality reflected firstly in out discussions of the labelling of polluting activities as 'criminal' or, in many cases, non-criminal. To this end we have examined how some commentators have drawn on Marxist or neo-Marxist perspectives to explain how environmental legal and regulatory systems in practice often seem to *facilitate* rather than *threaten* or otherwise curtail the aspirations of powerful actors in a capitalist society, including corporations and states themselves. Indeed, in Chapter 5 this volume has discussed the role of states in facilitating and perpetuating environmental harms and considered the possibility that such actions and inactions constitute an 'abuse of power'. We also saw arguments in Chapter 4 that it is in fact *corporations* rather than state actors which constitute the principal organs through which such power is exercised – and environmental harm constructed – within a capitalist society.

By contrast, we have seen how those humans and non-humans falling victim to the most immediate effects of much environmental harm also tend to be the poorer and disempowered elements of societies at a national and global level. Although Williams (1996) has argued that the assumption of the powerless as environmental victims and the powerful as environmental victimisers represents 'a stereotyped view that omits the victimisation of those with power and wealth' (p.201), the overriding evidence now points to endemic inequality in the distribution of the environmental harms. We have seen how this inequality plays out both in terms of a redistribution of environmental harms (and risk of harms) from the global rich to the global poor but also how it impacts upon groups of certain ethnic origins and, according to eco-feminists, reflects further fundamental power inequalities between men and women in all societies, and in particular how – contrary to the principles of environmental justice (see p.18) – such groups are also excluded from decision making process which impact upon them and their environments.

In Chapter 5 we discussed Mol's (2013) argument that (green) criminology needs to incorporate extensive examinations of the mechanisms by which power flows through green issues. The majority of this volume clearly supports this basic assertion. Thus, before green criminologists even reach the point of gathering data on specific environmental harms and their impacts (knowledge of which is itself reflective of power inequalities in the presentation of 'science' and knowledge), there are considerable debates to be had concerning the power inequalities behind the classification of such activities as crimes (or not) and the enforcement of environmental law and regulatory provisions regionally, national and internationally.

The identification, management and distribution of risk

Give the often uncertain legal position of many of the activities fostering environmental harms set out in this volume, it has become clear that much of green criminological study actually concerns *risk* rather than crime itself. Strategies of focusing on risk and risk management have also been adopted by many regulatory agencies, including the Environment Agency in the United Kingdom and the Environmental Protection Agency in the United States, with the associated use of Environmental Impact Assessments. Risk here includes both the management and avoidance of environmental risks, but also its distribution on a national and an intentional scale. Indeed we have seen that the redistribution of risk is closely associated with the power inequalities discussed above and the outcome is that some groups and societies bear the risks (and then feel the impacts) of environmental harm more than others. This 'power' is in fact often the power *to shift* environmental risk. This book has demonstrated that 'risk' here includes natural risks, such as the risk of typhoons, tsunamis and hurricanes but also man-made 'manufactured' risks such as the potential harm of oil spills, nuclear power, and carbon capture and storage. Significantly, green criminologists have also been concerned with how risk is identified and measured which, as we have seen in Chapter 1, raises questions about the objectivity of scientific date (given the power dynamics described in the last section) and the interaction of physical science (and in particular, its inherent uncertainty (Ruggiero and South, 2010a)) with the social context of regulation, law and capitalism.

A more eco-centric perspective?

In Chapter 1 I drew a tentative distinction between 'mainstream' criminologies of climate change and environmental crime and 'green criminology' as being essentially a matter of the latter adopting a far more eco-centric perspective compared with the almost exclusively anthropocentric position taken in most other areas of criminological investigation. Nevertheless, we have seen that even those criminologists broadly associating themselves with the 'green' movement have often in practice tended to emphasise more anthropocentric concerns. One example of this would be the work that has been carried out on the development of environmental mediation schemes, discussed in Chapter 3, where almost none of the research considers the place of non-human animals or the environment itself within those processes. Nevertheless we have also seen that many commentators feel that a less human-centred perspective is vital to the development of a distinct 'green criminology' because the environment and non-human animals have value independent of that afforded to them by humans or the benefit that humans can extract from them. We saw philosophical and moral arguments to this effect in Chapter 8.

Recently Munro (2012) has commented on the absence of animal protection discussions within social science literature, arguing that social scientists may in fact have more to contribute to animal movements than philosophers: philosophy up until recently being the main academic discipline to engage with this area. Furthermore, we can appreciate the considerable overlap that exists between eco-centric concerns and the arguments set out above regarding the apportioning of power and risk. In the case of power this is because we know the non-human aspects of the environment have little representation in most decision which impact upon them. In the case of risk this is because damage to the environment and no-human animals is seen in many cases as a more 'acceptable' risk than harm to humans. Even from an anthropocentric position, harms vested on the environment and animals cannot be separated from impacts on humans and human concerns. This was made especially clear in Chapter 2, where we discussed the many connections between environmental change and societal change, and the criminogenic outcomes in particular.

The above notwithstanding, any insistence that 'real' green criminology is never anthropocentric risks isolating the subject from more mainstream criminology and indeed from other disciplines when, as argued at numerous points in this book, a core concern of green criminology needs to be towards building interdisciplinary bridges. Consequently White's perspective that one is 'doing' green criminology if one thinks one is may actually be more helpful for the establishment and development of the area as a whole. Certainly we must be wary here of trying to force what (as we've seen) are essentially social phenomena into false chronologies and compartmentalisations (Kearon and Godfrey, 2007). That said, criminologists need not wholly subscribe to the argument that non-humans have intrinsic worth or any of the more activist-inspired/associated perspectives (concerning animal rights, animal abuse and so on) to appreciate the value of incorporating the effects on the (non-human) environment into their research, if only for the more instrumental purposes of establishing how those effects might also impact on humans, crime and law.

As such, there is a strong theme in much of the prevailing literature that green criminology, if not entirely or consistently eco-centric, most often incorporates elements that a *far more* eco-centric than those found typically in mainstream criminological discussions. In other words, rather than approaching the issue in terms of a binary distinction between 'anthropocentric' and 'eco-centric' methodologies, one must appreciate that between these two extreme positions there stretches a continuum. While the discussions put forward in this book might lead us to the conclusion that much of green criminology is distinguishable by reason of resting further along the continuum in the direction of eco-centricism than is typical of most other areas of criminology, this is far from a universal 'rule'.

The cultures of regulation

Many of the discussions in this book have touched upon the mechanisms through which different sectors, corporations, government and non-government agencies, as well as states themselves, respond to environmental harm and the risk of environmental harm. We saw in chapters 3 and 6 how in many developed countries a large proportion of these responses do not in fact rely on or involve the criminal justice process: partly because in many cases the nature of illegal environmentally damaging activities do not lend themselves to the conventions inherent to most criminal justice systems. Consequently, in many instances criminologists studying these issues will find themselves far more concerned with understanding the nuances of *regulation* rather than *criminalisation*. Of course we know that the apparently stark distinction between these two concepts is much cloudier than it may first appear: a fact commented on in detail in much of the wider literature on regulation (Muncie and McLaughlin, 2013). Thus, as we saw in Chapter 6, questions concerning policing, regulation, enforcement, sentencing and prevention all overlap, especially in the environmental sphere.

Throughout this book (see in particular pages 77 and 131) it has been demonstrated that the actual operation of regulatory schemes (ostensibly) aimed at protecting the environment tends to be highly dependent on the working practices, cultures and attitudes of regulators themselves as well as those (corporations, individuals and states) being regulated. Generally the trend demonstrated in Chapter 3 and Chapter 4 suggests greater moves towards less compulsive forms of regulation, and towards self-regulation in many sectors which impact upon the environment. How these systems operate in practice is again often greatly dependent on understandings reached between regulators and regulated. This is why the heading above refers to the *culture* of regulation. Of course, occupational culture is also a key determinant of how *criminal* justice systems respond to environmental crime and thus we have seen discussions in this volume centred on the occupational practices of police; prosecution agencies and the judiciary in relation to environmental harms.

COMBINING THEMES WITH THEORY

In examining the above themes it is clear that each of them have considerable antecedents within the wider body of more mainstream criminological investigation. Importantly, in each case mainstream criminology certainly offers a diverse range of theoretical frameworks on which to base further research. So, for example, in the case of the identification, management and distribution of risk we have discussed Beck's (1992) description of the 'risk society' (Chapter 1) as well as Giddens' (1990) modifications to this approach. Occupational culture has developed an extensive theoretical background, largely in the field of police research (Reiner, 2010). Regulation too has received considerable theoretical attention (and then application) by criminologists such as Braithwaite (2000b), Shearing (1993) and Crawford (2006). Even the eco-centric perspective owes much to theoretical and critical discussions of social harm borrowed from criminologists as well as the broader literature in the field of zemiology (Hillyard and Toombs, 2003).

In light of the above points, we can appreciate that while there may indeed be no overriding or consistent 'theory of green criminology', green criminologists in fact may (and indeed must) draw on the considerable theoretical work that has been carried out, by criminologists and others, concerning most of its key themes. Of course, methodologically speaking this generally pragmatic impetus may be criticised for constituting a 'pick and mix' approach (Grbich, 2012). What is important however is to emphasise that as green criminology continues to develop, commentators will be called upon to *adapt* such established theories to meet the many new challenges thrown up by environmental harm as a (still) novel subject of criminological enquiry. Consequently, just because no single theory captures all the work that is currently calling itself (or is labelled by others as) 'green criminology' does not mean that green criminologists don't draw extensively on theory both from within mainstream criminology and beyond it. In short, therefore, while green criminology itself represents a new and quickly evolving subject of enquiry, the themes it has raised so far will be familiar territory to many in the wider criminological world.

DEVELOPING A 'GREEN' METHODOLOGY

Given the interdisciplinary nature of the area, just as trying to artificially impose a set theoretical perspective/perspectives on the subject would be restrictive, so too would any suggestion that green criminologists 'must' follow any specific methodological precepts, including those set down in this volume.

The above notwithstanding, many of the examples, case studies and broader discussions found in previous chapters support the assertion made in chapters 1 and 2 of this book that environmental harm and environmental crime both need to be understood in their broader social, political economic and scientific contexts. The same is clearly true of the *responses* to such problems within civil society. For example, we saw in Chapter 5 how while corporations are essentially legal creations, their characteristics and in particular the power attributed to them are products both of the workings of the economy (investors need confidence and protection to invest, therefore the development of the corporate veil, see p.100) and broader societal perspectives (that which is done by corporations is judged to a different moral standard than the same activities carried out by individuals, p.92).

We saw in Chapter 5 how states' reaction to the challenges of environmental harms and climate change specifically (in terms of what becomes criminalised, what international agreements they enter into and so on) is heavily politicised. Similarly, the definition of what counts as 'environmental victimisation' depends greatly on social constructions of harm, including how alleged (human) victims themselves feel about what has happened to them.

Given the above dimensions of green criminological study, as well as the overlapping themes discussed in the last section, research which incorporates to a large extent social constructivist methodologies, as set out in Chapter 2, still seem particularly appropriate. That is not to say that a more positivistic perspective will not sometimes be required and indeed can yield important findings. Ultimately however if we are to approach the environment *as criminologists* there must be some acknowledgement that environmental harms take place within a constantly evolving nexus of shifting views and interpretations by different actors (with different interests) concerning the relative social good and social ills derived from such activities.

Of course this is partly because the 'objective' nature of the risks involved is still unclear. Furthermore, as argued in the last section, a key theme of green criminological discussion is often the design and application of *regulatory* systems. Criminologists have long accepted that the operation of the formal criminal justice system is still heavily influenced by the cultures and occupational practices of criminal justice actors even when dealing with well established and widely accepted crimes (in terms of their labelling as such). We have seen in chapters 3 and 6 that *regulatory* systems are often far more variable in their operation for the same reasons. Once again, therefore, to understand environmental regulatory processes one must have some appreciation for the wider social drivers behind those processes, how they are constructed in the eyes of those tasked with applying them, and how they shift and vary with time.

Of course, despite the above arguments, social constructivism arguably places too much emphasis on the anthropocentric approach, whereby the value of non-human animals, the environment itself and the harms vested upon these is defined entirely by human perspectives. That said, in the more eco-centric sense much of the focus of environmental law is dependent on prevalent attitudes (if only among social elites) towards non-human animals and the environment itself. Again we come back to the notion of socially constructed processes informing the creation and operation of such laws. So, to give one example, even ten years ago it might have been fanciful to speak of a serious attempt to create a declaration of rights for dolphins but now, as we have seen in Chapter 8, this movement has gained some very real momentum. Thus, while Nagel may be correct to suggest that we can never really know 'what it is like' to be a bat (Nagel, 1974), green criminologists do have a key role to play in understanding what socio-political factors influence the harming of bats and the protection afforded to them by humans (or lack thereof). Inevitably the greater focus on non-humans poses some of the greatest challenges to mainstream criminological positions and to the operation of traditional criminal justice process, both of which are very much grounded in human actions and harms *to* humans. As we saw in chapters 7 and 8, the further incorporation of animal rights and animal abuse perspectives within criminology may also run the risk of compromising the alleged objectivity of our research, and lean towards social activism. In terms of methodology however we have also seen in Chapter 1 that objectivism as an ontological position is increasingly being questioned and the conscious acknowledgement of the researcher's values is being emphasised.

Green criminology may also challenge the traditional ways in which data are collected, as well as analysed. Williams (2013) has recently commented on the diversification of data sources in the study and enforcement of environmental law and regulation, largely as a result of developments in technology. One key example is the use of satellite imagery to chart the growth in waste dumps. Purdy (2010) has thus argued that high quality satellite imagery has already become a vital component of the successful enforcement of environmental law. Such images have also been used to monitor the tipping of waste into the sea off the South Korean coast (Hong et al., 2012) and the technology has already been used to achieve prosecutions by the Environment Agency in the United Kingdom (Brosnan, 2013). In other examples, unmanned drones are now being employed to monitor air quality in India (Think India Foundation, 2011). Such developments in data capture do not necessarily involve cutting edge technology. Thus we saw in Chapter 6 how local communities in the United States are forming 'Bucket Brigades' using inexpensive home-made equipment ('buckets') to assist authorities in monitoring air omissions near industrial facilities. This last example is particularly significant not just because the data are being collected through new methods, but because they are being collected *by* members of the public rather than professional researchers or environmental enforcement officers. Indeed, often those interested in collecting these data – frequently for the express purposes of providing evidence at criminal or regulatory proceedings – are in fact representatives of the activist community. Take for example the activities of one United Kingdom-based charity, the League Against Cruel Sports, discussed in Box 1.

Box 1: The League against Cruel Sports: Charitable regulation?

The League against Cruel Sports was established in 1924 and has a stated mission to 'expose and end the cruelty inflicted on animals in the name of sport'. The League are active opponents of shooting, snaring and dog-fighting sports but were particularly instrumental in the banning of hunting with dogs (in particular the hunting and killing of foxes with packs of specially bred and trained foxhounds). Such bans were introduced in Scotland in the 2002 Protection of Wild Mammals (Scotland) Act and in England and Wales under the Hunting Act 2004. Since then, efforts of the League have turned to supporting prosecutions of those who defy or otherwise circumvent the ban. In terms of its successes the League maintain:

> Through our investigations and legal team we have worked closely with the police and CPS to ensure those who illegally hunt animals for sport are brought to justice. To date there has been at least one conviction every two weeks since the ban began in 2005. (League against Cruel Sports, 2014)

The emergence of a charity as a key investigator and enforcer of national criminal law is clearly significant from a criminological perspective. What is also significant for researchers however is that a portion of the data and evidence (including photographs and filming of alleged illegal hunting activities) collected by the League is done through covert operations. Such operations challenge traditional notions of informed consent employed in most mainstream research ethics statements. They would also almost certainly not be permitted under the Police and Criminal Evidence Act 1984. Notably the League's strategy also relies on recruiting the public to gather information about illegal hunting activities, calling on their website for the public to 'be our eyes and ears in the countryside' (League against Cruel Sports, 2014). Of course the actions of the League are testament to the enforcement gap, which sees a ban on hunting with dogs passed into law by parliament but has left the police services with significant practical and resourcing difficulties when it comes to actually investigating breaches of that law.

In keeping with the methodological points discussed above, the kind of NGO/activist involvement in both criminal justice processes and research activities described in Box 1 may raise questions concerning objectivity of the research outputs.

Munro (2012) provides a concise review of arguments for and against greater cooperation and interaction between academics (specifically social movement scholars) and social activists in many areas, but within the animal rights sphere in a particular. Despite the numerous practical and theoretical hurdles, Munro's conclusion is that:

> [T]heir [social movement scholars] academic 'tool kit' might prove to be more useful than the philosopher's more abstract concepts and reasoning; this would certainly be the case in the everyday practice of activism where strategy and tactics are of paramount importance…It is surely logical that social movement theories and concepts are enhanced by a scholar's engagement with activists whose 'practical knowledge' provides empirical credibility for what otherwise is often perceived as esoteric, abstract theory. (p.515)

In a broader sense, this move towards gathering large amounts of information from multiple, diverse sources may see green criminology moving further in the direction of so-called big data, whereby very large datasets are amassed from multiple (often online) repositories. As noted by Boyd and Crawford (2012):

> The era of Big Data has begun. Computer scientists, physicists, economists, mathematicians, political scientists, bio-informaticists, sociologists, and many others are clamoring for access to the massive quantities of information produced by and about people, things, and their interactions. Diverse groups argue about the potential benefits and costs of analyzing information from Twitter, Google, Verizon, 23andMe, Facebook, Wikipedia, and every space where large groups of people leave digital traces and deposit data. (p.1)

The practicalities, merits and ethics of big data are presently being debated across both the physical and social sciences but given that, as noted many times in this book, green criminology tends to be a criminology of 'groups' (of both victims and offenders) rather than individuals, and also tends to consider effects stretching across vast geographical areas (irrespective of state borders), it seems likely that big data will have an important role to play in the further development of green criminology as a research topic.

GREEN CRIMINOLOGY AS A NEW RENDEZVOUS DISCIPLINE?

It is important to appreciate that the kind of interdisciplinary approach taken to green criminology outlined throughout this volume and summarised in the above discussion is in in fact not so manifestly different from the growth and operation of wider branches of criminology. Criminology has often itself been conceptualised as a 'rendezvous' discipline (Rock and Holdaway 1997) of other subject areas (sociology, law, politics and so on) rather than constituting a true 'discipline' in its own right. South et al. (2013) have noted that 'rendezvous' 'is particularly appropriate as a description of criminology's engagement with environmental issues' (p.28). I have frequently emphasised the importance of such an interdisciplinary approach throughout this book: presenting it as not just a desirable aspect of green criminology, but a vital one.

What should be emphasised in this section is that – following the above discussions on green criminology themes, theories and methodologies – green criminologists need not only look to other *academic* disciplines (from the physical and social sciences) but must also consider the contributions to be made by other *sectors*. Thus an intersectoral approach may be as important to green criminology as an interdisciplinary one. The link to the work of NGO/charitable organisations discussed above is an important case in point. Engagement with industrial actors seems another likely feature of green criminological research, although this will obviously raise significant ethical questions. Of course, such ethical dilemmas are nothing new to criminologists and particularly to those who advocate and employ participant observation or ethnographic means of studying offenders in the field.

It seems likely that, as green criminology continues to develop, its reach and impact beyond its engagement with the traditional academic disciplines will extend further and further. Ethical questions aside, it is submitted that this can only be a good thing both in terms of the quality of the research produced but also the potential for the work of green criminologists to effect real change. Indeed green criminology is coming to prominence at a time when academic researchers (especially in the social sciences) are being increasingly challenged in most developed countries to demonstrate the practical application of their work and its positive impacts on real-world problems (see Flyvbjerg et al., 2012). This context, coupled with the increasing prevalence of climate change and environmental pollution as *a* (perhaps *the*) major global issue to be addressed by all sectors of international society in the 21st century puts green criminology in a strong position as a developing area of research and debate.

TENSIONS BETWEEN THE MACRO AND THE MICRO

In addition to the broad themes discussed above, another significant dynamic demonstrated in the previous chapters is the debate to be had between macro and micro perspectives in green criminology. By this I mean individual green criminologists must decide on the proper balance between broad societal trends probably extending to the international level (where topics include: the operation of capitalism in late modernity; state/corporate interactions; developing perspectives on harm; international law; and human/animal rights) and more 'micro' perspective focusing on specific states, specific crimes; specific plants and the individual 'man with the van' described by Bell and McGillivray (2008). Much of this volume has focused on the former of these two options: drawing on broader social constructivist perspectives to explore trends in environmental harm and the responses of the international community. Inevitably this has also fostered a focus on state-level actors and very large multinational corporations. As we have seen, there is clear evidence that such 'macro level' actors are indeed responsible for the largest and most far-reaching individual environmental disasters, whether this be the Gulf of Mexico Oil Spill, the exploitation of Oil Sands in Alberta or the Indian Bhopal disaster.

The above notwithstanding, an alternative view on the question of environmental harm is that, as discussed in Chapter 1, the more creeping impacts of systemic, smaller-scale, polluting activities perpetrated illegally by individuals and more localised businesses are in fact the more pressing issue for green criminologists to address rather than the major, headline-grabbing international disaster events discussed elsewhere in this volume. This is an argument recently made by Agnew (2013), who begins his analysis by identifying what he calls 'ordinary acts' that contribute to ecocide which are 'widely and regularly performed by individuals as part of their routine activities; they are generally viewed as acceptable, even desirable; and they collectively have a substantial impact on environmental problems' (p.59). Agnew sees green criminologists' tendency to underplay or simply ignore such 'ordinary harms' as understandable given the tremendous damage caused to the environment by states, corporations and organised crime groups. Nevertheless, for Agnew ordinary harms and the headline-grabbing disaster events may in fact be interrelated, with one driving the other because 'the harmful behavior of individuals is a function of larger social forces' (p.69). Thus, ordinary harms must also be a key focus for green criminology. In fact, Agnew goes on to demonstrate that such ordinary harms perpetrated mainly by individuals can be subject to persuasive explanation by many standard criminological perspectives including: strain theory; social control and rational choice perspectives. In summation Agnew notes:

> Taken together, the crime theories point to multiple reasons why ordinary harms are so common (and environmentally responsible behaviours are uncommon). (p.69)

What this means is that, as Agnew discusses, while thus far a great deal of green criminology has been based around notions of critical criminology – invoking harm caused, facilitated or permitted by the powerful – more individualistic criminological theories can also be applied to the issue of environmental harms. From here we can see that, just as in more established areas of criminology, an important task of green criminologists is thus to examine and explain how broader social and structural factors as indicated by the critical school may themselves prompt more individualistic 'ordinary harms' (and perhaps vice versa).

GREEN CRIMINOLOGY AND VICTIMOLOGY?

It seems fitting at this point to empathise the interconnectivity between criminology, green criminology and victimology. The study of victims of environmental harms (human and non-human) has been discussed in some detail in Chapter 7 and we saw there that the construction of environmental victimisation, just as is the case with other forms of 'criminal victimisation', is a deeply integrative social process. Much as victims of more recognised and researched criminal behaviours were ignored by criminologists for many years, so too have the victims of environmental harm tended to receive significantly less attention in the green criminological literature so far, especially non-human victims. It is argued that green criminology as it continues to develop needs to be much more in tune with the victimological approach to the questions it is raising than was the case during the development of most other, more established, areas of criminological discussion. This is because fundamentally green criminology, as we have seen throughout this volume, is often concerned with environmental *harms*. As such, study of how those harms occur, to whom (or 'what') and their impacts is central to the exercise. Furthermore, we have seen that many of the theoretical perspectives driving green criminology actually derive from a victimisation perspective. So, for example, concepts like environmental racism (Chapter 1) and more generally Marxist-inspired observations that environmental harm is perpetrated by the powerful at the expense of the powerless necessitate detailed study of the victimised. Furthermore, the eco-centric perspective itself focuses attention on the *recipients* of harm rather than its perpetrators.

More generally victimological theory and research has over the years developed a number of tools and ideas that may be especially applicable to the area of environmental harm, its criminalisation and its regulation. For example, while we have seen in Chapter 6 that the present reality of an international human right to a clean environment is questionable, much work has been done on the development of rights for victims of crime and wider social harms, including – as we have seen in Chapter 7 – victims of abuse of power. Thus, seen from the perspective of victimisation there is scope for further discussion and debate around the application of existing victim reforms to the environment and those affected by environmental harm: for example under principles and laws developed from the 1985 UN Declaration of Basic Principles for Victims of Crime and Abuse of Power.

Following on from the above, victimological study has also demonstrated that non-binding instruments at the national and international levels (what some international lawyers call 'soft law') can add real impetus and drive to a reform agenda (exerting genuine impact on the actions of states) despite them having little compulsive power. The 1985 UN Declaration on Victims of Crime and Abuse of Power is a classic example. This implies that 'hard law' and especially full criminalisation is not the only mechanism of addressing environmental harm or developing responses to it (politically or legally). In addition one of the key areas explored by victimologists is how notions of 'victim rights' can be grounded in general human rights (Doak, 2007). Increasingly, we saw in Chapter 5 how international environmental lawyers are turning to similar arguments in attributing liability to states for the impacts of climate change and other environmental harms on individuals.

In short, therefore, there is a compulsive case for far more involvement of the victim perspective at an earlier stage in the development of green criminology than was every the case in most other established areas of craniological thought. This of course makes the reality outlined in Chapter 8, that environmental victims still seem to lag behind the main vanguard of green criminology, all the more concerning.

GREEN CRIMINOLOGY AS MAINSTREAM CRIMINOLOGY

In concluding this chapter, and this volume, I wish to reflect on the observation made a number of times in previous chapters and again in the above discussion: that in many ways green criminology does not appear such a radical departure from state of the art developments occurring in wider criminology. Throughout this book I have avoided referring to green criminology as a 'discipline' because in fact it probably at most represents an extension of criminological thought (and there is much debate to be had about the conceptualisation of criminology itself as a separate discipline). This in fact represents a strength of the subject given that it gives green criminologist the opportunity to utilise and build on theoretical and methodological positions which are already tried and tested in other areas. So we have seen earlier in this chapter Agnew's (2013) application of traditional criminological positions to environmental crimes. At the same time, it has been noted throughout this volume that the application of a critical perspective to environmental harms is very much consistent with the now well-established umbrella of critical criminology, albeit critical criminologists have largely ignored environmental issues until relatively recently.

Methodologically too the approaches now being taken in many green criminological writings have also gained increased prominence in recent years among criminologists interested in other subjects. Social construction-ist perspectives for example are a common tool in the criminologist's arsenal, as are mixed methods forms of research. Also in terms of methodology it is certainly nothing new for criminologists (representing a 'rendezvous dis-cipline', see above) to embrace the proposition that multidisciplinary work often yields the most meaningful results. Criminologists more generally are also becoming aware of the power of big data (discussed above). One recent example is the funding by the UK government of projects aiming to utilise social media as a means of predicting civil disturbances in the wake of the 2011 London riots (Procter et al., 2013). More controversially perhaps criminologists interested in issues *other than* environmental concerns have made cases in their research for a more pragmatic approach acknowledg-ing less concern about achieving idealised standards of objectivity in their ontological positioning (see Turner, 2013).

Indeed, if one looks at the above list of suggested themes for green criminology, one can immediately appreciate that the cultures of regulation and power inequalities are equally key drivers of much wider criminological discussion and research that does not focus specifically on *environmental* harm. As noted above, while one way of distinguishing green criminology is to argue that it follows an eco-centric approach not generally adopted by other criminologists, we have also seen how green criminology itself has not (and need not) always adopt such a perspective, which in any case exists on a continuum between anthro- and eco-centricism rather than constituting absolute values.

In sum, therefore, it is submitted that 'green criminology' does not in fact represent a vast diversion from developments already occurring in the work of criminologists who do not associate themselves directly with any 'green' movement. What we have seen in this volume is that while environ-mental harm itself it still under-researched by criminologists, the overlaps between the social changes which lead to (other kids of) crime and harm and those that directly or indirectly impact upon the environment are sig-nificant such that these issues cannot be neatly separated into those of interest only to 'green criminologists' and those of concern to 'mainstream criminologists'. This becomes all the more apparent when environmental harm is in fact also officially recognised as in breach of the criminal law. Ultimately therefore, the importance of green criminology lies not exclu-sively in what this subject can contribute to tacking the key environmental issues of the 21st century, but also what it might add to wider criminological project.

Summary

Green criminology does not come with a predetermined set of specific theoretical positions or methodological traditions. At the same time however, the subject area does build on well-established themes of risk, regulation and critical engagement that will be familiar to many other criminologists. While the predominantly critical impetus of green criminology so far suggests a constructivist methodology, there is also scope within the area for systematic application of more traditional criminological approaches to the questions raised by environmental harm. At the same time, green criminologists would do well to consider the perspectives on harm, suffering and redress that have been developed by victimologists for the last 30 years. Ultimately green criminology can (and arguably should) be conceived not as an eccentric or minority sub-topic, separated from wider (anthropocentric) criminological debates, but an integral part of those debates: raising questions concerning crime, deviance and harm applicable to many areas of broader criminological thought.

Review questions

1) To what extent does green criminology represent (alternatively) an extension of existing criminological theories or the creation of new ones?
2) Is green criminology properly thought of as a 'discipline'?
3) What is the role of studying victimisation as a component of green criminology?
4) Is green criminology 'all about' eco-centricism?

Further reading

Hall, M. (2013), *Victims of Environmental Harm: Rights, recognition and redress under national and international law*, Abingdon: Routledge.

- Offers detailed analysis not only on the question of environmental victimisation but on the future development of green criminology and victimology as a whole.

Lynch, M., Long, M., Barrett, K., Stretesky, P. (2013), 'Is It a Crime to Produce Ecological Disorganization? Why Green Criminology and Political Economy Matter in the Analysis of Global Ecological Harms', *British Journal of Criminology*, **53**(6): 997–1016.

- Conceptualises green criminology from an alternative perspective, that of 'ecological disorganization'.

Natali, L. (2013), 'The Contemporary Horizon of Green Criminology'. In: N. South and A. Brisman (eds.), *Routledge International Handbook of Green Criminology*, Abingdon: Routledge, pp.73–84.

- Forward-looking piece offering analysis of the future directions of green criminology.

White, R. (2013), *Environmental Harm: An Eco-justice Perspective*, Bristol: Policy Press.

- White's adoption of an eco-justice perspective is likely to continue to exert significant influence on the development of green criminology.

Glossary

Administrative remedies – Used to denote remedies and enforcement procedures operated (sometimes under statue) by non-court and non-legal actors. These are often regulating bodies such as the Environment Agency in the United Kingdom and the Environmental Protection Agency in the United States. Such mechanisms usually require a standard of proof similar to or less than the civil standard.

Civil legal remedies – Used to denote a group of court-based legal mechanisms usually reserved to resolve private disputes between individuals (lawsuits, etc.) Require a lower standard of proof than criminal remedies.

Criminal remedies – Denotes the use of criminal proceedings and outcomes/punishments imposed by criminal courts. Such remedies are usually reserved for disputes that have a more public character or social consequences. Require a higher standard of proof than civil or administrative remedies.

Criminogenic outcomes – Leading to criminal activities or further criminal activities.

Customary international law – The International Court of Justice Statute recognises custom as a primary source of international law and defines customary international law in Article 38(1)(b) as 'evidence of a general practice accepted as law'. It is a body of law that becomes binding on international actors through general acceptance. The exact content of customary international law is often the topic of debate.

ECHR – Refers to The European Convention on Human Rights. This is the key human rights instrument of the Council of Europe and de facto of the European Union as well given that all Council of Europe members must become contracting parties to the Convention and thus agree to adhere to its principles, in addition all members of the European Union must be members of the Council of Europe and therefore also sign up to the Convention.

ECtHR – Refers to The European Court of Human Rights. This is the body which hears allegations from Council of Europe member states to the effect that their rights guaranteed under the European Convention on Human Rights have been.

EU Directive – Directives are key legislative tool of the European Union in the sense that they require member states to achieve the objectives set down in them, although they do not proscribe the exact means by which these objectives must be achieved. Thus they must be transposed in national law by individual legislation in member states.

EU Regulation – Unlike EU Directives, EU Regulations are directly enforceable in domestic courts of EU member states.

Precautionary principle – The belief that society should seek to avoid environmental damage through forward planning and blocking the flow of potentially damaging activities despite an absence of full scientific certainty on the matter. Sometimes argued to be an established principle of customary international law.

Restorative justice – Has been variously defined but generally presented as a more inclusive alternative to more adversarial forms of dispute settlement. One of the most widely used understanding coming from Marshall (1999): 'Restorative justice is a process whereby all the parties with a stake in a particular offense come together to resolve collectively how to deal with the aftermath of the offense and its implications for the future' (p.5).

Standard of proof – The degree to which a finder of fact in a legal or administrative process must be convinced of the truth of an accusation in order for it to be considered 'proven'. It is usually higher for criminal proceedings, where the standard is typically 'beyond reasonable doubt' compared with civil proceedings, where the standard is typically 'on the balance of probabilities'.

Strict liability – A category of criminal offence for which no moral blameworthiness, 'guilty frame of mind', negligence or fault on the part of the defendant or operator need be proven in order to achieve a conviction.

References

Adam, B., Allan, S. and Carter, C. (2003), *Environmental Risks and the Media*, Abington: Routledge.

Adleman, J. and Okada, Y. (2013), *Tepco's Shareholders Decline to Pursue GE for Fukushima Claims* [online]. Available at: http://www.bloomberg.com/news/2013-06-26/tepco-s-shareholders-decline-to-pursue-ge-for-fukushima-claims.html (accessed 21.03.14).

Agnew, R. (2011), *Toward a Unified Criminology: Integrating Assumptions about Crime, People, and Society*, New York: New York University Press.

Agnew, R. (2012), 'Dire Forecast: A Theoretical Model of the Impact of Climate Change on Crime', *Theoretical Criminology*, 16(1): 21–42.

Agnew, R. (2013), 'The Ordinary Acts that Contribute to Ecocide: A Criminological Analysis'. In N. South and A Brisman (eds.), *The Routledge International Handbook of Green Criminology*, Abingdon: Routledge, 58–72.

Ali, A. (2013), 'Food Safety and Public Health Issues in Bangladesh', *European Food and Feed Law Review*, 8(1): 31–40.

Alston, D. and Brown, N. (1993), 'Global Threats to People of Color'. In D. Bullard (ed.), *Confronting Environmental Racism: Voices from the Grassroots*, Cambridge: South End Press, 179–194.

Amy, D. (1983), 'The Politics of Environmental Mediation', *Ecology Law Quarterly*, 11(1): 1–19.

Anderson, A. (1997), *Media, Culture, and the Environment*, New Brunswick: Rutgers University Press.

Anderson, H. (2012), 'Challenging the Limited Liability of Parent Companies: A Reform Agenda for Piercing the Corporate Veil', *Australian Accounting Review*, 22(2):129–141.

AoL Travel (2013), *Smuggling Drug Gangs Caught Force-feeding Dogs with Cocaine* [online]. Available at: http://travel.aol.co.uk/2013/03/20/smuggling-drug-gangs-caught-force-feeding-dogs-cocaine-airport-italy/ (accessed 21.03.14).

Arluke, A. and Sanders, C. (1996), *Regarding Animals*, Philadelphia: Temple University Press.

Asal, V., Sommer, U. and Harwood, P. (2013), 'Original Sin: A Cross-National Study of the Legality of Homosexual Acts', *Comparative Political Studies*, 46(3): 320–351.

Association of Chief Police Officers (2008), *Guidance on Investigating Domestic Abuse*, London: National Police Improvement Agency.

Athanasiou, T. (1996), 'The Age of Greenwashing', *Capitalism Nature Socialism*, 7(1): 1–36.

Aulette, J. and Michalowski, R. (1993), 'Fire in Hamlet: A Case Study of a State-Corporate Crime'. In K. Tunnell (ed.), *Political Crime in Contemporary America: A Critical Approach*, New York: Garland, 171–206.

Australian Federal Police (2014), *What Is Environmental Crime?* [online]. Available at: http://www.afp.gov.au/policing/environmental-crime. aspx#whatisenvironmentalcrime (accessed 21.03.04).

Ayres, I. and Braithwaite, J. (1997), *Responsive Regulation: Transcending the Deregulation Debate*, Oxford: Oxford University Press.

Azzopardi, T. (2012), *Managing Chile's Water Resources* [online]. Available at: http://www.businesschile.cl/en/content/managing-chile%E2%80%99s-water-resources (accessed 21.03.14).

Bailey, K. (1994), *Methods of Social Research*, 4th Edition, New York: Free Press.

Bakan, J. (2005), *The Corporation: The Pathological Pursuit of Profit and Power*, London: Robinson Publishing.

Bakker, K. (2012), 'Water Security: Research Challenges and Opportunities', *Science*, 337(6097): 914–915.

Banerji, D. and Singh, L. (1985), 'Bhopal Gas Tragedy-An Epidemiological and Sociological Study', *JNU News*, April: 1–12.

Basiron, Y. (2007), 'Palm Oil Production Through Sustainable Plantations', *European Journal of Lipid Science and Technology*, 109(4): 289–295.

Baumer, E., Messner, S. and Rosenfeld, R. (2003), 'Explaining Spatial Variation in Support for Capital Punishment: A Multi-Level Analysis', *American Journal of Sociology*, 108: 844–875.

BBC, (2013), *Oil Spill Compensation System Abused, Says BP* [online]. Available at: http://www.bbc.co.uk/news/business-22559427 (accessed 17.03.14).

Bean, P. (2013), *Madness and Crime*, Cullompton: Willan.

Beck, U. (1992), *Risk Society: Towards a New Modernity*, New Delhi: Sage.

Beirne, P. (2007), 'Animal Rights, Animal Abuse and Green Criminology'. In P. Beirne and N. South (eds.), *Issues in Green Criminology: Confronting Harms Against Environments, Humanity and Other Animals*, Cullompton: Willan Publishing, 55–86.

Beirne, P. and South, N. (2007), *Issues in Green Criminology: Confronting Harms Against Environments, Humanity and Other Animals*, Cullompton: Willan Publishing.

Beirne, P., Boyle, A. and Redgwell, C. (2009), *International Law and the Environment*, 3rd Edition, Oxford: Oxford University Press.

Bell, S. and McGillivray, D. (2008), *Environmental Law*, 7th Edition, Oxford: Oxford University Press.

Bell, S., McGillivray, D. and Pedersen, O. (2013), *Environmental Law*, 8th Edition, Oxford: Oxford University Press.

Benton, T. (1996), *The Greening of Marxism*, New York: Guilford Press.

Benton, T. (2007), 'Ecology, Community and Justice: The Meaning of Green'. In P. Beirne and N. South (eds.), *Issues in Green Criminology: Confronting Harms Against Environments, Humanity and Other Animals*, Cullompton; Willan, 3–31.

Berrittella, M., Bigano, A., Roson, R. and Tol, R. (2006), 'A General Equilibrium Analysis of Climate Change Impacts on Tourism', *Tourism Management*, 27(5): 913–992.

Bisschop, L. (2010), 'Corporate Environmental Responsibility and Criminology', *Crime, Law and Social Change*, 53(4): 349–364.

Bisschop, L. (2012), 'Is It All Going to Waste? Illegal Transports of E-waste in a European Trade Hub', *Crime, Law and Social Change*, 58(3): 221–249.

Bisschop, L. and Vande Walle, G. (2013), 'Environmental Victimisation and Conflict Resolution: A Case Study of e-Waste'. In R. Walters, D. Westerhuisand and T. Wyatt (eds.), *Emerging Issues in Green Criminology: Exploring Power, Justice and Harm*, Basingstoke: Palgrave Macmillan, 34–56.

Block, A. (1985), *Poisoning for Profit – The Mafia and Toxic Waste in America*, New York: William Morrow & Co.

Blowfield, M. and Murray, A. (2011), *Corporate Responsibility*, Oxford: Oxford University Press.

Boer, J., Pastor, J., Sadd, L and Snyder, L. (1997), 'Is There Environmental Racism? The Demographics of Hazardous Waste in Los Angeles County', *Social Science Quarterly*, 78(4): 793–810.

Boutellier, H. (2000), *Crime and Morality: The Significance of Criminal Justice in Post-Modern Culture*, AA Dordrecht: Kluwer.

Bowman, M. (2002), 'The Definition and Valuation of Environmental Harm: An Overview'. In M. Bowman and A. Boyle (eds.), *Environmental Damage in International and Comparative Law*, Oxford: OUP: 1–17.

Bowman, A. and Kearney, R. (2010), *State and Local Government*, Andover: Cengage Learning.

Boyd, D. and Crawford, K. (2012), 'Six Provocations for Big Data', Presented at the Decade in Internet Time: Symposium on the Dynamics of the Internet and Society, September 2011 [online]. Available at: http://papers.ssrn.com/sol3/papers.cfm?abstract_id=1926431 (accessed 21.03.14).

BP (2010), *BP Establishes $20 Billion Claims Fund for Deepwater Horizon Spill and Outlines Dividend Decisions*, Press Release of June 2010 [online]. Available at: http://www.bp.com/genericarticle.do?categoryId=2012968&contentId=7062966 (accessed 05.03.14).

Braithwaite, J. (1991), 'Poverty, Power, White-collar Crime and the Paradoxes of Criminological Theory', *Australian & New Zealand Journal of Criminology*, 24(1): 40–58.

Braithwaite, J. (2000a), 'The New Regulatory State and the Transformation of Criminology'. In D. Garland and R. Sparks (eds.), *Criminology and Social Theory*, Oxford: Oxford University Press, 47–70.

Braithwaite, J. (2000b), 'The New Regulatory State and the Transformation of Criminology', *British Journal of Criminology*, 40(2): 222–238.

Braithwaite, J. (2002), *Restorative Justice and Responsive Regulation*, New York: Oxford University Press.

Braithwaite, J. and Fisse, B. (1987), 'Self-Regulation and the Control of Corporate Crime'. In C. Shearing and P. Stenning (eds.), *Private Policing*, Thousand Oaks: Sage, 14–34.

Braithwaite, J, and Makkai, T. (1991), 'Testing an Expected Utility Model of Corporate Deterrence', *Law and Society Review*, 25(7): 7–40.

Brickey, K. (1982), 'Criminal Liability of Corporate Officers for Strict Liability Offenses – Another View', *Vanderbilt Law Review*, 35: 1337–1381.

Brickey, K. (2013), 'Environmental Crime at the Crossroads: The Intersection of Environmental and Criminal Law Theory', *Tulane Law. Review*, 71: 507–111.

Brickey, K. (2013), 'Perspectives on Corporate Criminal Liability'. In G. Bruinsma and D. Weisburd (eds.), *Encyclopedia of Criminology and Criminal Justice*, New York: Springer Publishing, 120–121.

Brisman, A. (2006), 'Meth Chic and the Tyranny of the Immediate: Reflections on the Culture-Drug/Drug-Crime Relationships', *North Dakota Law Review*, 82(4): 1273–1396.

Brisman, A. (2012), 'Toward a Unified Criminology: Integrating Assumptions About Crime, People, and Society: A Commentary', *Journal of Theoretical and Philosophical Criminology*, 4(2): 54–64.

Brisman, A. (2013), 'Not a Bedtime Story: Climate Change, Neoliberalism, and the Future of the Arctic', *Michigan State International Law Review*, 22(1): 241–289.

Brisman, A. (2013), 'Environmental and Human Rights'. In Gerben Bruinsma and David Weisburd (eds.), *Encyclopedia of Criminology and Criminal Justice*, Vol.3, New York: Springer Verlag, 1344–1345.

Brody, A., Demetriades, J. and Esplen, E. (2008), *Gender and Climate Change: Mapping the Linkages – A Scoping Study on Knowledge and Gaps*, Sussex: BRIDGE Institute of Development Studies.

Brosnan, A. (2013), 'Prosecuting Environmental Crime'. Paper Presented at the *ICOSS Climate Change, Law and Victimisation Seminar*, 30th October, University of Sheffield.

Brown, C. (2008), *Green Tax Revolt: Britons will not Foot Bill to Save Planet* [online]. Available at: http://tinyurl.com/5flsml (accessed 26.02.14).

Brown, K., Turner, R., Hameed, H. and Bateman., I. (1997), 'Environmental Carrying Capacity and Tourism Development in the Maldives and Nepal', Environmental *Conservation*, 24(4): 316–325.

Brunnèe, J. (1995), 'Environmental Security in the Twenty-First Century: New Momentum for the Development of International Environmental Law?', *Fordham International Law Journal*, 18: 1742–1747.

Bryant, B. (1995), *Environmental Justice*, Boston: Island Press.

Bryman, A. (2012), *Social Research Methods*, 4th Edition, Oxford: Oxford University Press.

Burley, A.-M. and Mattli, W. (1993), 'Europe Before the Court: A Political Theory of Legal Integration', *International Organization*, 47: 41–76.

Burr, V. (2003), *Social Constructivism*, Abingdon: Routledge.

Byrne, D. (1999), *Social Exclusion*, Buckingham: Open University Press.

Cable, S. and Benson, M. (1993), 'Acting Locally: Environmental Injustice and the Emergence of Grass-Roots Environmental Organizations', *Social Problems*, 40(4): 464–477.

Campbell, R., Patterson, D. and Bybee, D. (2011), 'Using Mixed Methods to Evaluate a Community Intervention for Sexual Assault Survivors: A Methodological Tale', *Violence Against Women*, 17(3): 376–388.

Canadian Department of Justice (2012), *Victim Surcharge, Restitution Orders and Compensation* [online]. Available at: http://www.justice.gc.ca/eng/contact/comm6.html (accessed 05.03.14).

Čapek, S. (1993), 'The Environmental Justice Frame: A Conceptual Discussion and an Application', *Social Problems*, 40(1): 5–24.

Carrabine, E., Cox, P., Fussey, P., Hobbs, D., South, N., Thiel, D. and Turton, J. (2014), *Criminology: A Sociological Introduction*, 3rd Edition, Abingdon: Routledge.

Carrington, D. (2014), *Queen's Speech: Fracking to Get Boost from Trespass Law Changes* [online]. Available at: http://www.theguardian.com/environment/2014/jun/04/queens-speech-fracking-trespass-law-changes (accessed 12.06.14).

Carrington, K., McIntosh, A., Hogg, R. and Scott, J. (2013), 'Rural Masculinities and the Internalisation of Violence in Agricultural Communities'. *International Journal of Rural Criminology*, 2(1): 3–24.

Carroll, A. and Shabana, K. (2010), 'The Business Case for Corporate Social Responsibility: A Review of Concepts, Research and Practice', *International Journal of Management Reviews*, 12(1): 85–105.

Carter, T. (1998), 'Policing the Environment'. In M. Clifford (ed.), *Environmental Crime: Enforcement, Policy, and Social Responsibility*, Aspen Publishers: New York, 169–198.

Carter, S. (1999), 'Ascent of the Corporate Model in Environmental-Organized Crime', *Crime, Law and Social Change*, 31(1): 1–30.

Castle, P. (1996), *Study of Civil Liability Systems for Remedying Environmental Damage*, London: CMS Cameron McKenna.

Cazaux, G. (1999), 'Beauty and the Beast: Animal Abuse from a Non-speciesist Criminological Perspective', *Crime, Law & Social Change*, 31: 105–126.

Chalecki, E. (2001), 'A New Vigilance: Identifying and Reducing the Risks of Environmental Terrorism', *Global Environmental Politics*, 2(1): 46–64.

Chan, J. (1996), 'Changing Police Culture', *British Journal of Criminology*, 36(1): 109–134.

Chiricos, T., Hogan, M. and Gertz, M. (1997), 'Racial Composition of Neighbourhood and Fear of Crime', *Criminology*, 35(1): 107–131.

Chivian, E., McGally M., Hu, H. and Haines, A. (1993), *Critical Condition: Human Health and the Environment*, Cambridge: MIT Press.

Christie, N. (1977), 'Conflicts as Property', *British Journal of Criminology*, 17: 1–15.

Christie, N. (1986), 'The Ideal Victim'. In E. Fattah (ed.), *From Crime Policy to Victim Policy*, Basingstoke: Macmillan, 17–30.

CNTV Chinese Network Television (2011), *China Passes Amendments to Criminal Law* [online]. Available at: http://english.cntv.cn/program/china24/20110226/107569.shtml (accessed 26.02.14).

Cohen, S. (1985), *Visions of Social Control*, Cambridge: Polity Press.

Cook, P., Machin, S., Marie, O. and Mastrobuoni, G. (2012), 'Lessons from the Economics of Crime'. In P. Cook, S Machin and G. Mastrobuoni (eds.), *Lessons from the Economics of Crime*, Cambridge: MIT Press, 1–14.

Coomans, F. (2003), 'The Ogoni Case Before the African Commission on Human and Peoples' Rights', *The International and Comparative Law Quarterly*, 52(3): 749–760.

Cotterell, R. (2006), *Law, Culture and Society: Legal Ideas in the Mirror of Society*, Farnham: Ashgate.

Council of Europe (1998), *Convention on the Protection of the Environment Through Criminal Law: Explanatory Report*, ETS n.172 [online]. Available at: http://www.conventions.coe.int/Treaty/en/Reports/Html/172.htm (accessed: 22.03.14).

Crank, J. (2004), *Understanding Police Culture*, 2nd Edition, Cincinnati: Anderson.

Crawford, A. (2006), 'Networked Governance and the Post-regulatory State? Steering, Rowing and Anchoring the Provision of Policing and Security', *Theoretical Criminology*, 10(4): 449–479.

Crawford, A., Lewis, S. and Traynor, P. (2013), *Anti-Social Behaviour Interventions with Young People*, Bristol: Policy Press.

Cressey, D. (1986), 'Research Implications of Conflicting Conceptions of Victimology'. In E. Fattah (ed.), *Towards a Critical Victimology*, London: Macmillan, 43–54.

Critharis, M. (1990), 'Third World Nations Are Down in the Dumps: The Exportation', *Brooklyn Journal of International Law*, 16: 311–340.

Croall, H. (2001), *Understanding White Collar Crime*, Buckingham: Open University Press.

Cross, F. (1989), *Environmentally Induced Cancer and the Law: Risks, Regulation, and Victim Compensation*, Santa Barbara: Greenwood Press.

Cullinan, P., Acquilla, S. and Dhara, V. (1996), 'Long Term Morbidity in Survivors of the 1984 Bhopal Gas Leak', *National Medical Journal of India*, 9(1): 5–10.

Dal Bó, E. (2006), 'Regulatory Capture: A Review', *Oxford Review of Economic Policy*, 22(2): 203–225.

D'Amato, A. (1982), 'The Concept of Human Rights in International Law', *Columbia Law Review*, 82(6): 1110–1159.

Daston, L. and Mitman, G. (2005), *Thinking with Animals: New Perspectives on Anthropomorphism*, New York: Columbia University Press.

Davies, P. (2013), 'Green Crime and Victimisation: Tensions Between Social and Ecological Justice'. Paper Presented at the *ICOSS Climate Change, Law and Victimisation Seminar*, 30th October, University of Sheffield.

Davis, J.-D. (2005), *State Responsibility for Global Climate Change: The Case of the Maldives*, Medford: Tufts Fletcher School.

De Geer, M. (2002), *Biopiracy: The Appropriation of Indigenous Peoples' Cultural Knowledge* [online]. Available at: http://www.nesl.edu/userfiles/file/nejicl/vol9/degeer.pdf (accessed 19.03.14).

De Jongh, P. and Morissette, L. (1996), 'The Netherlands' Approach to Environmental Policy Integration', Washington, DC: Centre for Strategic and International Studies.

DeMerieux, M. (2001), 'Deriving Environmental Rights from the European Convention for the Protection of Human Rights and Fundamental Freedoms', *Oxford Journal of Legal Studies*, 21(3): 521–561.

Department of Health (UK) (1998), *Quantification of the Effects of Air Pollution on Health in the United Kingdom Committee on the Medical Effects of Air Pollutants*, London: The Stationary Office.

Deschênes, O. and Greenstone, M. (2007), 'The Economic Impacts of Climate Change: Evidence from Agricultural Output and Random Fluctuations in Weather', *The American Economic Review*, 97(1): 354–385.

Dhavan, R. (1985), 'For Whom? and for What? Reflections on the Legal Aftermath of Bhopal', *Texas International Law Journal*, 20: 295–316.

Dignan, J. (2002), 'Restorative Justice and the Law: The Case for an Integrated, Systemic Approach'. In L. Walgrave (ed.), *Restorative Justice and the Law*, Cullompton: Willan Publishing, 168–190.

Dignan, J. (2004), *Understanding Victims and Restorative Justice*, Maidenhead: Open University Press.

Dillon, L. (2012), 'Book Review: Slow Violence and the Environmentalism of the Poor', *Progress in Human Geography*, 36(6): 830–831.

Doak, J. (2007), *Victims' Rights, Human Rights and Criminal Justice: Reconceiving the Role of the Third Parties*, Oxford: Hart.

Dobash, R. and Dobash, R. E. (2000), 'Evaluating Criminal Justice Interventions for Domestic Violence', *Crime & Delinquency*, 46(2): 252–270.

Docherty, B. and Giannini, T. (2009), 'Confronting a Rising Tide: A Proposal for a Convention on Climate Change Refugees', *Harvard Environmental Law Review*, 33: 349–403.

Dow Chemical (2012), *Agent Orange* [online]. Available at: http://www.dow.com/sustainability/debates/agentorange/ (accessed 17.03.14).

Downs, F. (2013), *Rule of Law and Environmental Justice in the Forests the Challenge of Strong Law Enforcement in Corrupt Conditions*, Bergen: U4 Anti Corruption Resource Centre.

Doyle, C. (2008), *Crime Victims' Rights Act*, Hauppauge: Novinka.

Drewitt, A. and Langston, R. (2006), 'Assessing the Impacts of Wind Farms on Birds', *IBIS International Journal of Avian Science*, 148(S1): 29–42.

Dryzek, J. and Hunter, S. (1987), 'Environmental Mediation for International Problems', *International Studies Quarterly*, 31(1): 87–102.

D'Silva, T. (2006), *The Black Box of Bhopal: A Closer Look at the World's Deadliest Industrial Disaster*, Bloomington: Trafford Publishing.

Dupont-Morales, M. (1998), 'Constructing the Case Study in Victimology', *Journal of Criminal Justice Education*, 9(2): 293–302.

Du Rées, H. (2001), 'Can criminal Law Protect the Environment', *Journal of Scandinavian Studies in Criminology and Crime Prevention*, 2: 109–126. Reprinted In R. White (ed., 2009), *Environmental Crime: A Reader*, Cullompton: Willan Publishing, 638–655.

Dyupina, E. and van Amstel, A. (2013), 'Arctic Methane', *Journal of Integrative Environmental Sciences*, 10(2): 93–105.

Dwernychuck, L., Cau, H., Hatfield, C., Boivin, T., Hung, T., Dung, P. and Thai, N. (2002), 'Dioxin reservoirs in Southern Viet Nam – A Legacy of Agent Orange', *Chemosphere*, 47: 117–137.

Earthrights International (2014), *Sahu v Union Carbide* [online]. Available at: http://www.earth rights.org/legal/sahu-v-union-carbide (accessed 21.03.14).

Ebeku, K. (2003), 'Judicial Attitudes to Redress for Oil-Related Environmental Damage in Nigeria', *Review of European Community & International Environmental Law*, 12(2): 199–208.

Economy, E. (2007), 'The great leap backward? The costs of China's environmental crisis', *Foreign Affairs*, Sept: 38–59.

Edwards, H (1985), 'Alternative Dispute Resolution: Panacea or Anathema', *Harvard Law Review*, 99: 668–684.

Edwards, I. (2004), 'An Ambiguous Participant: The Crime Victim and Criminal Justice Decision-Making', *British Journal of Criminology*, 44: 967–982.

Elias, R. (1983), *Victims of the System: Crime Victims and Compensation in American Politics and Criminal Justice*, New Brunswick: Transaction.

Environment (2013), *Reporting Incidents: Environmental Crime Reporting – South Africa* [online]. Available at: http://www.environment.co.za/crime-reporting/reporting-incidents-environmental-crime-reporting-south-africa-2.html (accessed 19.03.14).

Environment Agency (2012), *Civil Sanctions* [online]. Available at: http://a0768b4a8a31e106d8b0-50dc802554eb38a24458b98ff72d550b.r19.cf3.rackcdn.com/geho0512bupt-e-e.pdf (accessed 21.03.14).

Environment Agency (2014a), *Civil Sanctions* [online]. Available at: http://www.environment-agency.gov.uk/business/regulation/116844.aspx (accessed 17.03.14).

Environment Agency (2014b), *Environmental Risk Assessment and Management* [online]. Available at: http://www.environment-agency.gov.uk/research/policy/40179.aspx (accessed 17.03.14).

Environmental Investigation Agency (2007), *Upholding The Law: The Challenge of Effective Enforcement* [online]. Available at: http://www.eia-international.org/upholding-the-law-briefing (accessed 21.03.14).

Environmental Leader (2013), *Death to Polluters: China's New Threat* [online]. Available at: http://www.environmentalleader.com/2013/06/20/death-to-polluters-chinas-new-threat/ (accessed 19.03.14).

Environmental Protection Agency (2003), *Epa Issues Unilateral Administrative Order to General Electric Company in Rome, Georgia* [online]. Available at: http://yosemite.epa.gov/opa/admpress.nsf/6427a6b7538955c585257359003 f0230/5592f5848c70b2858525731b00674e9c!OpenDocument D (accessed 21.03.14).

Environmental Protection Agency (2010), *Cleaning Up Electronic Waste (E-Waste)* [online]. Available at: http://www.epa.gov/international/toxics/ewaste/index.html (accessed 15.03.14).

Environmental Protection Agency (2012a), *Basic Information About Environmental Risk* [online]. Available at: http://www.epa.gov/risk_assessment/basicinformation. htm (accessed 21.03.14).

Environmental Protection Agency (2012b), *Criminal Enforcement: What Is an Environmental Crime?* [online]. Available at: http://www2.epa.gov/enforcement/ criminal-enforcement-what-environmental-crime (accessed 17.03.14).

Eradicating Ecocide (2012), *The Problem* [online]. Available at: http://www. eradicatingecocide.com/theproblem/ (accessed 02.02.14).

Escobar, J., Lora E., Venturini, O., Yáñez, E., Castillo, E. and Almazan, O. (2009), 'Biofuels: Environment, Technology and Food Security', *Renewable and Sustainable Energy Reviews*, 13(6): 1275–1287.

Evans-Pritchard, A. (2011), *Egypt and Tunisia Usher in the New Era of Global Food Revolutions* [online]. Available at: http://www.telegraph.co.uk/finance/comment/ ambroseevans_pritchard/8291470/Egypt-and-Tunisia-usher-in-the-new-era-of-global-food-revolutions.html (accessed 21.03.14).

Farber, D. (2007), 'Compensation for Victims of Climate Change', *University of Pennsylvania Law Review*, 155: 1605–1656.

Farrall, S., Jackson, J. and Gray, E. (2009), *Social Order and the Fear of Crime in Contemporary Times*, Oxford: Clarendon Studies in Criminology, Oxford University Press.

Faure, M. and Svatikova, K. (2012), 'Criminal or Administrative Law to Protect the Environment? Evidence from Western Europe', *Journal of Environmental Law*, 24(2): 253–286.

Faust, K. and Carlson, S. (2011), 'Devastation in the Aftermath of Hurricane Katrina as a State Crime: Social Audience Reactions', *Crime, Law and Social Change*, 55(1): 33–51.

Favre, D. (2004), 'Integrating Animal Interests into Our Legal System', *Animal Law*, 10: 87–97.

Feeley, M. and Simon, J. (1994), 'Actuarial Justice: The Emerging New Criminal Law'. In D. Nelken (ed.), *The Futures of Criminology*, New York: Sage, 173–201.

Fenwick, H. (1997), 'Procedural 'Rights' of Victims of Crime: Public or Private Ordering of the Criminal Justice Process?', *Modern Law Review*, 60(3): 317–333.

Fielding, N. (2010), 'Mixed Methods Research in the Real World', *International Journal of Social Research Methodology*, 13(2): 127–138.

Finnis, J. (2011), *Natural Law & Natural Rights*, 2nd Edition, Oxford: Oxford University Press.

Flyvbjerg, B., Landman, T. and Schram, S. (2012), *Real Social Science: Applied Phronesis*, Cambridge: Cambridge University Press.

Foster, P. (2011), *Climate Torts and Ecocide in the Context of Proposals for an International Environmental Court* [online]. Available at: http://digital-archives.ccny.cuny.edu/gallery/thesis/2011SpSs07.pdf (accessed 21.03.14).

Gaarder, E. (2013), 'Evading Responsibility for Green Harm: State-corporate Exploitation of Race, Class, and Gender-inequality'. In N. South and A. Brisman (eds.), *Routledge International Handbook of Green Criminology*, Abingdon: Routledge, 272–281.

Garkawe, S. (2004), 'Revisiting the Scope of Victimology – How Broad a Discipline Should It Be?', *International Review of Victimology*, 11: 275–294.

Garland, D. (2001), *The Culture of Control: Crime and Social Order in Contemporary Society*, Oxford: Oxford University Press.

Gedling Borough Council (2014), *Anti-Social Behaviour* [online]. Available at: http://www.gedling.gov.uk/community/communitycrimeprevention/anti-socialbehaviour/ (accessed 17.03.14).

George, R. (2001), *In Defense of Natural Law*, Oxford: Oxford University Press.

Gibbs, C., Gore, M., McGarrell, E. and Rivers, L. (2010), 'Introducing Conservation Criminology: Towards Interdisciplinary Scholarship on Environmental Crimes and Risks', *British Journal of Criminology*, 50(1): 124–144.

Giddens, A. (1990), *The Consequences of Modernity*, Cambridge: Polity Press.

Giles, M. and Buckner, M. (1993), 'David Duke and Black Threat: An Old Hypothesis Revisited', *Journal of Politics*, 55: 702–723.

Gill, P. (2002), 'Policing and Regulation: What Is the Difference?', *Social & Legal Studies*, 11: 523–546.

Giovanini, D. (2006), 'Taking Animal Trafficking Out of the Shadows: RENCTAS Uses the Internet to Combat a Multi-Billion Dollar Trade', *Innovations: Technology, Governance, Globalization*, 1(2): 25–35.

Girard, A., Day, S. and Snider, L. (2010), 'Tracking Environmental Crime Through CEPa: Canada's Environment Cops or Industry's Best Friend?', *Canadian Journal of Sociology*, 35(2): 219–241.

Glasbeek, H. (2004), *Wealth by Stealth: Corporate Crime, Corporate Law, and the Perversion of Democracy*, Toronto: Between the Lines.

Global Water Partnership (2013), *Chile* [online]. Available at: http://www.gwp.org/en/About-GWP/Country-Water-Partnerships/Chile/ (accessed 21.03.14).

Gobert, J. (2008), 'The Corporate Manslaughter and Corporate Homicide 2007: Thirteen Years in the Making But Was It Worth the Wait?', *Modern Law Review*, 71(3): 413–463.

Goff, L. (2012), 'Climate-Induced Migration from Northern Africa to Europe: Security Challenges and Opportunities', *Brown Journal of World Affairs*, 18(2): 1–21.

Goldberg, J. and Zipersky, B. (2011), 'Civil Recourse Revisited', *Florida State University Law Review*, 39: 341–371.

Goodstein, E. (1994), *Jobs and the Environment: The Myth of a National Trade-off*, Washington, DC: Economic Policy Institute.

Gottberg, A., Morris, J., Pollard, S., Mark-Herbert, C. and Cook, M. (2006), 'Producer Responsibility, Waste Minimisation and the WEEE Directive: Case Studies in Eco-design from the European Lighting Sector', *Science of the Total Environment*, 359: 38–56.

Grabosky, P. and Grant, F. (2000), *Improving Environmental Performance, Preventing Environmental Crime*, Research and Public Policy Series n.27, Canberra: Australian Institute of Criminology.

Grandin, T. (2006), 'Progress and Challenges in Animal Handling and Slaughter in the U.S.', *Applied Animal Behaviour Science*, 100(1–2): 129–139.

Gray, M. (1996), 'The International Crime of Ecocide', *California Western International Law Journal*, 26: 215–272.

Gray, M. and Coates, J. (2012), 'Environmental Ethics for Social Work: Social Work's Responsibility to the Non-human World', *International Journal of Social Welfare*, 21(3): 239–247.

Grbich, C. (2012), *Qualitative Data Analysis: An Introduction*, Thousand Oaks: Sage.

Green, M. (1992), 'Expert Witnesses and Sufficiency of Evidence in Toxic Substances Litigation: The Legacy of Agent Orange and Bendectin Litigation', *Northwestern University Law Review*, 86: 643.

Green, P. and Ward, T. (2004), *State Crime*, London: Pluto Press.

Greenberg, D. (1993), *Crime and Capitalism: Readings in Marxist Criminology*, Philadelphia: Temple University Press.

Groombridge, N. (1991), *Corporate Crime: An Environmental View* [online]. Available at: http://www.criminologyinpublic.com/greencriminology.html (accessed 25.02.14).

Guattari, F. (2008), *The Three Ecologies*, London: Continuum.

Guerrero, S. and Innes, R. (2013), 'Self-Policing Statutes: Do They Reduce Pollution and Save Regulatory Costs?', *Journal of Law, Economics, and Organization*, 29(3): 608–637.

Gupta, P. (2004), 'Pesticide Exposure – Indian Scene', *Toxicology*, 198(1–3): 83–90.

Hall, M. (2009), *Victims of Crime: Policy and Practice in Criminal Justice*, Cullompton: Willan Publishing.

Hall, M. (2010), *Victims and Policy Making: A Comparative Perspective*, Cullompton: Willan Publishing.

Hall, M. (2013), *Victims of Environmental Harm: Rights, Recognition and Redress Under National and International Law*, Abingdon: Routledge.

Hall, M. and Farrall, S. (2013), 'The Criminogenic Consequences of Climate Change: Blurring the Boundaries Between Offenders and Victims'. In N. South and A. Brisman (eds.), *The Routledge International Handbook of Green Criminology*, Abingdon: Routledge, 26–58.

Hall, M. and Shapland, J. (2013), 'International Responses to Victims in Criminal Justice: Progress and Challenges for the 21st Century'. In G. Bruinsma and D. Weisburd (eds.), *Encyclopedia of Criminology and Criminal Justice*, New York: Springer Publishing, 287–290.

Halsey, M. (2004), 'Against "Green" Criminology', *British Journal of Criminology*, 44(6): 833–853.

Halsey, M. and White, R. (1998), 'Crime, Ecophilosophy and Environmental Harm', *Theoretical Criminology*, 2(3): 345–371.

Hamilton, J. (1995), 'Testing for Environmental Racism: Prejudice, Profits, Political Power', *Journal of Policy Analysis and Management*, 14(1): 107–132.

Hansen, J, (2012), 'Comparing Public Engagement with Bio-objects: Implementing Co-existence Regiemes for GM Crops in Denmark, the UK and Germany'. In N. Vermeulen, S. Tamminen and A. Webster (eds.), *Bio-Objects: Life in the 21st Century*, Burlington: Ashgate, 85–102.

Harland, A. (1978), 'Compensating the Victim of Crime', *Criminal Law Bulletin*, 14: 203–224.

Harrison, N. and Bryner, G. (2004), *Science and Politics in the International Environment*, Lanham: Rowman & Littlefield Publishers.

Harvey, F. (2011), 'Climate Change Adviser Warns of Coming Test for Cameron's Green Credentials' [online]. Available at: http://www.guardian.co.uk/uk/2011/may/09/climate-defining-green-moment-cameron (accessed 26.03.14).

Harvie, P. and Manzi, T. (2011), 'Interpreting Multi-agency Partnerships: Ideology, Discourse and Domestic Violence', *Social & Legal Studies*, 20(1): 79–95.

Hawkins K. (1990), 'Compliance Strategy, Prosecution Policy and Aunt Sally: A Comment on Pearce and Tombs', *British Journal of Criminology*, 30(4): 444–466.

Hawkins, K. (1998), 'Law as Last Resort'. In R. Baldwin, C. Scott and C. Hood (eds.), *A Reader on Regulation*, Oxford: Oxford University Press, 288–306.

Heckler, H. (2011), *Peace and Sustainable Development Through Environmental Security*, The Hague: Institute for Environmental Security.

Helm, D. and Hepburn, C. (2009), *The Economics and Politics of Climate Change*, Oxford: Oxford University Press.

Herrick, C. (2004), 'Objectivity Versus Narrative Coherence: Science, Environmental Policy, and the US Data Quality Act', *Environmental Science & Policy*, 7(5): 419–433.

Higgins, R. (1978), 'Conceptual Thinking about the Individual in International Law', *British Journal of International Studies*, 4: 1–10.

Higgins, P., Short, D. and South, N. (2013), 'Protecting the Planet: A Proposal for a Law of Ecocide', *Crime, Law and Social Change*, 59: 251–266.

Hillyard, P. and Toombs, D. (2003), 'Introduction'. In P. Hillyard, D. Toombs and C. Pantazis (eds.), *Beyond Criminology: Taking Harm Seriously*, London: Pluto Press, 1–9.

Hirko, S. (2012), 'The Possible Overlap Between Plant Variety Protection and Patent: Approaches in Africa with Particular Reference to South Africa and Ethiopia', *Haramaya Law Review*, 1(1): 125–136.

Hiskes, R. (2008), *The Human Right to a Green Future: Environmental Rights and Intergenerational Justice*, Cambridge: Cambridge University Press.

Hofrichter, R. (1993), *Toxic Struggles: The Theory and Practice of Environmental Justice*, Philadelphia: New Society Publishers.

Holdaway, S. (1983), *Inside the British Police: A Force at Work*, Oxford: Blackwell Publishing.

Holder, J. (2004), *Environmental Assessment: The Regulation of Decision Making*, Oxford: Oxford University Press.

Hong, G., Yang, D., Lee, H.-M., Yang, S., Chung, H., Kim, C., Kim, Y.-I., Chung, C., Ahn, Y.-H., Park, Y.-J. and Moon, J.-E. (2012), 'Surveillance of Waste Disposal Activity at Sea Using Satellite Ocean Color Imagers: GOCI and MODIS', *Ocean Science Journal*, 47(3): 387–394.

Hooghe, M., Vannhoutte, W. and Bircan, T. (2011). 'Unemployment, Inequality, Poverty and Crime: Spatial Distribution Patterns of Criminal Acts in Belgium, 2001–06', *British Journal of Criminology*, 51(1): 1–20.

Houck, O. (2003), 'Tales from a Troubled Marriage: Science and Law in Environmental Policy', *Science*, 302: 1926.

Hough, P. (2012), *Environmental Security: An Introduction*, Abingdon: Routledge Publishing.

House, E. and Howe, K. (1999), *Values in Evaluation and Social Research*, Thousand Oaks: Sage Publishing.

House of Commons Environmental Audit Committee (2004), *Environmental Crime and the Courts: Sixth Report of Session 03–04*, London: The Stationary Office.

Hsiang, S., Burke, M. and Miguel, E. (2013), 'Quantifying the Influence of Climate Change on Human Conflict', *Science*, 341: para.6151.

Hue, P. and Anton, D. (2011), 'Introduction to the Declaration of Rights for Cetaceans: Whales and Dolphins', *Journal of International Wildlife Law & Policy*, 14(1): 76–77.

Hulsman, L. (1986), 'Critical Criminology and the Concept of Crime'. In H. Bianchi and R. van Swaaningen (eds.), *Abolitionism: Towards a Non-Repressive Approach to Crime*, Amsterdam: Free University Press, 35–49.

Hyoung-Ah, K., Eun-Mi, K., Yeong-Chul, P., Ji-Yeon, Y., Seung-Kwon, H., Seong-Hoon, J., Kui-Lea, P., Sook-Jin, H. and Yong, H. (2003), Immunotoxicological Effects of Agent Orange Exposure to the Vietnam War Korean Veterans', *Industrial Health*, 41: 158–166.

Indian Express (2010), *Under New Law, Life Imprisonment for Food Adulteration* [online]. Available at: http://www.indianexpress.com/news/under-new-law-life-imprisonment-for-food-adulteration/608835/ (accessed 21.03.14).

Indian Express (2013), *Walmart to Pay Over $110 for Environmental Crimes* [online]. Available at: http://www.indianexpress.com/news/walmart-to-pay-over--110-for-environmental-crimes/1122125/ (accessed 19.03.14).

International Association for the Study of Insurance Economics (2009), *The Insurance Industry and Climate Change – Contribution to the Global Debate*, Geneva: The Geneva Association.

International Law Commission (2006), *Draft Principles on the Allocation of Loss in the Case of Transboundary Harm Arising Out of Hazardous Activities, with Commentaries*, Report on the Work of the Fifty-eighth Session – 1 May to 9 June and 3 July to 11 August 2006, General Assembly Official Records Sixty-first Session Supplement No. 10 (A/61/10)).

INTERPOL (2014), *Environmental Crime* [online]. Available at: http://www.interpol.int/Crime-areas/Environmental-crime/Environmental-crime (accessed 21.03.14).

Irish Criminal Injuries Compensation Tribunal (2009), *Scheme of Compensation for Personal Injuries Criminally Inflicted – As Amended from 1 April 1986*, Dublin: Irish Criminal Injuries Compensation Tribunal.

Ivanic, M. and Martin, W. (2008), *Implications of Higher Global Food Prices for Poverty in Low-Income Countries*, World Bank Policy Research Working Paper No. 4594, Washington, DC: The World Bank.

Jackson, T. (2000), 'The Employment and Productivity Effects of Environmental Taxation: Additional Dividends or Added Distractions?', *Journal of Environmental Planning and Management*, 43(3): 389–406.

Jackson, J. (2004), 'Putting Victims at the Heart of Criminal Justice: The Gap Between Rhetoric and Reality'. In E. Cape (ed.), *Reconcilable Rights? Analysing the Tension Between Victims and Defendants*, London: Legal Action Group, 65–80.

Jaggi, B. and Freedman, M. (2006), 'An Examination of the Impact of Pollution Performance on Economic and Market Performance: Pulp and Paper Firms', *Journal of Business Finance & Accounting*, 19(5): 673–713.

Jarvis, R. (2012), 'Sinking Nations and Climate Change Adaptation Strategies', *Seattle Journal for Social Justice*, 9(1): 447–486.

Jasparro, C. and Taylor, J. (2008), 'Climate Change and Regional Vulnerability to Transnational Security Threats in Southeast Asia', *Geopolitics*, 13(2): 232–256.

Johnson, K. (2004), 'International Human Rights Class Actions: New Frontiers for Group Litigation', *Michigan State Law Review*, 3: 643–664.

Johnson, R. and Onwuegbuzie, A., (2004), 'Mixed Methods Research: A Research Paradigm Whose Time Has Come', *Educational Researcher*, 33(7): 14–26.

Johnston, A. (2012), *Governing Externalities: The Potential of Reflexive Corporate Social Responsibility*, Centre for Business Research, University of Cambridge, Working Paper No. 436.

Jones, S. (2013), *Criminology*, 5th Edition, Oxford: Oxford University Press.

Jordan, J. (2004), 'Beyond Belief? Police, Rape and Women's Credibility', *Criminal Justice*, 4: 29–59.

Jordan, A., Rüdiger, K. and Zito, A. (2005), 'The Rise of "New Policy" Instruments in Comparative Perspective: Has Governance Eclipsed Government?', *Political Studies*, 53: 477–496.

Jose, A. and Lee, S.-M. (2007), 'Environmental Reporting of Global Corporations: A Content Analysis Based on Website Disclosures', *Journal of Business Ethics*, 72: 307–321.

Karstedt, S. and Farrall, S. (2006), 'The Moral Economy of Everyday Crime: Markets, Consumers and Citizens', *British Journal of Criminology*, 46(6): 1011–1036.

Kasperson, J. and Kasperson, R. (2013), *Global Environmental Risk*, Abingdon: Routledge.

Katz, R. (2010), 'The Corporate Crimes of Dow Chemical and the Failure to Regulate Environmental Pollution', *Critical Criminology*, 18: 295–306.

Kauzlarich, D., Matthews, R. and Miller, W. (2001), *Critical Criminology*, 10: 173–194.

Kauzlarich, D., Mullins, C. and Matthews, R. (2003), 'A Complicity Continuum of State Crime', *Contemporary Justice Review*, 6(3): 241–254.

Kearon, T. and Godfrey, B. (2007), 'Setting the Scene: A Question of History'. In S. Walklate (ed.), *Handbook of Victims and Victimology*, Cullompton: Willan Publishing, 17–36.

Keith, M. (2005), *After the Cosmopolitan?: Multicultural Cities and the Future of Racism*, Abingdon: Routledge.

Khare, R. (1987), 'The Bhopal Industrial Accident: Anthropological and Civic Issues', *Anthropology Today*, 3(4): 4.

Kluin, M. (2013), 'Environmental Regulation in Chemical Corporations: Preliminary Results of a Case Study'. In R. Walters, D. Westerhuis and T. Wyatt (eds.), *Emerging Issues in Green Criminology: Exploring Power, Justice and Harm*, Basingstoke: Palgrave Macmillan, 145–172.

Kotzé, L. and Paterson, A. (2009), *The Role of the Judiciary in Environmental Governance: Comparative Perspectives*, Amsterdam: Wolters Kluwer.

Kramer, R. (2013), 'Carbon in the Atmosphere and Power in America: Climate Change as State-corporate Crime', *Journal of Crime and Justice*, 36(2): 153–170.

Kramer, R. and Michalowski, R. (1993), 'State-Corporate Crime'. In K. Tunnell (ed.), *Political Crime in Contemporary America: A Critical Approach*, New York: Garland, 101–120.

Kramer, R. and Michalowski, R. (2012), 'Is Global Warming a State-Corporate Crime?' In R. White (ed.), *Climate Change from a Criminological Perspective*, New York: Springer, 71–88.

Kramer, R., Michalowski, R. and Kauzlarich, D. (2002), The Origins and Develop of the Concept and Theory of State-corporate Crime', *Crime and Delinquency*, 48(2): 263–282.

Krauss, C. and Scwartz, J. (2012), *BP will Plead Guilty and Pay Over $4 Billion* [online]. Available at: http://www.nytimes.com/2012/11/16/business/global/16iht-bp16.html?_r=0 (accessed 21.03.14).

Kriebel, D., Tickner, J., Epstein, P., Lemons, J., Levins, R., Loechler, E. and Stoto, M. (2001), 'The Precautionary Principle in Environmental Science', *Environmental Health Perspectives*, 109(9): 871–892.

Kroneberg, C. and Kalter, F. (2012), 'Rational Choice Theory and Empirical Research: Methodological and Theoretical Contributions in Europe', *Annual Review of Sociology*, 38: 73–92.

Krzyzanowski, J. (2012), 'Environmental Pathways of Potential Impacts to Human Health from Oil and Gas Development in Northeast British Columbia, Canada', *Environmental Reviews*, 20(2): 122–134.

Kubasek, N., Browne, M. and Williamson, C. (2000), 'The Role of Criminal Enforcement in Attaining Environmental Compliance in the United States and Abroad', *University of Baltimore Journal of International Law*, 7(2): 122–160.

Larsen, G. (2013), 'The Most Serious Crime: Eco-Genocide and Eco-global Crimes: Concepts and Perspectives in Eco-Global Criminology'. In R. Ellefsen, G. Larsen and R Sollund (eds.), *Contemporary Problems and Future Challenges*, Farnham: Ashgate, 28–54.

Laufer, W. (2003), 'Social Accountability and Corporate Greenwashing', *Journal of Business Ethics*, 43(3): 253–261.

Laursen, L. (2012), 'Monsanto to Face Biopiracy Charges in India', *Nature Biotechnology*, 30: 11.

Lawrence, R. (2006), 'Research Dissemination: Activity Bringing the Research and Policy Worlds Together', *Evidence & Policy*, 2: 373–384.

League against Cruel Sports (2014), *Who we are* [online]. Available at: http://www. league.org.uk/who-we-are (accessed 21.03.14).

Lee, M. (2007), *Human Trafficking*, Cullompton: Willan Publishing.

Lee, M. and Blanchard, T. (2010), *Health Impacts of Deepwater Horizon Oil Disaster on Coastal Louisiana Residents*, Baton Rouge: Louisiana State University Press.

Lee, T.-P. (2009), *A Welfare Approach to Mitigating Environmental Injustice: Exploring Needs of Pollution Victims* [online]. Available at: http://www.welfareacademy. org/pubs/international/epckdi/2.pdf (accessed 22.02.14).

Leff, E. (1993), 'Marxism and the Environmental Question: From the Critical Theory of Production to an Environmental Rationality for Sustainable Development', *Capitalism Nature Socialism*, 4(1): 44–66.

Lenaerts, K. and Gutiérrez-Fons, A. (2010), 'The Constitutional Allocation of Powers and General Principles of EU Law', *Common Market Law Reports*, 47(6): 1640–1644.

Levinson, A. (1996), 'Environmental Regulations and Manufacturers' Location Choices: Evidence from the Census of Manufacture', *Journal of Public Economics*, 62: 5–29.

Li, J., Lopez N., Liu, L., Zhao, N., Yu, K. and Zheng, L. (2013), 'Regional or Global WEEE Recycling. Where to Go?'. *Waste Management*, 33(4): 923–934.

Liddick, D. (2010), 'The Traffic in Garbage and Hazardous Wastes: An Overview', *Trends in Organized Crime*, 13(2–3): 134–146.

Lin, A. (1998), 'Bridging Positivist and Interpretivist Approaches to Qualitative Methods', *Policy Studies Journal*, 26(1): 162–180.

Lin, A. (2005), 'Beyond Tort: Compensating Victims of Environmental Toxic Injury', *Southern California Law Review*, 78: 1439–1528.

Lindén, O. and Pålsson, J. (2013), 'Oil Contamination in Ogoniland, Niger Delta', *Ambio*, 42(6): 1–17.

Lobell, D., Schlenker, W. and Costa-Roberts, J. (2011), 'Climate Trends and Global Crop Production Since 1980', *Science*, 5th May: 1204531.

Loomes, G. (2007), 'Valuing Reductions in the Risks of Being a Victim of Crime: The "Willingness to Pay" Approach to Valuing the "Intangible" Consequences of Crime', *International Review of Victimology*, 14(2): 237–251.

Lowell, P. (2012), 'The Saga of Dow and Bhopal', *Chemical & Engineering News*, 90(22): 4.

Lury, C. and Wakeford, N. (2012), *Innovative Methods: The Happening of the Social*, Abingdon: Routledge.

Lynch, M. (1990), 'The Greening of Criminology', *Critical Criminologist*, 2: 1–5.

Lynch, M. and Stretesky, P. (2001), 'Toxic Crimes: Examining Corporate Victimization of the General Public Employing Medical and Epidemiological Evidence', *Critical Criminology*, 10: 153–172.

Lynch, M. and Stretesky, P. (2003), 'The Meaning of Green: Towards a Clarification of the Term Green and its Meaning for the Development of a Green Criminology', *Theoretical Criminology*, 7: 217–238.

Lynch, M. and Stretesky, P. (2007), 'Green Criminology in the United States'. In P. Beirne and N. South (eds.), *Issues in Green Criminology: Confronting Harms Against Environments, Humanity and Other Animals*, Cullompton: Willan Publishing, 248–269.

Lynch, M., Burns, R. and Stretesky, P. (2010), 'Global Warming and State-Corporate Crime: The Politicalization of Global Warming under the Bush Administration', *Crime, Law and Social Change*, 54(3–4): 213–239.

Macleod, A., Pautasso, M., Jeger, M. and Haines-Young, R. (2010), 'Evolution of the International Regulation of Plant Pests and Challenges for Future Plant Health', *Food Security*, 2: 49–70.

Macpherson (1999), *The Stephen Lawrence Inquiry: Report of an Inquiry by Sir William Macpherson of Cluny*, London: HMSO.

Maier-Katkin, D., Mears, D. and Bernard, T. (2009), 'Towards a Criminology of Crimes Against Humanity', *Theoretical Criminology*, 13: 227–255.

Maines, D. (1993), 'Narrative's Moment and Sociology's Phenomena: Toward a Narrative Sociology', *Sociological Quarterly*, 34: 17–38.

Maintenay, A. (2013), 'Environmentalism as Religion: A Fruitful Concept? A Roundtable Discussion', *Studies in Religion/Sciences Religieuses*, 42: 291–292.

Malarkey, T. (2003), 'Human Health Concerns with GM Crops', *Mutation Research/Reviews in Mutation Research*, 544(2–3): 217–221.

Mandalia, S. (2005), 'The Spice Traders' Tale', *New Statesman*, 7 March 2005: 14.

Mandiberg, S. and Faure, M. (2009), 'A Graduated Punishment Approach to Environmental Crimes: Beyond Vindication of Administrative Authority in the United States and Europe', *Columbia Journal of Environmental Law*, 34(2): 447–511.

Manhart, M., Amera, T. and Belay, M. (2013), *E-waste Country Study Ethiopia*, Bonn: StEP Initiative.

Mann, K. (1992), 'Punitive Civil Sanctions: The Middleground Between Criminal and Civil Law, *The Yale Law Journal*, 101(8): 1795–1873.

Mares, D. (2010), 'Criminalizing Ecological Harm: Crimes Against Carrying Capacity and the Criminalization of Eco-Sinners', *Critical Criminology*, 18: 279–293.

Marris, E. and Fairless, D. (2010), 'Wind Farms' Deadly Reputation Hard to Shift', *Nature*, 447: 126.

Marshall, T. (1999), *Restorative Justice: An Overview*, London: Home Office Research Statistics Directorate.

Martuzzi, F., Mitis, F., Bianchi, F., Minichilli, F., Comba, P. and Fazzo, L. (2009), 'Cancer mortality and Congenital Anomalies in a Region of Italy with Intense Environmental Pressure Due to Waste', *Occupational Environmental Medicine*, 66: 725–732.

Marzulla, R. and Kappel, B. (1991), 'Nowhere to Run, Nowhere to Hide: Criminal Liability for Violations of Environmental Statutes in the 1990s', *Columbia Journal of Environmental Law*, 16: 201–223.

Matsumoto, S. (2011), 'A Duration Analysis of Environmental Alternative Dispute Resolution in Japan', *Ecological Economics*, 70: 659–666.

Matthews, B. and Ross, L. (2010), *Research Methods: A Practical Guides for the Social Sciences*, London: Longman Publishing.

Matthews, R. and Kauzlarich, D. (2007), 'State Crimes and State Harms: A Tale of Two Definitional Frameworks', *Crime, Law and Social Change*, 48: 42–55.

McAdam, J. (2012), *Climate Change and Displacement: Multidisciplinary Perspectives*, Oxford: Hart Publishing.

McBarnet, D. (1983), 'Victim in the Witness Box – Confronting Victimology's Stereotype', *Crime, Law and Social Change*, 7: 293–303.

McEldowney, J. and McEldowney, S. (2011), 'Science and Environmental Law: Collaboration Across the Double Helix', *Environmental Law Review*, 13(3): 169–197.

McMulan, J. and Perrier, D. (2002), 'Lobster Poaching and the Ironies of Law Enforcement', *Law & Society Review*, 36(4): 679–720.

McMurray, R. and Ramsey, S. (1986), 'Environmental Crime: The Use of Criminal Sanctions in Enforcing Environmental Laws', *Loyola of Los Angeles Law Review*, 19: 1133–1169.

Mendelsohn, R., Dinar, A. and Williams, L. (2006), 'The Distributional Impact of Climate Change on Rich and Poor Countries', *Environment and Development Economics*, 11: 159–178.

Mernitz, S. (1980), *Mediation of Environmental Disputes*, New York: Praeger.

Merryman, J. (1968), 'The Public Law-Private Law Distinction in European and American Law', *Journal of Public Law*, 17: 3–19.

Miers, D. (1991), *Compensation for Criminal Injuries*, London: Butterworths.

Mies, M. (1993), 'Towards a Methodology for Feminist Research'. In M. Hammersley (ed.), *Social Research: Philosophy*, Politics and Practice, Thousand Oaks: Sage, 25–39.

Milton, D. (2011), 'Two Models of Corporate Social Responsibility', *Wake Forest Law Review*, 46: 523–540.

Mohamed, M. (2012), *Changing Reef Values: An Inquiry into the Use, Management and Governances of Reef Resources in Island Communities of the Maldives*, Unpublished Doctoral Thesis, Canterbury: University of Canterbury.

Mol, H. (2013), ' "A Gift from the Tropics to the World": Power, Harm and Palm Oil'. In R. Walters, D. Westerhuisand and T. Wyatt (eds.), *Emerging Issues in Green Criminology: Exploring Power, Justice and Harm*, Basingstoke: Palgrave Macmillan, 242–260.

Molloy, C. (2011), *Popular Media and Animals*, London: Palgrave Macmillan.

Monaghan, M., Pawson, R. and Wicker, K. (2012), 'The Precautionary Principle and Evidence-Based Policy', *Evidence & Policy: A Journal of Research, Debate and Practice*, 8(2): 171–191.

Mooney, C. (2011), 'ENERGY-The Truth About Fracking-What We Know, and Don't Know, About the Dangers of Hydraulic Fracturing', *Scientific American*, 80: 80–85.

Moreno-Riaño, G. (2005), 'Natural Law and Modern Economic Theory', *Journal of Market & Morality*, 8(3): 387–413.

Mörner, N.-A., Tooley, M. and Possnert, G. (2004), 'New Perspectives for the Future of the Maldives', *Global and Planetary Change*, 40(1–2): 177–182.

Morrow, K. (2013), 'Rio+ 20: A Critique–The Global Is Personal: The Personal Is Global', *Journal of Human Rights and the Environment*, 4(1): 1–5.

Morss, E. (1996), 'Clean Air Act Implementation: An Industry Perspective', *Pace Environmental Law Review*, 14(1): 63–68.

Mullier, E. (2010), 'The Emergence of Criminal Competence to Enforce EC Environmental Law: Directive 2008/99 in the Context of the Case-Law of the European Court of Justice', *Cambridge Student Law Review*, 6(1): 94–116.

Muncie, J. and McLaughlin, E. (2013), *Criminological Perspectives*, Thousand Oaks: Sage Publishing.

Munro, L. (2012), 'Teaching & Learning Guide for: The Animal Rights Movement in Theory and Practice: A Review of the Sociological Literature', *Sociology Compass*, 6(6): 511–518.

Myhill, A. and Bradford, B. (2013), 'Overcoming Cop Culture? Organizational Justice and Police Officers' Attitudes Toward the Public', *Policing: An International Journal of Police Strategies & Management*, 36(2): 338–356.

Mythen, G. and Walklate, S. (2006), Criminology and Terrorism: Which Thesis? Risk Society or Governmentality?, *British Journal of Criminology*, 46(3): 379–398.

Nagel, T. (1974), 'What Is It Like to Be a Bat?', *The Philosophical Review*, 83: 435–450.

Nagler, M. (2011), 'Negative Externalities, Competition and Consumer Choice', *The Journal of Industrial Economics*, 59(3): 396–421.

Nelken, D. (1994), 'White Collar Crime'. In M. Maguire, R. Morgan and R. Reiner (eds.), *The Oxford Handbook of Criminology*, 1st Edition, Oxford: Oxford University Press, 355–392.

Nemani, R., White, M., Cayan, D., Jones, G., Running, S., Coughlan, J. and Peterson, D. (2001), 'Asymmetric Warming Over Coastal California and its Impact on the Premium Wine Industry', *Climate Research*, 19: 25–34.

Newell, P. (2013), *Globalization and the Environment: Capitalism, Ecology and Power*, Cambridge: Polity Press.

Newburn, T. (1988), *The Use and Enforcement of Compensation Orders in Magistrates' Courts*, Home Office Research Study 102, London: Home Office.

Newburn, T. (2013), *Criminology*, 2nd edition, Abingdon: Routledge.

New York Post (2013), *Serious Polluters in China to be Given Death Penalty* [online]. Available at: http://www.nypost.com/p/news/international/serious_polluters_in_china_to_be_aw5xWCndtGIQ9UKxK5AM9N (accessed 19.03.14).

New Zealand Law Commission (2008), *Compensating Crime Victims*, Issues Paper 11, Wellington: New Zealand Law Commission.

New Zealand Law Commission (2012), *Civil Pecuniary Penalties*, Issues Paper 33. Wellington: New Zealand Law Commission.

Nolon, S. (2012), 'Do We Need Environmental Mediators? Indigenous Environmental Mediation: Exploring New Models for Resolving Environmental Disputes', *Indigenous Environmental Mediation: Exploring New Models for Resolving Environmental Disputes*, January 25.

Norgaard, K. (2006), 'People Want to Protect Themselves a Little Bit: Emotions, Denial and Social Movement Nonparticipation', *Sociological Inquiry*, 76(3): 372–396.

Northeast States for Coordinated Air Use Management (2011), *Economic Analysis of a Program to Promote Clean Transportation Fuels in the Northeast/Mid-Atlantic Region*, Boston: NESCAUM.

Nurse, A. (2013a), *Animal Harm: Perspective on Why People Harm and Kill Animals*, Farnham: Ashgate.

Nurse (2013b), 'Perspective on Criminality in Wildlife'. In R. Walters, D. Westerhuisand and T. Wyatt (eds.), *Emerging Issues in Green Criminology: Exploring Power, Justice and Harm*, Basingstoke: Palgrave Macmillan, 127–144.

Odorico, P., Bhattachan, A., Davis, K., Ravi, S. and Runyan, C. (2013), 'Global Desertification: Drivers and Feedbacks', *Advances in Water Resources*, 51: 326–344.

Ogus, A. and Abbot, C. (2013), 'Sanctions for Pollution: Do We have the Right Regime?, *Journal of Environmental Law*, 25(3): 283–298.

O'Hear, M. (2004), 'Sentencing the Green-Collar Offender: Punishment, Culpability, and Environmental Crime', *The Journal of Criminal Law and Criminology*, 95(1): 133–276.

Ojakorotu, V. and None, L. (2010), '8. Nigerian Leaders in the 1990s and Politics of Oil in the Niger Delta', *Anatomy of the Niger Delta Crisis: Causes, Consequences and Opportunities for Peace*, 3: 121.

O'Malley, P. (1992), 'Risk, Power and Crime Prevention', *Economy and Society*, 21(3): 252–275.

O'Malley, P. (2009), 'Risk and Criminology'. In G. Mythen and S. Walklate (eds.), *Critical Reflections on Risk and Human Security: Towards a Holistic Approach*, London: Mcgraw-Hill/Open University Press, 43–59.

Opotow, S. (1993), 'Animals and the Scope of Justice', *Journal of Social* Issues, 49(1): 71–85.

O'Rourke, D. and Macey, G. (2003), 'Community Environmental Policing: Assessing New Strategies of Public Participation in Environmental Regulation', *Journal of Policy Analysis and Management*, 22(3): 383–414.

Osborne, D. and Gaebler, T. (1992), *Reinventing Government: How the Entrepreneurial Spirit Is Transforming the Public Sector*, London: Longman.

Pandey, U. (2014), *Japan Can't Abandon Nuclear Power* [online]. Available at: http://www.bangkokpost.com/business/news/397951/japan-can-t-abandon-nuclear-power (accessed 17.03.14).

Paoline, E. (2003), 'Taking Stock: Toward a Richer Understanding of Police Culture', *Journal of Criminal Justice*, 31(3): 199–214.

Paradossos, J.-J. (2005), 'Planning Delays, Human Rights and Damages', *Environmental Law Review*, 7(2): 85.

Park, M. and Singer, S. (2012), 'The Globalization of Animal Welfare More Food Does Not Require More Suffering', *Foreign Affaires*, March/April: 1–4.

Passas, N. (2005), ' "Lawful But Awful": Legal Corporate Crimes', *Journal of Socio-Economics*, 24: 771–786.

Paternoster, R. and Simpson, S. (1996), 'Sanction Threats and Appeals to Morality: Testing a Rational Choice Model of Corporate Crime', *Law and Society Review*, 30(3): 549–583.

Patterson-Kane, E. and Piper, H. (2012), 'Animal Abuse and Cruelty'. In T. Shackelford and V. Weekes-Shackleford (eds.), *The Oxford Handbook of Evolutionary Perspectives on Violence, Homicide, and War*, Oxford: Oxford University Press, 254–269.

Patz, J., McGeehin, M., Bernard, S., Ebi, K., Epstein, P., Grambsch, A., Gubler, D., Reiter, P., Romieu, I., Rose, J., Samet, J. and Trtanf, J. (2000), 'The Potential Health Impacts of Climate Variability and Change for the United States: Executive Summary of the Report of the Health Sector of the U.S. National Assessment', *Environmental Health Perspectives*, 108(4): 367–376.

Pearce, F. and Tombs, S. (1990), 'Ideology, Hegemony and Empiricism: Compliance Theories of Regulation', *British Journal of Criminology*, 30(4): 423–444.

Pederson, O. (2013), 'Environmental Enforcement Undertakings and Possible Implications: Responsive, Smarter or Rent Seeking?', *Modern Law Review*, 76(2): 319–345.

Pegg, S. and Zabbey, N. (2013), 'Oil and Water: The Bodo Spills and the Destruction of Traditional Livelihood Structures in the Niger Delta', *Community Development Journal*, 48(3): 391–405.

Perry, A., Low, P., Ellis, J. and Reynolds, J. (2005), 'Climate Change and Distribution Shifts in Marine Fishes', *Science*, 308(5730): 1912–1915.

Peterson, J., and Bomberg, E. (1999), *Decision-Making in the European Union*, New York: Palgrave Macmillan.

Phillips, C. and Bowling, B. (2012), 'Ethnicities, Racism, Crime and Criminal Justice'. In M. Maguire, R. Morgan and R. Reinder (eds.), *The Oxford Handbook of Criminology*, 5th Edition) Oxford: Oxford University Press, 370–397.

Pickering, S., McCulloch, J. and Wright-Neville, D. (2008), *Counter-terrorism Policing*, New York: Springer.

Pinstrup-Andersen, P. (2009), 'Food Security: Definition and Measurement', *Food Security*, 1: 5–7.

Piquero, N., Tibbetts, S. and Blankenship, M. (2005), 'Examining the Role of Differential Association and Techniques of Neutralization in Explaining Corporate Crime', *Deviant Behaviour*, 26(2): 159–188.

Political Economy Research Institute (2003), *General Electric Co.* [online]. Available at: http://web.archive.org/web/20070927204419/http://www.rtknet.org/new/tox100/toxic100.php?database=t1&detail=1&datype=T&reptype=a&company1=&company2=8337&chemfac=fac&advbasic=bas (accessed 21.03.14).

Potter, G. (2012), 'Pushing the Boundaries of (a) Green Criminology: Environmental Harm as a Cause of Crime', *Green Criminology Monthly*, 3: 1–5.

Prechel, H. and Zheng, L. (2012), 'Corporate Characteristics, Political Embeddedness and Environmental Pollution by Large US Corporations', *Social Forces*, 90(3): 947–970.

Procter, R., Crump, J., Karstedt, S., Voss, A. and Cantijoch, M. (2013), 'Reading the Riots: What were the Police Doing on Twitter?', *Policing and Society*, 23(4): 413–436.

Pulido, L. (2000), 'Rethinking Environmental Racism: White Privilege and Urban Development in Southern California', *Annals of the Association of American Geographers*, 90(1): 12–40.

Purdy, R. (2010), 'Using Earth Observation Technologies for Better Regulatory Compliance and Enforcement of Environmental Laws', *Journal of Environmental Law*, 22(1): 59–87.

Rawls, J. (1999), *A Theory of Justice*, Cambridge: Harvard University Press.

Redgwell, C. (2014), 'International Environmental Law'. In M. Evans (ed.), *International Law*, 4th Edition, Oxford: Oxford University Press, 688–726.

Reiner, R. (2010), *The Politics of the Police*, 4th Edition, Oxford: Oxford University Press.

Reiner, R. (2012), *In Praise of Fire Brigade Policing: Contra Common Sense Conceptions of the Police Role*, London: The Howard League for Penal Reform.

Richardson, N. (2010), *Deepwater Horizon and the Patchwork of Oil Spill Liability Law*, Washington, DC: Resources for the Future.

Ritchie, M., Dawkins, K. and Vallianatos, M. (2012), 'Intellectual Property Rights and Biodiversity: The Industrialization of Natural Resources and Traditional Knowledge', *Journal of Civil Rights and Economic Development*, 11(2): 431–261.

Rivers, L. (2012), 'Shareholder Return- a 'Nuremberg Defence'? Ecocide and Restorative Justice', *Environmental Law & Management*, 24(1): 17–19.

Robson, R. (2010), 'Crime and Punishment: Rehabilitating Retribution as a Justification for Organizational Criminal Liability', *American Business Law Journal*, 47(1): 109–144.

Robson, C. (2011), *Real World Research: A Resource for Users of Social Research Methods in Applied Settings*, Chichester: Wiley.

Rock, P. (1986), *A View from the Shadows: the Ministry of the Solicitor General of Canada and the Making of the Justice for Victims of Crime Initiative*, Oxford: Clarendon Press.

Rock, P. (1990), *Helping Victims of Crime: The Home Office and the Rise of Victim Support in England and Wales*, Oxford: Oxford University Press.

Rock, P. (1998), *After Homicide: Practical and Political Responses to Bereavement*, Oxford: Clarendon Press.

Rock, P. and Holdaway, S. (1997), *Thinking About Criminology*, London: University College London Press.

Rothe, D. (2010), 'Global e-waste Trade: The Need for Formal Regulation and Accountability Beyond the Organization', *Criminology and Public Policy*, 9(3): 561–567.

Rothe, D., Ross, J., Mullins, C., Friedrichs, D., Michalowski, R., Barak, G., Kauzlarich, D. and Kramer, R. (2009), 'That Was Then, This Is Now, What About Tomorrow? Future Directions in State Crime Studies', *Critical Criminology*, 17(1): 3–13.

Roughton, G. (2007), 'The Ancient and the Modern: Environmental Law and Governance in Islam', *Colombia Journal of Environmental Law*, 32: 99–140.

Royal Borough of Greenwich (2014), *Environmental Crime* [online]. Available at: http://www.royalgreenwich.gov.uk/info/200089/street_care_and_cleaning/216/environmental_crime (accessed 21.03.14).

Ruggiero, V. and South, N. (2010a), 'Critical Criminology and Crimes Against the Environment', *Critical Criminology*, 18: 245–250.

Ruggiero, V. and South, N. (2010b) 'Green Criminology and Dirty Collar Crime', *Critical Criminology*, 18(4): 251–262.

Ruggiero, V. and South, N. (2013), 'Green Criminology and Crimes of the Economy: Theory, Research and Praxis', *Critical Criminology*, 21(3): 359–373.

Russia Today (2013), *Polluting to Death: China Introduces Execution for Environmental Offenders* [online]. Available at: http://rt.com/news/china-execution-environmental-offenders-967/ (accessed 19.03.14).

Saint, S. (2008), 'A Critical Discourse Analysis of Corporate Environmental Harm', *Internet Journal of Criminology* [online]. Available at: http://www.internet journalofcriminology.com/Saint%20-%20A%20CRITICAL%20DISCOURSE% 20ANALYSIS%20OF%20CORPORATE%20ENVIRONMENTAL%20HARM. pdf (accessed 21.03.12).

Sampson, R. (2008), 'Rethinking Crime and Immigration', *Contexts*, 7(1): 28–33.

Sampson, A., Stubbs, P. and Smith, G. (1988), 'Crime, Localities and the Multi-agency Approach', *British Journal of Criminology*, 28(4): 478–493.

Sands, P. and Peel, J. (2012), *Principles of International Environmental Law*, Cambridge: Cambridge University Press.

Saro-Wiwa, K. (1992), *Genocide in Nigeria: The Ogoni Tragedy*, London: Saros.

Schanbacher, W. (2010), *The Politics of Food: The Global Conflict Between Food Security and Food Sovereignty*, Santa Barbara: Praeger Security International.

Schofield, T. (1999), 'The Environment as an Ideological Weapon: A Proposal to Criminalize Environmental Terrorism', *Boston College Environmental Affairs Law Review*, 26(3): 619–647.

Schur, E. (1969), *Our Criminal Society*, Englewood Cliffs, NJ: Prentice Hall.

Schwartz, D. (1998), 'Environmental Terrorism: Analyzing the Concept', *Journal of Peace Research*, 35(4): 483–496.

Seis, M. (1999), 'A Community-Based Criminology of the Environment', *Criminal Justice Policy Review*, 10(2): 291–312.

Sentencing Council for England and Wales (2014), *Environmental Offences: Definitive Guidelines*, London: Sentencing Council.

Shantz, J. (2012), *Green Syndicalism: An Alternative Red/Green Vision*, New York: Syracuse University Press.

Shapiro, S. (2012a), 'Blowout: Legal Legacy of the Deepwater Horizon Catastrophe: The Complexity of Regulatory Capture: Diagnosis, Causality, and Remediation', *Roger Williams University Law Review*, 17: 221–256.

Shapiro, S. (2012b), 'The Complexity of Regulatory Capture: Diagnosis, Causality and Remediation', *Roger Williams University Law Review*, 102(1): 101–172.

Shapland, J. (2003), 'Bringing Victims in from the Cold: Victims' Role in Criminal Justice'. In J. Jackson and K. Quinn (eds.), *Criminal Justice Reform: Looking to the Future*, Belfast: Institute of Criminology and Criminal Justice, Queens University Belfast, 48–69.

Shapland, J. and Hall, M. (2007), 'What Do We Know About the Effect of Crime on Victims?', *International Review of Victimology*, 14: 175–217.

Shapland, J., Robinson, G. and Sorsby, A. (2011), *Restorative Justice in Practice*, Abingdon: Routledge.

Shapland, J., Willmore, J. and Duff, P. (1985), *Victims and the Criminal Justice System*, Aldershot: Gower.

Shapland, J., Atkinson, A., Atkinson, H., Chapman, B., Colledge, E., Dignan, J., Howes, M., Johnstone, J., Robinson, G. and Sorsby, A. (2006), *Restorative Justice in Practice – Findings from the Second Phase of the Evaluation of Three Schemes*, Home Office Research Findings 274, London: Home Office.

Shearing, C. (1993), *A Constitutive Conception of Regulation. Business Regulation and Australia's Future*, Canberra: Australian Institute of Criminology.

Shelley, L. (2007), 'Human Trafficking as a Form of Transnational Crime'. In Lee, M. (ed.), *Human Trafficking*, Cullompton: Willan Publishing, 116–137.

Shifferd, K. (1972), 'Kar Marx and the Environment', *Journal of Environmental Education*, 3(4): 39–42.

Shiva, V. (1997), *Biopiracy: The Plunder of Nature and Knowledge*, Dehra Dun: Natraj Publishers.

Shmueli, D. and Kaufman, S. (2006), *Environmental Mediation*, The Center for Environmental Policy Studies Series no. 24, Jerusalem: Center for Environmental Studies.

Sierra Club Legal Defence Fund (1993), *Human Rights and the Environment: The Legal Basis for Human Rights to the Environment' Report to the UN Sub-Commission on the Prevention of Discrimination and Protection*, San Francisco: Sierra Club.

Simon, D. (2000), 'Corporate Environmental Crimes and Social Inequality New Directions for Environmental Justice Research', *American Behavioral Scientist*, 43(4): 633–645.

Simon, D. (2005), 'General Electric'. In L. Salinger (ed.), *Encyclopaedia of White Collar & Corporate Crime*, Thousand Oaks: Sage, 257.

Sipe, N. (2007), 'An Empirical Analysis of Environmental Mediation', *Journal of the American Planning Association*, 64(2): 275–285.

Situ, Y. and Emmons, D. (2000), *Environmental Crime: The Criminal Justice System's Role in Protecting the Environment*, Thousand Oaks: Sage.

Skinnider, E. (2011), *Victims of Environmental Crime – Mapping the Issues*, Vancouver: The International Centre for Criminal Law Reform and Criminal Justice Policy.

Smandych, R. and Kuenman, R. (2009), 'Ecological Criminology? Recasting the Role of Criminology in Responding to Humanly Created Ecological Harm'. Invited Paper Presented at the Institute of Criminology School of Social and Cultural Studies, Victoria University of Wellington, Wellington, New Zealand.

Smandych, R. and Kueneman, R. (2010), 'The Canadian-Alberta Tar Sands: A Case Study of State-Corporate Environmental Crime'. In R. White (ed.) *Global Environmental Harm*. Cullompton: Willan.

Snider, L. (2000), 'The Sociology of Corporate Crime: An Obituary (Or: Whose Knowledge Claims Have Legs?)', *Theoretical Criminology*, 4(2): 169–206.

Soothill, K., Fitzpatrick, C. and Francis, B. (2013), *Understanding Criminal Careers*, Abingdon: Routledge.

South, N. (1998), 'A Green Field for Criminology: A Proposal for a Perspective', *Theoretical Criminology*, 2(2): 211–233.

South, N. (2007), 'The "Corporate Colonisation of Nature": Bio-prospecting, Bio-piracy and the Development of Green Criminology'. In P. Beirne and N. South (eds.), *Issues in Green Criminology: Confronting Harms Against Environments, Humanity and Other Animals*, Cullompton: Willan, 230–247.

South, N. (2010), 'The Ecocidal Tendencies of Late Modernity: Polnational Crime, Social Exclusion, Victims and Rights'. In R. White (ed.), *Global Environmental Harm: Criminological Perspectives*, Cullompton: Willan Publishing, 236–240.

South, N. and Beirne, P. (2006), *Green Criminology*, London: Ashgate.

South, N., Brisman, A. and Beirne, P. (2013), 'A Guide to Green Criminology'. In N. South and A. Brisman (eds.), *Routledge International Handbook of Green Criminology*, Abingdon: Routledge, 27–47.

Spalek, B. (2006), *Crime Victims: Theory, Policy and Practice*, New York: Palgrave Macmillan.

Spencer, D. and Fitzgerald, A. (2013), 'Three Ecologies, Transversality and Victimization: The Case of the British Petroleum Oil Spill', *Crime, Law and Social Change*, 59(3): 209–223.

Spencer, M., Garratt, A., Hockman, E., Bryant, B. and Kohn-Wood, L. (2011), 'Environmental Justice and the Well-being of Poor Children of Color', *Communities, Neighborhoods and Health*, 1(3): 219–233.

Stafford, S. (2003), *Does Self-Policing Help the Environment? EPA's Audit Policy and Hazardous Waste Compliance*, Williamsburg: William & Mary College.

Starr, J., Flack, B. and Foley, A. (2008), 'New Intersection: Environmental Crimes and Victims' Rights', *Natural Resources & Environment*, 24: 41–52.

Stebbins, K. (1993), 'Garbage Imperialism: Health Implications of Dumping Hazardous Wastes in Third World Countries', *Medical Anthropology*, 15(1): 81–102.

Steinberg, T. (2008), *Down to Earth: Nature's Role in American History*, Oxford: Oxford University Press.

Stewart, R. (1993), 'Environmental Regulation and International Competitiveness', *Yale Law Journal*, 102(8): 2039–2106.

Stone, C. (2010), *Should Trees Have Standing?*, New York: Oxford University Press.

Strauss, A., Schatzman, L., Ehrich, D., Bucher, R. and Sabshin, M. (1963), 'The Hospital and Its Negotiated Order'. In E. Freidson (ed.), *The Hospital in Modern Society*, New York: Free Press of Glenoce, 147–169.

Stretesky, P. (2006), 'Corporate Self-policing and the Environment', *Criminology*, 44(3): 671–708.

Stretesky, P. and Knight, O. (2013), 'The Uneven Geography of Environmental Enforcement INGOs'. In R. Walters, D. Westerhuisand and T. Wyatt (eds.), *Emerging Issues in Green Criminology: Exploring Power, Justice and Harm*, Basingstoke: Palgrave Macmillan, 145–172.

Sutherland, E. (1949), *White Collar Crime*, New York: Dryden.

Sutherland, E. and Cressey, D. (1974), *Principles of Criminology*, 4th Edition, Lanham: AltaMira Press.

Sykes, G. and Matza, D. (1957), 'Techniques of Neutralization: A Theory of Delinquency', *American Sociological Review*, 22: 664–670.

Szasz, A. (2006), 'Corporations, Organized Crime, and the Disposal of Hazardous Waste: An Examination of the Making of a Criminogenic Regulatory Structure', *Criminology*, 24(1): 1–27.

Szasz, A. and Meuser, M. (1997), 'Environmental Inequalities: Literature Review and Proposals for New Direction in Research and Theory', *Social Problems*, 33: 200–217.

Tabbach, A. (2012), 'Wealth Redistribution and the Scope and Costs of Crime and Law Enforcement'. In A. Harel and K. Hylton (eds.), *Research Handbook on the Economics of Criminal Law*, Cheltenham: Edward Elgar Publishing, 97–121.

Takemura, N. (2007), ' "Criticality of Environmental Crises" and Prospect of "Complexity Green Criminology" ', *Toxin University of Yokohama Research Bulletin*, 17: 12–25.

Taylor, D. (1997), 'American Environmentalism: The Role of Race, Class and Gender in Shaping Activism', *Race, Gender and Class*, 5(1): 16–62.

Taylor, D. (1998), 'The Urban Environment: The Intersection of White Middle Class and White Working Class Environmentalism', *Advances in Human Ecology*, 7: 207–292.

The Telegraph (2009), Maldives Government Holds Underwater Cabinet Meeting [online]. Available at: http://www.telegraph.co.uk/news/newstopics/howaboutthat/6356036/Maldives-government-holds-underwater-cabinet-meeting.html (accessed 21.03.14).

Squires and Anast, (2009), *Greek Immigration Crisis Spawns Shanty Towns and Squats* [online]. Available at: http://www.telegraph.co.uk/news/worldnews/europe/greece/6147072/Greek-immigration-crisis-spawns-shanty-towns-and-squats.html (accessed 20.03.14).

The Daily Telegraph (2011), 'Egypt and Tunisia Usher in the New Era of Global Food Revolutions', 30th January, 2011.

The Economist (2004), *The Lunatic You Work for*, 6th May at 12.

Think India Foundation (2011), Now, a UAV to Monitor Air Quality [online]. Available at: http://www.thinkindia.net.in/2011/09/now-a-uav-to-monitor-air-quality.html (accessed 21.03.14).

Thirlway, H. (2010), 'The Sources of International Law'. In M. Evans (ed.), *International Law*, 3rd Edition, Oxford: Oxford University Press, 95–121.

Thompson, E. (1991), *Customs in Common*, London: Penguin Books.

Tilburg Law School (2013), *Master's Programs* [online]. Available at: http://www.tilburguniversity.edu/education/masters-programmes/victimology-and-criminal-justice/ (accessed 21.03.14).

Tobey, J. and Smets, H. (1996), 'The Polluter-Pays Principle in the Context of Agriculture and the Environment', *The World Economy*, 19: 63–87.

Tolman, C. (2008), 'Karl Marx, Alienation, and the Mastery of Nature', *Environmental Ethics*, 3(1): 63–74.

Tombs, S. and Whyte, D. (2007), 'Researching White Collar and Corporate Crime in and Era of Neo-Liberalism. In H. Pontell and G. Geis (eds.), *International Handbook of White Collar and Corporate Crime*, New York: Springer Publishing, 125–147.

Tomkins, K. (2005), 'Police, Law Enforcement and the Environment', *Current Issues in Criminal Justice*, 16(3): 294–306.

Tonsor, G. and Olynk, N. (2010), *U.S. Meat Demand: The Influence of Animal Welfare Media Coverage* [online]. Available at: http://www.ksre.ksu.edu/bookstore/pubs/MF2951.pdf (accessed 20/03/14).

TRAFFIC (2013), *Endangered Animal Trafficking Officially Criminalised in Russia* [online]. Available at: http://www.traffic.org/home/2013/6/21/endangered-animal-trafficking-officially-criminalised-in-rus.html (accessed 19.03.14).

Turner, E. (2013), 'Beyond "Facts" and "Values" Rethinking Some Recent Debates About the Public Role of Criminology', *British Journal of* Criminology, 53(1): 149–166.

Tyler, T. (1990), *Why People Obey the Law*, New Haven: Yale University Press.

Tyler, T. (2009), 'Self-Regulatory Approaches to White-Collar Crime: The Importance of Legitimacy and Procedural Justice', In S. Simpson and D. Weisburd (eds.), *The Criminology of White-Collar Crime*, New York: Springer, 195–216.

Tyler, T. and Mentovich's (2010), *Punishing Collective Entitles*, New Haven: Yale Law School.

Uhlmann, D. (2011), 'After the Spill Is Gone: The Gulf of Mexico, Environmental Crime, and the Criminal Law', *Michigan Law Review*, 109: 1413–1462.

Ullman, R. (1983), 'Redefining Security', *International Security*, 8(1): 129–153.

United Kingdom Environmental Law Association (2011), *The State of UK Environmental Legislation in 2011 – is There a Case for Reform?* [online]. Available at: http://www.ukela.org/?id=10&pressid=59 (accessed 21.03.14).

United Nations Development Programme (2010), *Millennium Development Goals and Climate Change Adaptation*, NewYork: UNDP-GEF.

United Nations Environment Programme (2011), *UNEP Ogoniland Oil Assessment Reveals Extent of Environmental Contamination and Threats to Human Health* [online]. Available at: http://www.unep.org/newscentre/Default.aspx?DocumentID=2649&ArticleID=8827&l =en (accessed 22.03.14).

United Nations Food and Agriculture Organization (2010), *Special Programme for Food Security* [online]. Available at: www.fao.org/spfs (accessed 26.03.14).

US Department of the Interior (2010), *The Deepwater Horizon Tragedy*, Washington, DC: US Department of the Interior.

van Kammen, J., de Savigny, D. and Sewankambo, N. (2006), 'Using Knowledge Brokering to Promote Evidence-based Policy-making: The Need for Support Structures', *Bulletin of the World Health Organization*, 84(8): 608–612.

Van Tassell, K. (2011), *Compensating Victims of Environmental Disasters* [online]. Available at: http://lawprofessors.typepad.com/healthlawprof_blog/2011/01/compensating-victims-of-environmental-disasters.html (accessed 06.03.14).

Varner, G. (2002), *In Nature's Interests? Interests, Animal Rights, and Environmental Ethics*, Oxford: Oxford University Press.

Verheyen, R. (2005), *Climate Change Damage and International Law: Prevention Duties and State Responsibility,* Boston: Martinus Nijhoff Publishers.

Verry, J., Heffernan, F. and Fisher, R. (2005), *Restorative Justice Approaches in the Context of Environmental Prosecution*, Griffith: Australian Institute of Criminology.

Vidal, J. (2013), *Congo's Rare Mountain Gorillas Could Become Victims of Oil Exploration* [online]. Available at: http://www.theguardian.com/environment/2013/aug/01/congo-mountain-gorillas-virunga-wwf (accessed 21.03.14).

Vito, G. and Mahhs, J. (2012), *Criminology: Theory, Research and Policy*, London: Jones & Bartlett Learning.

Vogel, D. (2003), 'The Hare and the Tortoise Revisited: The New Politics of Consumer and Environmental Regulation in Europe', *British Journal of Political Science*, 33: 557–580.

Von Lewinski, S. (2008), *Indigenous Heritage and Intellectual Property: Genetic Resources, Traditional Knowledge and Folklore*, The Hague: Kluwer Law International.

Wachholz, S. (2007), ' "At risk": Climate Change and its Bearing on Women's Vulnerability to Male Violence'. In P. Beirne and N. South (eds.), *Issues in Green Criminology: Confronting Harms Against Environments, Humanity and Other Animals*, Cullompton: Willan, 161–185.

Walsh, A. and Ellis, L. (2007), *Criminology: An Interdisciplinary Approach*, Thousand Oaks: Sage.

Walters, R. (2006), 'Crime, Bio-agriculture and the Exploitation of Hunger', *British Journal of Criminology*, 46(1): 26–45.

Walters, R. (2009), 'Bhopal, Corporate Crime and Harms of the Powerful', *Global Social Policy*, 9: 324–327.

Walters, R. (2010), 'Toxic Atmospheres: Air Pollution and the Politics of Regulation', *Critical Criminology*, 18(4): 307–323.

Walters, R. and Westerhuis, D. (2013), 'Green Crime and the Role of Environmental Courts', *Crime, Law and Social Change*, 59: 279–290.

Wang, Q. and Chen, X. (2012), ' Regulatory Failures for Nuclear Safety – the Bad Example of Japan – Implication for the Rest of World', *Renewable and Sustainable Energy Reviews*, 16(5): 2610–2617.

Warner, K., Afifi, T., Dun, O., Stal, M. and Schmidl, S. (2008), *Human Security, Climate Change and Environmentally Induced Migration*, Bonn: United Nations University – Institute for Environment and Human Security.

Watts, J. (2010), 'In China's "Cancer Villages", Residents Pay the Price for a Dirty Revolution', *The Guardian*, Tuesday, 8th June, 21.

Wellsmith, M. (2010), 'The Applicability of Crime Prevention to Problems of Environmental Harm: A Consideration of Illicit Trade in Endangered Species'. In R. White (ed.), *Global Environmental Harm: Criminological perspectives*, Cullompton: Willan, 132–149.

Weisslitz, M. (2002), 'Rethinking the Equitable Principle of Common but Differentiated Responsibility: Differential Versus Absolute Norms of Compliance and Contribution in the Global Climate Change Context', *Colorado Journal of International Environmental Law & Policy*, 13: 473–502.

Wheatley, M. (1997), 'Social and Cultural Impacts of Mercury Pollution on Aboriginal Peoples in Canada', *Water, Air & Soil Pollution*, 97(1–2): 85–90.

White, R. (2007), 'Green Criminology and the Pursuit of Social and Ecological Justice'. In P. Beirne and N. South (eds.), *Issues in Green Criminology: Confronting Harms Against Environments, Humanity and Other Animals*, Cullompton: Willan, 32–54.

White, R. (2008a), *Crimes Against Nature: Environmental Criminology and Ecological Justice*, Cullompton: Willan Publishing.

White, R. (2008b), 'Depleted Uranium, State Crime and the Politics of Knowing', *Theoretical Criminology*, 12(1): 31–54.

White, R. (2009), *Environmental Crime: A Reader*, Cullompton: Willan Publishing.

White, R. (2010), *Global Environmental Harm: Criminological Perspectives*, Cullompton: Willan Publishing.

White, R. (2011), *Transnational Environmental Crime: Towards an Eco-global Criminology*, Abingdon: Routledge Publishing.

White, R. (2013a), 'Eco-global Criminology and the Political Economy of Environmental Harm'. In N. South and A. Brisman (eds.), *Routledge International Handbook of Green Criminology*, Abingdon: Routledge, 243–260.

White, R. (2013b), 'The Conceptual Contours of Green Criminology'. In R. Walters, D. Westerhuisand and T. Wyatt (eds.), *Emerging Issues in Green Criminology: Exploring Power, Justice and Harm*, Basingstoke: Palgrave Macmillan, 17–33.

Williams, C. (1996), 'An Environmental Victimology', *Social Science*, 23(1): 16–40. Reprinted in White, R. (ed.), (2009), *Environmental Crime: A Reader*, Cullompton: Willan Publishing, 200–222.

Williams, C. (2013), 'Research Methodologies in Examining Climate Change Law and Victimisation'. Paper Presented at the *ICOSS Climate Change, Law and Victimisation Seminar*, 30th October, University of Sheffield.

Wilson, G. (2011), *Human Rights and Environment: The Case Law of the European Court of Human Rights in Environmental Cases*, Brno: Justice and Environment.

Woods, M. (2005), *UKELA Litigation Working Party Position Paper on Environmental Civil Penalties*, Dorking: UKELA.

Woods, M. and Macrory, R. (2003), *Environmental Civil Penalties: A More Proportionate Response to Regulatory Breach*, London: University College London.

Women's News Network (2010), *Climate Change, Poverty and Tourists Put Maasai Daughters at Risk* [online]. Available at: http://womennewsnetwork.net/2010/04/16/kenya-climatechange-trafficking-892/ (accessed 25.02.14).

World Health Organization (2008), *Quantification of the Health Effects of Exposure to Air Pollution Report of a WHO Working Group*, Bilthoven: WHO Regional Office for Europe.

World Wildlife Foundation (2013), *Japan and Russia Increase Penalties for Wildlife Crimes* [online]. Available at: http://wwf.panda.org/?208304/Japan-and-Russia-increase-penalties-for-wildlife-crimes (19.03.14).

Woynillowicz, D. and Severson-Baker, C. (2009), *Oil Sands Fever-The Environmental Implications of Canada's Oil Sands Rush*, Toronto: The Pembina Institute for Appropriate Development.

Wyatt, J. (2010), 'Law-making at the Intersection of International Environmental, Humanitarian and Criminal Law: The Issue of Damage to the Environment in International Armed Conflict', *International Review of the Red Cross*, 92(879): 593–646.

Young, M. (1997), 'Victim Rights and Services: A Modern Saga'. In R. Davis, A. Lurigio and W. Skogan (eds.), *Victims of Crime*, 2nd Edition, Thousand Oaks: Sage Publications, 194–210.

Young, W., Hwang, K., McDonald, S. and Oates, C. (2010), 'Sustainable Consumption: Green Consumer Behaviour When Purchasing Products', *Sustainable Development*, 18(1): 20–31.

Yun, K., Lurie, M. and Hyde, P. (2010), 'Moving Mental Health into the Disaster-Preparedness Spotlight', *The New England Journal of Medicine*, 263: 1193–1195.

Zimmerman, M. (2003), 'The Black Market for Wildlife: Combating Transnational Organized Crime in the Illegal Wildlife Trade', *Vanderbilt Journal of Transnational Law*, 36: 1657–1689.

Index

Note: Page references with 'b' and 'f' notation refer to boxes and figures cited in the text.

wealth, 9, 15, 87–8, 151–2, 168, 211
welfare approach to environmental
    harms, 174
Western societies, 14
wetlands, 59–60
whales, 190b
white-collar crime, 4, 81, 85–7, 90, 96,
    135, 159
'white' environmental harm, 17
Wikipedia, 220
wildlife crime, 5, 34–6, 40, 42, 68, 76,
    153b, 154–5, 170–1, 219b
Wildlife Crime Working Group,
    INTERPOL, 137b
wildlife products, illegal trade, 153b
wildlife resources, 154, 171
wildlife trafficking, 5, 34–6, 40, 42
wind farms, 53
wine industry, 40

win-win-win solution, 156
women, impact of environmental
    degradation on, 169–70
women's empowerment, 170
working cultures, 133, 135
workload increase of women, 170
World Food Summit of 1996, 46
World Health Organization, 165
World Heritage, 59
World Society of Victimology, 173
World Wide Fund for Nature (WWF),
    35–6
W.R Grace & Co. case, 162b
WW II, 114b

xenophobia, 39

Zambia, 172
Zander v *Swedeni*, 201